Contemporary Chinese Economy

The Chinese economy has been regarded as one of the most dazzling phenomena in the current world economy. A systematic, objective and academic analysis on the contemporary Chinese economy, however, is still lacking. This book, written by an excellent native Chinese scholar, fills this void, in many respects, lucidly.

The book gives a systematic analysis of the modern Chinese economy since China's economic reform and its opening up in 1978. It also includes analytical comparisons on differences between China and the West, and illustrates how these differences, in terms of economic structure, financial and administrative systems, and the governance of the economy, attributed to the growth and economic performance of China. The book also provides a deep economic analysis of China's future difficulties and challenges in development. The book provides a strategic consideration on how China should meet with these challenges and difficulties.

Since China is an example of the successful rise of a developing nation in the current world, this book is an innovative contribution to academics in the field of macroeconomics for developing economies. The book illustrates the success from a new perspective. It makes an excellent choice as a textbook for related courses on Chinese economy in universities, and also serves as an excellent reference for understanding and researching contemporary Chinese economy.

Gong Gang gained his PhD in Economics from New School University in the US. He is Professor in the School of Economics, Nankai University in China. He has published four books, published by Princeton University Press and Oxford University Press, and has also published more than 40 academic papers in English and in Chinese. Currently, he is on the advisory board of Metroeconomica.

Contemporary Chinese Economy

Gong Gang

Routledge
Taylor & Francis Group

LONDON AND NEW YORK

First published 2012
by Routledge
2 Park Square, Milton Park, Abingdon, Oxfordshire OX14 4RN

Simultaneously published in the USA and Canada
by Routledge
711 Third Avenue, New York, NY 10017

First issued in paperback 2014

Routledge is an imprint of the Taylor & Francis Group, an informa company

British Library Cataloguing in Publication Data
A catalogue record for this book is available from the British Library

Library of Congress Cataloging in Publication Data
Gong, Gang, 1959–
   Contemporary Chinese economy/by Gang Gong.
   p. cm.
   Includes bibliographical references and index.
   1. China–Economic policy–2000– 2. China–Economic
   conditions–2000– I. Title.
   HC427.95.G65 2012
   330.951–dc23

                                                    2011037310

ISBN 13: 978-0-415-61690-4 (hbk)
ISBN 13: 978-0-415-70517-2 (pbk)

Typeset in Times New Roman
by Wearset Ltd, Boldon, Tyne and Wear

Contents

Figures and tables

Figures

Tables

Part I

Introduction and preparation

1 Introduction

1.1 The "mysterious" in Chinese economy

"China fever"

At 8 p.m. on August 8, 2008, the world's attention and numerous flashlights were focused on the "Bird Nest" stadium in Beijing. More than 80 national leaders gathered in Beijing to attend the opening ceremony of the Olympic Games, including US President George W. Bush, Japanese Prime Minister Yasuo Tomita and French President Nicolas Sarkozy. This created a new historical record for the number of national leaders attending the Olympic opening ceremony. It showed the respect that the leaders of many countries have not only for the Olympic spirit, but also for Beijing and even for China. Meanwhile, the world witnessed the successful practice of China's "harmonious world" concept.

Recently, the US Magazine *Times* published a list of the "World's Most Influential People" in 2008, and the Chinese President Hu Jintao was again on the list. Furthermore, the Hamburg-based fashion magazine *Park Avenue* announced its list of the "World's 100 Most Influential People", which also included President Hu Jintao. The rise of China makes the world proud of it, and the growing trend has been irresistible. Even some Western strategists have to admit that the rise of China, as a great power, is the most definite trend in the international relations of the 21st century.

With global "China fever" blooming, Confucius Institutes, the carriers of Chinese culture, are springing up widely around the world. In just two years from the end of 2004, when the first Confucius Institute was formally opened in South Korea, more than 140 Confucius Institutes were established in 50 countries and regions.

At the same time, "China Week", "China Festival" and new "Chinatown" are also held in all parts of the world. In the United Kingdom, it is said that the word "China" appears in the media so often that it is second only to the word "British". It has been reported that there is a piece of news about China in the world every eight minutes. There is no exaggeration in saying that China has seized the world's attention, and that "China fever" is booming all over the world.

The "mysteries" of the Chinese economy

Needless to say, the source of "China fever" lies in the fabulously high and stable growth of the Chinese economy since the reform and opening up launched 30 years ago. Following this, the Chinese economy began sliding onto an unprecedented fast track, and China has become one of the world's most promising countries. In the 21st century, the Chinese economy has still maintained a nearly double-digit growth. That miracle has earned China great esteem from the world. Without doubt, China is increasingly becoming the dazzling growth point of the global economy that people cannot help but watch.

It is safe to say that today's interest in China is a common phenomenon in Western society, and that research on the Chinese economy has developed vigorously. In fact, the enthusiasm of and motivation for foreign scholars to study the Chinese economy originate not only from "seeing it through", but also from being "unable to see it through". Over the years, the variety of "mysteries" permeating the Chinese economy have always brought a number of explorers to "appreciate the flowers in the mist", and thus spurred the impulse to unveil the mysteries of Chinese economy.

In the eyes of Western scholars, or according to the mainstream economics in Western academy, the economic development of China is full of "contradiction", "impossibility", "uncommonness" and "anti-logic". Here are some examples.

In the year 1997, China entered into a long period of deflation: the price index in China continued to decline for the next five years. However, China's growth rate was still kept miraculously high at the level of about 8 percent. That level was among the highest in the world at that time. This high growth accompanied by deflation has puzzled many economists both at home and abroad. A new economics term, "deflationary expansion", was even created to represent the situation. Unraveling the mystery of "deflationary expansion" was once the research focus for many economists, and some foreign economists even suspected the reliability of official statistics announced from China.

The system of state-owned commercial banks in China has injected a lot of money into the rapidly growing Chinese economy. In many cases, loans from state-owned commercial banks can be obtained easily and at a very low cost. As

Table 1.1 Comparison of financial resources of China and some OECD countries

	China	*USA*	*Germany*	*France*
Real interest rate (%)	2.1418	3.4757	4.1092	4.5654
	(1980–2001)	(1964–2003)	(1970–2003)	(1980–2003)
Growth rate in money supply (%)	20.06	7.12	6.26	6.01
	(1985–2001)	(1964–2003)	(1975–2003)	(1980–2003)
Growth rate in nominal GDP (%)	16.06	7.25	5.64	6.19
	(1981–2001)	(1964–2003)	(1970–2003)	(1980–2003)

Data regarding the United States, Germany and France are from the OECD (2004); data regarding China are from the National Bureau of Statistics in China (2004). Figures in brackets are for years.

seen in Table 1.1, the loan rate in China has been far lower than that in Western countries. At the same time, over a very long period, the growth rate of money supply in China has been as high as 20 percent – significantly higher than the growth rate of nominal GDP of 16 percent. According to the prevailing theory of monetary economics and the experiences of developed countries, the growth rate of money supply should be approximately equal to the growth rate of nominal GDP. Clearly, such a high rate of money growth in China should logically have spelled worsened inflation. However, there was actually no inflation at that time; instead, China witnessed deflation in a magic way (see Figure 1.1).

At the same time, when the growth of the money supply (or loans) was too high, the state-owned commercial banks in China also suffered from huge non-performing loans. In China, non-performing loans of state-owned commercial banks had once reached one-third of total assets. Such a high proportion of non-performing loans led some foreign economists to make a bold prediction: the financial system in China would be bound to collapse. However, this forecast again proved to be inaccurate. The financial system in China showed no signs of failure, but the financial system in US and European countries has collapsed recently.

Although the Chinese economy as a whole shows the trend of a sustained high growth, a variety of discordances, unbalances and even contradictions have continued to attract the attention from foreign media. This is one of the reasons why Western economists have doubts about Chinese economy. Their confusion springs from the shabby bungalow the *Der Spiegel* reporter captured under the shadow of modern skyscrapers in Shanghai; from the earth-built dwellings in the

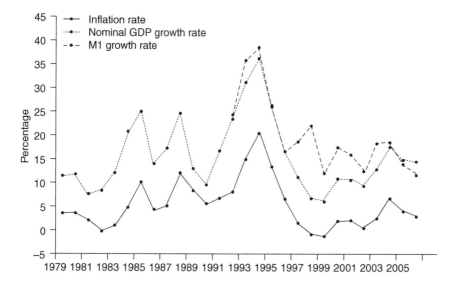

Figure 1.1 Inflation rate, growth rate in nominal GDP and in money supply (M1). Data are from the National Bureau of Statistics in China (2007); money supply (M1) is measured from the value at the beginning of the year.

rural areas in western China which are silhouetted against the neon lights of eastern coastal cities; from the figures of weather-beaten peasants in mountainous areas compared with those rich people who are constantly traveling overseas and purchasing luxuries; and from the black joke "an old ox is pulling a truck", which once widespread on the Internet.

What exactly happened to the Chinese economy? Is China's economy really so confusing? Is the operation of the Chinese economy really outside the basic laws of economics?

1.2 Economic theories and the analytical framework of economics

In fact, Western scholars' confusion about the Chinese economy can be more accurately expressed as "The Western scholars lack understanding of Chinese economy because the theories they use to explain the phenomenon of the Chinese economy are established on the developed market economies".

This drives us to wonder, when facing an economic phenomenon, what basic tool should be used? Should it be the available economic theory or the basic framework of economic analysis? Undoubtedly, the answer is the latter. Existing economic theory itself arises from the analytical framework: economic theory is a summary of the laws and relations acquired from utilizing the basic framework of economic analysis to study specific economic phenomena. For example, Western economic theories are summaries of the economic operation of Western economy that are obtained by using the basic framework of economic analysis. In this sense, an economic theory is only an interpretation of economic phenomena under certain conditions, but the basic framework of economic analysis is universal and is for analyzing all economic phenomena.

So what is the basic analytical framework of modern economics? On this issue, Qian (2003) and Tian (2005) provide a good discussion. Here, our discussion begins with the basic question: What is economics as a science?

First, we must recognize that economic analysis often relies on optimization. This seems to suggest that economics should be a science to explore what the best economic choice to achieve certain objectives is. Such a way to understand economics is to regard economics as being a normative discipline that tells how people make choices (what should we do?). Yet, economics should also be regarded as being a positive science. As a positive science, economics studies should be of the economic phenomena, or what happens under certain conditions (what will happen?). For instance, when the price of a product rises, will the market demand for the product increase or decrease? When money supply increases, will inflation occur? What are the possible economic effects of government spending on the economy? And so on. Thus, we can define economics as a positive science as follows:

> Economics is a science to study economic operation or the determination of economic variables under a certain economic environment.

However, the research on economic operation or the determination of economic variables must comply with a certain analytical framework.

First, the determination of economic variables is usually the integrated result of various economic activities of many economic agents, and therefore the behavior analysis of economic agents is the starting point for economic research. To some extent, economics is a science for studying the behavior of economic agents.[1]

Second, there is a basic hypothesis regarding the behavior of economic agents in economic research, involving "self-interest" and "rationality". The so-called "self-interest" refers to the fact that economic agents always pursue their own interests without considering the benefits of others when engaging in economic activities.[2] The so-called "rationality" means that economic agents are wise, and know how to achieve optimal results. The optimization models often existing in economics research actually reflect the assumption of the rationality of economic agents. Such a behavior hypothesis of economic agents was imposed to some extent by Adam Smith 200 years ago.

Third, no matter how rational, wise, selfish or greedy economic agents may be, their actions, after all, are always restricted by the economic environment within which they operate (a more specific discussion on the economic environment will be given in the next section). Therefore, economic research is the study of the economic operation or the determination of economic variables under a certain economic environment.

The previous discussion allows us to summarize the analytical framework of modern economics into a trilogy:

- specifying the economic environment;
- defining the behavioral objectives of economic agents (reflecting the self-interest and rationality); and
- analyzing economic operation (the overall performance from various economics agents).

The aforementioned trilogy can be understood as a standard paradigm of economic analysis, and every reasonable economic analysis should follow such a paradigm. Of course, reasonable economic analysis does not mean it is qualified. According to different research contents, readers and precision requirements, some researches may be extremely complicated. For instance, in order to complete this trilogy, economists may establish a mathematical model and use some mathematical tools for analysis. At the same time, in order to make their researches more convincing, economists may also use the data for a test.

It can be safe to say that this analytical framework of modern economics is universal and general. It will not change with time or because of different regions. Therefore, as far as the analytical framework of modern economics is concerned, there are no such concepts as "Western economics" and "Eastern economics". However, the analytical framework of modern economics does not exclude the possible different schools of economics and economic theories adaptable to a specific region in a specific period.

Different schools of economics or different economic theories are often derived from different economic environments. As noted earlier, the economic environment restricts the behavior and the choice of economic agents, creating different ways to determine economic variables. For instance, "Keynesian" and "neoclassical" are regarded as the two major schools of economics, both of which originated from the Western developed countries, and hence both of them regarded the developed market economy as its economic environment. Nevertheless, understanding and observing the developed market economy are not the same in the two schools. It is these different observations leading to different specifications of economic environment that create "Keynesian" and "neoclassical" – the two schools of current mainstream economics.

Thus, when people use the basic framework of economic analysis to study hypothetically different economies or the economies with hypothetically different environments, they will have different economic theories. Similarly, the current economic theories dominating classroom teaching throughout the world stem from research on the developed market economy of Western countries. Consequently, when we use those economic theories, produced under a completely different economic environment, to examine the Chinese economy, we are bound to feel "confused" and "anti-logical".

Finally, when we emphasize the positive role of economics, we cannot ignore the normative role of economics. However, the normative role of economics must be based on its positive research. Obviously, only when we have fully studied the economic operation or the determination of economic variables can we propose the corresponding policy and recommendations. Yet the role of qualified economists is by no means to put forward policies and proposals to achieve some kind of targets recognized by societies and governments, even if these proposals are made on the basis of adequate understanding of the economic operation. In fact, economists must also tell people the possible effects of such policy recommendations on the economy. For example, for a policy recommendation to reduce unemployment, an economist should tell people not only that policy may reduce unemployment, but also that it could possibly generate inflation.[3] This seems to bring us back to the positive definition of economics.

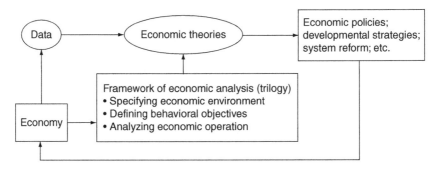

Figure 1.2 Economic theories and the framework of economic analysis.

The previous discussion on economic theories and the framework of economic analysis is summarized in Figure 1.2.

1.3 Economic resources and the economic system

It's already known that economic environment restricts the behavior and the choice of economic agents. Yet, what is the economic environment? Clearly, the economic environment is a very broad concept. Here, we only discuss the two most important components of economic environment, namely economic resources and the economic system. First of all, let's discuss economic resources.

Economic resources

Although I am very familiar with Europe, I still cannot help marveling at the fresh air, beautiful surroundings, exquisite castles and modern facilities whenever I set foot on the continent. However, what initially impressed me most was people's more relaxed demeanour and greater opportunities for leisure in Western countries. Here, people are enjoying their life, while the term "hardworking" has a different meaning to that in China. I cannot help but think emotionally of my own father and mother, who've worked hard for a lifetime, and of the Chinese people, especially farmers. We have been always emphasized that China has a vast territory with abundant resources, and that the Chinese people are industrious people. However, why don't our hard work and rich resources bring us the due quality of life?

When I taught at the University of Leiden in The Netherlands in 2005, I had an opportunity to listen to a wonderful speech given by Zheng Bijian. He said:

> Many problems in China can be represented by two math problems: one is the multiplication, which means that any minor number multiplied by 1.3 billion would be huge; another is the division, which means that any astronomical figure, divided by 1.3 billion, would become negligible.

In view of this, even if China has a vast territory with abundant resources, as long as the resources are apportioned by its population, they absolutely cannot be called "abundant".

In fact, speaking of resources, the problem is far from simple. Indeed, resources are not confined to those physical geographies given by God, as is understood usually; more of the resources are created and accumulated by the economic activities of human beings. These non-God-given resources include not only capital equipment like plants, machineries and infrastructure (roads, parks, etc.), but also the intangible human capital and knowledge capital related to technology. Among these, machinery and equipment are created by investment in fixed assets by enterprises; infrastructure is usually built by governments. From the individual point of view, human capital comprises the knowledge, skills, abilities and health acquired by an individual. From the social point of view, it means the citizen quality of a country. Its accumulation comes from investment in education and health. Knowledge capital is accumulated from investment in scientific research and development (R&D), which can be represented by a variety of academic papers, monographs, designs and patents. All in all, the economic resources in a country include not only the natural ones, but also the tangible and intangible resources created by the economic activities of human beings.

There is no doubt that the resources in a nation – or, to be more exact, the resources per capita – determine the living quality of its inhabitants. This determination is obviously through influencing and restricting the behavior choice of economic agents. When people have more resources, they have more economic activities to choose from, and thus their effectiveness and quality of life will be better. In China, the life quality of farmers is far less than that of urban residents, and the development of western regions is far behind that of the eastern cities. This is linked with the resources they possess. As far as farmers are concerned, they have almost nothing but a small piece of land that they depend on for survival and necessary means of production (including inadequate human capital). Thus, even if they are allowed to enter the cities and search for jobs since the reform and opening up of China, their choices are still extremely limited because of their low human capital and the lack of additional resources. They can only be employed in those low-paid jobs with little technological content. Similarly, the backwardness of western regions in China, to a large extent, is also due to their lack of economic resources.

Indeed, to some extent, the major difference between developed and developing countries consists in their possession of per capita resources, while per capita resources determine per capita GDP, thus affecting the life quality of people in a country.

Here, what we also need to stress is that although resources can be generated, created and accumulated, at the same time they can also be damaged, wasted and destroyed. The creation and generation of economic resources brings to developing countries the hope of catching up with developed countries. Meanwhile, destruction of resources requires us to protect them. War and unrest usually destroy resources. In China, the Great Leap Forward and the Cultural Revolution seriously slowed down the pace of resource accumulation. Even today, we still find in China that many economic activities aiming to create one type of resources have destroyed many other types of resources.

Economic system

Next, we will discuss the economic system. Clearly, the economic system must be one of the factors restricting the behavior choice of economic agents. But what is the economic system? How can we distinguish between different economic systems? I think that a country's economic system can be basically identified from the following two aspects: one is its allocation (operation) mechanism of economic resources; the other is its enterprise system.

With regard to the operation mechanism, there are two major kinds: market economy and planned economy. As far as the enterprise system is concerned, it leans largely on ownership. It must be explained that while the enterprise system relies on its ownership form, the same ownership form can have different types of enterprise system. For example, since the reform and opening up of the country, state-owned enterprises in China have evolved in different systems, and some enterprise systems even have mixed forms of ownership. Nevertheless, we still cannot deny that the ownership form (or the system of property rights) restricts the enterprise system to a large extent.

The impact of the enterprise system on the economy is mainly represented by a firm's behavior, or the goals pursued by enterprises. Take a collective enterprise, for example. If the firm's CEO is elected by his or her employees, then the behavior of the firm is more likely to include the pursuit of workers' welfare. This pattern of behavior could have an impact on the firm's decisions in investment, employment and output.

The impact of the enterprise system on a firm's behavior has already attracted attention from economists. For example, Kalbraith (1985) pointed out, in his *New Industrial State*, that in a new industrial era some large stock companies dominate the market, and because of the wide dispersal of the stock shares, firms' decision-makers do not completely represent the interests of shareholders. Those decision-makers are often well-educated professional managers. Therefore, the objectives they pursue are more likely to be stable corporate growth or market share under certain profitability conditions.

Here, we might ask a question: Is there a conflict between the two main aspects constituting the economic system (i.e., operation mechanism and enterprise system)? We believe that this problem is clearly there. For instance, as a mechanism of resource allocation, the success of market operation relies on the actions of market participants or traders. When a price increases, the supply of corresponding output is assumed to be increased while the demand is assumed to be decreased. If the market traders were to be unresponsive or make an opposing decision because of the restrictions from the enterprise system, it is difficult to imagine that such a market would be able allocate economic resources efficiently. Similarly, it is difficult to imagine that the existing enterprise system in Western countries would be able to work in a planned economy.

Economic reform in China, in particular the reform of the state-owned enterprise system, can be interpreted to a large extent as the process in which the two main aspects constituting the economic system are constantly being adjusted to make them work with each other. This is discussed further in Chapter 3.

1.4 Objectives, content and methods

In this book, we will study the contemporary Chinese economy. Our goal is to explain the operation of the contemporary Chinese economy, or how the economic variables in the contemporary Chinese economy are determined. The topics of our discussion will cover economic growth, economic fluctuations and the government behavior in managing the Chinese economy, among others. At the same time, we will also discuss the problems arising from the contemporary Chinese economy, and probe into the future of the Chinese economy on this basis.

The basic content of this book can be divided into three parts. The first three chapters constitute the "Introduction and Preparation". Chapter 2 discusses the socialist economy of traditional China. This discussion is very necessary. In fact, even now we still find that the Chinese economy is shadowed by many socialist traditions. Chapter 3 describes economic reform in China. This gives us a better idea of China's current institutional environment and economic development level, thus paving the way for the environment specification required by the second part of the book.

The second part of this book, "Reading the Brilliance", is composed of Chapters 4, 5, 6 and 7. It explores the operation of the contemporary Chinese economy. Chapter 4 investigates the Chinese economy from the perspective of statistical data, and tries to answer the question: Is the volatility of the major macroeconomic variables in China consistent with the law embodied in typical market economies as in Western developed countries? Chapter 5 discusses the higher growth in contemporary Chinese economy. We will try to show how the Chinese economy can grow so fast. We will also try to explain why the neoclassical growth theory that dominates scholarship throughout the world is unable to explain China's high economic growth. Chapter 6 introduces the economic reform and the current institutional properties of the financial sector in China. Chapter 7 depicts business cycles in the Chinese economy, and tries to explain how the Chinese government implements demand management in response to economic fluctuations. We will see that there are great differences in the approaches to dealing with business cycles between China and developed countries.

The third part of this book, "Challenges in the Future", comprises Chapters 8, 9 and 10. This part regards the future of the Chinese economy. Among them, Chapter 8 analyzes the quality of China's high economic growth and the future changes in domestic and international environments. It sets forward the proposition that the mode of economic growth must be transformed in contemporary Chinese economy in order to sustain economic growth in the future. That proposition will run through the remainder of the book. Chapter 9 studies China's technological progress, which is the key to the transformation of the growth mode. We will examine the difficulties and barriers that China must overcome for technological progress. As we will find, this requires further institutional reform in addition to the probable fiscal support from the government. Chapter 10 discusses the external pressures that China will be confronted with. These external pressures may include increased demands from the international community for trade balance and RMB appreciation, and the increased demand for non-substitutable resources (such as oil), among others. We find that to meet with these pressures, the only solution is to internationalize RMB. We then discuss the difficulties and the possible risks for RMB internationalization. This may include opening up the capital market, among others.

It needs to be noted that the study of economics usually requires the help of mathematical tools. However, in order to serve more readers, the main body of this book is basically easy to understand without the requirement for academic training in economics and mathematics. More advanced economic theories and research involving math are contained in the four appendices, A–D, which are an important part of this book.

Discussion and questions

1 Many economic phenomena in China can be considered as being a "mystery". Give some examples.
2 What is positive economics? What is normative economics? How do you understand the relationship between the two?
3 What is the basic analytical framework of economics? How does it relate to general economic theory?
4 What is the basic assumption regarding the behavior of economic agents? How do you understand the optimization problem in economics?
5 What is the economic environment? What role does it play in economics? How do you define the economic environment?
6 What are economic resources? Could you distinguish different types of economic resources? How are different types of economic resources created or accumulated? In what ways could economic resources be destroyed?
7 What is the economic system? How do you distinguish different economic systems? Give an example illustrating how the economic system affects the behavior of firms.

2 The Chinese economy before reform and opening up

October 1, 1949 opened a new era in the history of China. The establishment of the new China allowed the country to become independent, and the Chinese people have "stood up" ever since. However, it is no exaggeration to say that the Chinese people were initially standing on a disastrous ruin following almost half a century of wars.

So, how did the Communist Party of China (CPC) lead the Chinese people to build their own homes on their war-torn ruin? What was their development strategy? How do you appraise such a development strategy?

2.1 Historical background and development strategies

The old Chinese economy

Compared with the year 1936, heavy industry production in China in 1949 had declined by 70 percent, light industry production by 30 percent, and agricultural production by 25 percent.[1] At the same time, inflation was like a runaway horse. In the years before 1949, the prices of general consumption goods in China had risen several times, several hundred times, or even several thousand times per year. According to an ironic report from Associated Press on July 24, 1947, 100 yuan *fabi* (the currency circulated at that time) could buy two heads of cattle in 1937, a pig in 1941, an egg in 1946, and one-third of a matchbox in 1947. The "Gold Yuan Certificate"[2] issued in 1948 was initially assumed to be a gold reserve, but soon become waste paper. Some people even used the "Gold Yuan" as wallpaper.

Before 1949, China was a semi-colonial and semi-feudal society. Old China had very low social productivity. Industry accounted for a very small portion of the whole economy, and modern industry was even weaker. In 1949, gross industrial output accounted for 30.1 percent of total output, of which modern industry was only 23.2 percent.[3]

The agricultural production in old China was also backward. In 1949, the average production per *mu* (a Chinese unit of area) was 68.5 kilograms of grain, or 10.5 kilograms of cotton. Although more than 80 percent of population was engaged in agricultural production, which made China as an agricultural economy, large amounts of grain and cotton had to be imported from abroad every year. In the meantime, landlords and rich peasants comprised less than 10 percent of the rural population, but occupied 70–80 percent of rural land. This indicates that most farmers did not possess their own land and thus had to rent farmland from landlords for their livelihood. The landlord charged for rent, which was usually 50 percent, or even 70–80 percent, of a farmer's harvest.[4]

The lifeline of the old Chinese economy was fully controlled by foreign monopoly capital and bureaucratic capital. For example, on the eve of the Second Sino-Japanese War between 1937 and 1945, the foreign monopoly capital comprised 41 percent of industrial capital. It monopolized 64 percent of iron production, 57 percent of cigarette production, 69.5 percent of the shipping industry and 90 percent of the railway industry.[5] The bureaucratic capital of old China, represented by Chiang, Soong, Kung, and Chen, the so-called the "Four Big Families", was the monopoly capital, with strong connections to the state power. They directly used the strength of state power for the collection of 10–20 billion US dollars. By the eve of the Chinese Civil War, two-thirds of the total banks were controlled by bureaucratic capital. Bureaucratic capital reached two-thirds of the total industrial capital in the country. It stood at 80 percent of the fixed assets of industry, controlled 90 percent of the national steel output, 33 percent of coal production, 67 percent of electricity production, 45 percent of cement production, and all the oil and non-ferrous metals production.[6]

Problems faced by the CPC after the founding of new China

The absolutely low level of productivity and the extremely unequal resource allocation were typical properties of the old Chinese economy. The Communist Party of China (CPC) took over the war-torn country and the heavy burden of economic development on such a disastrous ruin. After the founding of New China, the CPC faced, among others, the following problems in the economy:

- how to solve the basic problems of living, such as food and clothing, for the large majority of people in China who were still living below the poverty line;
- how to lead the Chinese people, who were very grateful to and had great hopes of the CPC, to go on with economic development after they became masters of the country;
- how to resist the economic blockade against China imposed by the US-led Western countries.
- how to deal with the US military threat, especially that from the Korean War (1950–1953), to economic development and social stability.

"Trinity" development strategies

Confronted with those challenges, the Communist Party of China formulated a set of "trinity" development strategies:[7]

- prioritizing the development of heavy industry;
- choosing the planned economy as the allocation mechanism of economic resources;
- selecting public ownership as the ownership form.

Three reasons urged the CPC to opt for prioritizing the development of heavy industry as a basic state policy. The first was the experience of the Soviet Union. China lacked the experience of socialist construction, and the success achieved by the Soviet Union in giving priority to heavy industry obviously persuaded the CPC to adopt this strategy.

The second reason was the international environment that the new China confronted. At that time, Western countries, led by the United States, took a hostile attitude towards the new China, initiating an economic blockade and posing a military threat to the country. Prioritization of heavy industry allowed progress of China's military production.

The Hoffmann theorem was the third reason, from the perspective of economic theory. In the early 1930s, Hoffmann (1931) carried out a statistical analysis on the change of relative position in the consumer goods and capital goods industries (i.e., heavy industry) during the process of industrialization in Western countries. His conclusion was as follows: no matter when industrialization began, the tendency was the same – that is, with the progress of industrialization, the ratio of the output from the capital goods industry to the output from the consumer goods industry shows a gradually upward trend. This trend was known as the "heavy industrialization" trend. The Hoffmann theorem indicates that giving priority to heavy industry could accelerate industrialization.[8]

Prioritizing heavy industry as a forging-ahead strategy surely meant that the country would choose the planned economy in terms of the mechanism of allocating economic resources.[9] In a country with a low level of development and a shortage of capital, this strategy only factitiously lowers the prices of production means (e.g., energy, raw materials and the labor force) in order to reduce the threshold of capital formation for heavy industry. Therefore, this development strategy requires great distortion of prices. Since the market mechanism could not ensure that scarce resources would flow into heavy industry, allocation of economic resources according to plans and administrative orders was necessary.

Furthermore, for enforcing plans and orders, an enterprise needs to be established that aims at completing planned tasks. It can be said that the public ownership is the inevitable choice of a planned economy: it allows the plan to be implemented easily, and thus helps the central government to mobilize economic resources for the fast development of heavy industry.

Therefore, once the forging-ahead strategy had been chosen, with prioritization of heavy industry as the goal, the choice of a planned economy and public ownership became inevitable.

2.2 The socialist reform in ownership

After the Communist Party of China had established its own development strategies, it quickly pressed on with socialist reform in ownership. As previously mentioned, socialist public ownership was an important part of the "trinity" of development strategies. Prior to the establishment of socialist ownership, New China had experienced a period called the "new democratic economy", featuring the market and private ownership economy under the leadership of the CPC. Even though the party and state leaders (including Mao Zedong) repeatedly pointed out that the new democratic economy would last for a long period of time, the reform to China's socialist ownership was soon launched, in 1953, under the promotion of the "trinity" development strategies.

It needs to be stated that in the period of the new democratic economy, the CPC had already implemented the land reform that allowed peasants to possess their own land. The economic power of foreign monopoly capital and bureaucratic capital in China were either eliminated or confiscated by the state. This indicates that the lifeline industries such as banks and transportation, among others, had already been controlled by the state. The so-called socialist reform was only for agriculture in rural areas, and for handicrafts, manufacturing and commerce industries in urban areas.

Socialist reform in rural areas

Socialist reform in rural China can be divided into two phases: the first was from 1953 to 1956, when the agricultural cooperative movement was basically completed; the second was referred to the "Great Leap Forward" and the people's commune movement, which began in 1958.

The rural cooperative movement experienced the development from temporary, seasonal mutual aid teams into perennial ones, and then the evolution from primary cooperative communes into advanced ones. Primary cooperative communes are organizations that transform farmers' individual economies into a collective economy, characterized by farmers offering land and other production means to cooperative communes for unified management. Appropriate remuneration was given to the commune members according to the offered quality and quantity of land and other production means; at the same time, a labor reward was also granted. Primary cooperative communes generally consisted of 20–30 families. By the second half of 1955, the country had basically succeeded in setting up the primary cooperative commune movement in rural China.

In advanced cooperative communes, not only are farming activities unified in management; the main production means (e.g., land, farming animals, etc.) are also fully owned collectively, thus abolishing the land dividend. The distribution was then fully in line with the principle of "each according to ability and each according to his work". At the same time, these communes were larger than primary cooperative communes in size. Advanced cooperative communes in rural areas were basically established in 1956.

People's communes

The establishment of advanced cooperative communes indicated that China had completed the socialist reform in its rural area. In 1958, however, along with the arrival of the "Great Leap Forward", China's rural areas started another more vigorous movement named "people's communes". The main characteristic of people's communes is that they are "large in size and collective in nature". The "large in size" aspect refers to combining smaller cooperative communes into larger ones, or people's communes. "Collective in nature" refers to the more thorough public ownership of socialism – namely, removing all remnants of capitalism. For instance, any private plots and livestock must be contributed to the commune. With regard to distribution, people's communes implemented commune-level unified accounting marked by the "big pot and communal dining".[10] Such a distribution system completely negated the distribution principle "according to work and ability". This extreme egalitarianism significantly inhibited the farmers' enthusiasm for productivity.

The people's commune system and the Great Leap Forward caused great damage to the economy. China's grain output in 1959 was only 170 billion kilograms, a decrease of 15 percent from 1958; grain output in 1960 was further reduced to 143.5 billion kilograms, falling to the level of 1951.[11]

To address the problems of the people's commune system, the state again had to begin to reform the it. In 1962, the CPC Central Committee issued *Instructions on the Change of Basic Accounting Units in Rural People's Communes*, and established a guideline for people's communes to be "divided into three levels and team-based" accounting units – that is, transforming the former commune-level accounting into three levels (i.e., commune, production brigade, and production team), with the production team as the basic accounting unit. At the same time, the "big pot and communal dining" were scrapped, and the principle of distribution according to work points was enforced.

Obviously, such a reform inhibited, to some extent, the disadvantages exposed by the "large in size and collective in nature" system in the early period of building people's communes. Yet it did not fundamentally change features, such as the egalitarian allocation and lack of incentives embodied in the traditional socialist system. Distribution according to work points seemed to equate to distribution according to work, but actually it could not distinguish between labor quantity and labor quality. The reformed people's commune system continued for nearly 20 years in China, until the reform and opening up was launched in 1978.

Socialist reform in the handicraft industry

The socialist reform of urban artisans (or the handicraft industry) was fully introduced following the third national conference on handicraft production cooperation held in November, 1953. The concrete steps of reform included, starting from collective supply and marketing, the transition from small to large and from lower to higher levels. Handicraft production cooperatives were an advanced form of handicraft cooperation. This was a collective economy with the nature of socialism. The principle of voluntariness and mutual benefit was adhered to when it came to members' admission. In addition to paying a certain amount of entrance fees, their main production tools and equipment were bought, at a discount, and owned by the cooperative as shared property. Cooperative members were directly involved in collective production, thus changing the old employment relationship between master and apprentice existing in the individual handicraft workshops. Their wage took the form of work remuneration. Part of the net revenue of cooperatives was used for tax payment, and the remainder was regarded as a variety of funds and shared reserves.

By the end of December 1956, the socialist reform of the handicraft industry had been basically completed. Nationwide, 91.7 percent of handicraft workers joined in handicraft cooperatives.

Socialist reform in manufacturing and commerce industries

In January 1954, socialist reform in manufacturing and commence industries was proposed, to take place in two steps. First, the capitalist economy in manufacturing and commerce industries needed to be transformed into the state capitalist economy; then, the state capitalist economy was to be converted into the socialist economy.

Here, state capitalism did not indicate an independent form of ownership. It referred to the fact that private manufacturing and commerce firms were related to the state economy in various forms under guidance from the government. In the practice of this transformation, state capitalism was divided into two stages: primary and advanced forms. In the primary form, a private enterprise entered into a contract with the state economy; thus, its production had to some extent been incorporated into national plans, though the production processes were still managed by the private enterprise. The state capitalism economy in the primary form mainly included acquisition, processing, ordering, purchasing, and underwriting.

State capitalism in the advanced form was the public–private partnership. The public–private partnership ensured that socialist components flowed into firms' interior production processes, so that the firms' production relationships underwent fundamental changes. The public–private partnership went through two stages in its development process: the pre-1955 public–private partnership of individual companies, and the post-1955 public–private partnership of the whole industry. In fact, the public–private partnership of the whole industry made the state capitalist economy develop into the socialist economy.

In the public–private partnership of the whole industry, capitalists handed all means of production over to the state, and the state paid fixed interest to the capitalists through audit of the assets in a given period (not assigning an interest rate). Capitalists and capitalist agents who had held various positions in their enterprise were appointed according to their talent, and were rewarded by the principle that they should be taken good care of. All of them were offered an appropriate post, and their high salaries were retained. Capitalists were no longer masters of the capital, but were engaged in the enterprise management as staff working for the state. By the end of 1956, 99 percent of private manufacturing firms and 82 percent of private commerce firms had achieved the ownership transformation, which marked the basic completion of socialist reform in these industries.

2.3 The traditional planning system

The formation of China's traditional planning system took about eight years to be completed. In the early days of founding New China, the Administration Council set up a Planning Bureau, which was the first national planning organization. With the progress in economic recovery and the growth of state-owned economy, the National Planning Commission was founded in the late 1952 to meet the requirements from implementing large-scale economic construction and the first five-year plan. By 1957, the highly integrated planning system in China had been basically established.

The basic contents of the planned economy

With regard to the planned economy, *Chinese Encyclopedia* gives the following definition:[12]

> The planned economy refers to the fact that the socialist state manages and regulates the national economy through the compulsory and instructive plan, according to the requirements of objective economic laws, particularly the law of planned and proportional development, based on the public ownership of production means, and on the premise of socialized production. It is not only a method and system of managing the national economy, but also an economic system and one of the basic characteristics of a socialist society.

In the planned economy system, the production, consumption and allocation of economic resources are all implemented according to the plan drawn in advance. Specifically, the three major problems of economics – what to produce, how to produce it, and for whom – are all solved according to the plan (not through the market). Plans are formulated by the government, and most of them are *compulsory* (occasionally instructive); all economic activities (especially by firms) are carried out according to the plan.

It needs to be stated that, under the traditional system of planned economy, the scope of the plan can be all-inclusive. Here, details of what and how much firms produce are required by the plan; corporate investment, sales, hiring, finance, wages and prices are all included in the plan. As for families, people's daily necessities (i.e., grain, oil, meat, and clothing) are planned and managed through issuing the related coupons by the state.

Preparation for the plan

Extensive preparation for the national economic plan was made, in compliance with the process called "two transitions to the lower, one reporting to the upper".

The first transition to the lower: the State Planning Commission set down the planned control figures and then issued the figures to ministries and local authorities. These figures were the basic requirements and outlines for ministries and local authorities when preparing their plan draft. The planning units of ministries and local authorities then developed a more detailed plan draft and issued this to subordinate departments or enterprises, on the basis of their actual situation. Such a process would run through the whole economy until it reached the grass-roots enterprises.

Reporting to the upper: the respective grass-roots enterprises made necessary amendments and adjustments to the plan drafts issued by their superiors, according to their actual situation. This process can be regarded as a bargaining process. The revised plan drafts then underwent layers of reporting until they reached the State Planning Committee.

The second transition to the lower: the State Planning Commission summarized and balanced those indicators based on the plan drafts from various sectors and regions, and then developed a nationwide plan for the approval of the State Council and the National People's Congress. After approval from the National People's Congress, a formal plan was set down for the various sectors and regions. The plan then permeated down through the economy until it reached the grass roots of enterprises.

The basic method of preparation for the national economic plan is the comprehensive balance method. This method mainly refers to the balance between social production and social needs, the balance between labor, finance, materials and production. Through such balances, all individual units in the economy are linked and are kept in appropriate proportions. Among those balances, the heavy industry indicators (e.g., steel production growth rate) are usually predetermined as a starting point of balance. Here, we can cite a passage from Mao Zedong in June, 1964, when discussing the third five-year-plan:[13]

> In the past the method of developing plan was learned essentially from the Soviet Union: first set the number of steel, then calculate how many coal, electricity and transport are needed on this basis, and again calculate how much urban population and welfare will be increased; the decrease in steel output cuts down others. This is the way to use a calculator, which does not conform to the reality and won't work. This way of calculations does not contain the effect of some uncertain factors. For instance, if natural disasters led to the lack of food supply and the urban population did not increase as expected, anything else would come to nothing.

Implementation of the plan

The preparation, implementation and the possible adjustment of the plan needed a set of organizational mechanisms to provide a guarantee. Clearly, a public-owned (including state-owned and collectively owned) economy established by the socialist reform in the 1950s is the fundamental guarantee for the planned economy. In practice, such a mechanism can be represented as a pyramidal organizational structure of administrative power (see Figure 2.1).

It needs to be explained that local governments, as seen in Figure 2.1, can be further subdivided (for example, into provinces, cities and counties), and each local government has its own functional bureau (such as the Industrial Development Bureau and the Commence Bureau) and manages its subordinate businesses. Thus, even if all enterprises are owned by the state, some subtle differences still exist in the ownership by the state at the county, municipal, provincial and central levels (central-level enterprises are managed directly by related ministries). As a result, the corporate leaders should have the appropriate administrative rank. For example, the administrative rank of a leader in a provincial-level enterprise may be equal to that of county head. In addition, under this administrative organizational structure, each local functional bureau is normally under dual leadership. This means that on the issue of business operation each functional bureau is under the guidance of a superior functional bureau (up to the level of the ministries). Meanwhile, it is subject to restriction from the same level of local government on personnel and financial issues.

Clearly, in such a planned economy and administrative organizational structure, a firm is not a real business unit: it is only an administrative unit executing command (which, in China, is known as the failure to separate the function of government from those of enterprises). The business incentive mechanism is mainly reflected in the promotion of the relevant leaders due to their completion of plans. In fact, in the traditional system, when a leading cadre (or office-holder)

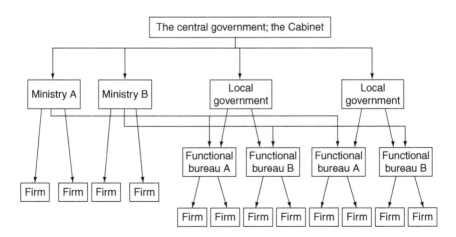

Figure 2.1 Administrative organizational structure under the planned economic system.

was identified as a training object, that cadre was continuously transposed between business and government positions, and his or her position spiraled upwards in the ongoing cursory transpositions. Experiences gained by leading cadres in enterprises were often dubbed the "understanding of the economy". As a result, cadres were usually all-rounders who understood not only politics but also business; who served either as entrepreneurs or as politicians; and who were factory directors, managers or presidents, and also county heads, magistrates or mayors.[14]

The aforementioned discussion on plan implementation focuses mainly on urban areas. In rural areas, largely because of the presence of collective ownership, the agricultural plan of basically depending on estimates was arbitrary to a considerable extent. The plan neither had an accurate and reliable statistical basis, nor served as an indicator for assessing the performance of rural grassroots units.[15]

2.4 Evaluation of the "trinity" strategies

With regard to the traditional socialist planned economy, economists have offered an almost unanimously negative evaluation. What we do here is simply review and summarize these studies.

Should heavy industrialization be prioritized?

The system of China's traditional planned economy was established with the forging-ahead strategy of "prioritizing the development of heavy industry". Our first point, then, is whether such a strategy in itself is reasonable.

First of all, the Hoffmann theorem is only an empirical study based on the change in industrial structure during the early stages of capitalist industrialization, and the current industrial structure does not necessarily change according to the theorem.[16] For example, it can be seen from the current experience of developed countries that the proportion of modern service industries seems to be growing. This excessive emphasis on judging development according to the proportion of the industrial structure ignores the most basic criterion determining the level of economic development: technology. The concept and importance of technology will be explored in Chapter 9.

Second, the Hoffman theorem itself does not explain why prioritizing the development of heavy industry – namely, raising the proportion of heavy industry in the national economy – will be able to speed up the process of industrialization. At least, we do not know where the mechanism lies.

Third, more importantly, such a forging-ahead strategy is clearly out of line with the "comparative advantage" principle in economics. In accordance with the comparative advantage theory, every country has its own comparative advantage industry, even if the absolute level of productivity in all industries is lower than that of other countries. For instance, countries with capital scarcity but that are relatively rich in labor are bound to possess a comparative advantage in labor-intensive industries. A good development strategy must follow the comparative advantage principle; namely, conforming to the comparative advantage decided by the factor endowment structure for selecting their industrial development.[17] For a long time, the dual economic structure in China has determined that the comparative advantage industries in China are not capital-intensive heavy industry, but labor-intensive industries.

According to Lin (2003), economies that follow the comparative advantage for their development have enterprises which possess viability in the market economy. Enterprise viability means that a business will usually get a socially acceptable normal profit in a free, open and competitive market. Whether an enterprise can survive by relying on its own ability without external supports hinges on the industry it exists in and whether its use of production technology is in line with this economy's comparative advantage. The company set up with a breach of comparative advantage has no viability, and its survival can only count on governmental support. In China, such support is embodied in the severe distortion of price, administrative allocation of resources and soft budget constraint under the traditional planned economy.[18]

The difference between developed and developing countries is largely reflected in that of factor endowments. In general, developed countries are relatively rich in capital and have relatively scarce labor, while developing countries are the opposite. Nevertheless, with the development of the economy, developing countries can have an enhanced structure of factor endowments, which means that a country will be increasingly affluent and shortages of labor will gradually appear. According to Lin (2007), however, the speed of such enhancement depends on the return on capital of the overall economy. Only when the enterprise in the economy has viability can the rate of capital return be maximized, and so the factor endowment structure is likely to be promoted the fastest. Thus, the "trinity" development strategies, and prioritizing the development of heavy industry as the driving force, would not really achieve the forging-ahead goal for China.

Huge transaction costs

It has already been explained that in the forging-ahead strategy of heavy industrialization, the enterprise has no viability and its existence can only bank on governmental support through the traditional planning system. We also point out that the results of such support will be sure to lead to inefficient enterprises. For the economy as a whole, this also means low efficiency of resource allocation, low return on capital, and a slow pace of capital accumulation, thus negatively affecting the enhancement of the factor endowment structure.

Why, then, will the economy be normally inefficient under the traditional planned economy? We can sum this up in two reasons:[19] the first is that the system of planned economy has huge transaction costs in the course of its operation; the other is the lack of incentives.

The so-called transaction costs are incurred when people are interacting with each other and making a deal. They are the essential relationship costs between people, as opposed to general production costs (between man and nature).[20] According to Pejovich (2000), the huge transaction costs of a planned economy include the following:

1 the costs of making rational economic planning;
2 the costs of carrying out the plan;
3 the costs of maintaining and supporting various authorities needed for the planning system to run;
4 the costs caused by the fraud and false information offered by the grassroots enterprises that lead the central planning authorities to develop wrong planning schema.

Here, there is no need to expand upon all the aforementioned transaction costs at length; however, there can be some discussion about the transaction costs of the plan preparation process as previously described. We know that the plan preparation process can basically be summed up as "two transitions to the lower, one reporting to the upper". At the same time, the completion of plans is seen as a major (or even the only) criterion for performance evaluation of the state-owned enterprises. In order for plans to be easily completed, firms make full use of "one reporting to the upper" in the plan preparation process to bargain with their superiors, such as requiring a reduction in output or an increase in input (e.g., manpower, equipment and raw materials). Meanwhile, once the plan is developed, even if firms are able to do better than was planned, they generally have no incentive to do so. If firms make the effort to do better than was planned, their superior departments will be provided with more genuine information, thus increasing the difficulties for the firms in completing their plans in the following year.

No incentives

The traditional system of planned economy uses highly centralized, large bureaucracy as a guarantee to develop and implement the plans. Such a system conflicts with the nature of economic agents who maximize their own interests, and thus leaves the whole economy lacking in incentives.

In the traditional planned economy, individuals' employment and income are distributed solely by the state. They can neither choose their own favorite work, nor receive more returns due to their own efforts. This makes them lose their ambition when engaged in economic activities, and thus they can only be a tool for completing the tasks they are assigned. Once people become a tool, without ambition, they lose energy as well as their initiative. Of course, it must be noted that, in the traditional planned economy, motivation for individuals does not vanish at all; motivation is mainly represented by spiritual rewards and promotions.

As for enterprises, the soft budget constraint as occurs in the traditional planned economy severely restricts innovation. According to Schumpeter (1942), innovation is the fundamental driving force for technological progress and economic development. Economic development is mainly embodied in the fact that old products and technologies are phased out as a result of continuous innovation, which is known as "creative destruction".

Here, we would like to note that innovation is not a purely technical concept. It is the process of transforming existing knowledge (or inventions) into productivity. Therefore, it is the business of entrepreneurs. In the market economy, competition forces companies to continue to innovate and maintain the process of transforming existing knowledge into productivity. However, in a traditional planned economy, because of the presence of soft budget constraints, there is a lack of incentive for innovation in the business. Accordingly, despite the ability to concentrate national resources to develop some high, refined and sophisticated technologies in particular fields (e.g., the military), the transformation of new knowledge into productivity was obviously slow for the economy as a whole. Obsolete equipment could be seen everywhere in general production. Ma and Cao (2002) showed that prior to the reform and opening up, technological progress had contributed only 10 percent to China's economic growth while that proportion had reached 60 percent in some developed countries.

Discussion and questions

1   What was the Chinese economy like at the beginning of the new China? What were the difficulties faced by the Communist Party of China?
2   What are the "trinity" development strategies? Why did the Chinese Communist Party take such a development strategy?
3   What kind of economy did the Chinese economy belong to from 1949 to 1953? During this period, what reforms or revolutions did the Communist Party of China carry out? What were the implications of these reforms or revolutions on the subsequent socialist reform?
4   How did Communist Party of China conduct its three socialist reforms?
5   Regarding people's communes and the Great Leap Forward, what kind of damage did they cause to the accumulation of economic resources in China? What kind of adjustments did the system of people's communes go through later on?
6   What is the planned economy? How are the plans prepared in China? How are they executed?
7   What is the Hoffman theorem? What are transaction costs? What is the soft budget constraint?
8   How do you assess the "trinity" development strategies?

3   Economic reform in China

The traditional socialist system of China and the development strategy of prioritizing heavy industry did not bring China prosperity and allow the country to forge ahead as envisaged. Instead, such a system and the development strategy, together with the political campaigns that frequently occurred (such as the Great Leap Forward and the Cultural Revolution), caused a great deal of damage to the Chinese economy. At the same time, the success of Japan and the Four Asian Tigers[1] seems to symbolize the superiority of another economic system. Clearly, in the peaceful competition of the different economic systems between the East and the West, the West had overtaken the East. Thus, in 1978, the Communist Party of China did not hesitate to learn from the West, launching unprecedented reforms in economic system.

The system reform of Chinese economy has already lasted more than 30 years, and is still continuing. In this chapter, we will describe the reform of the economic system. This will enable us to understand the current institutional environment of the Chinese economy, thus preparing for the study of contemporary Chinese economy in the next chapter.

3.1 "Progressive", "opening" and "spontaneous" – three features of economic reform in China

In December 1978, the Third Plenary Session of the 11th Central Committee of the Communist Party of China (CPC) passed a resolution on the reform of the economic system and opening up. This marked the advent of a new historical period in China – the period of economic reform and opening up. The economic reform and opening up in China did not go at all smoothly. It was involved much debate on "socialism" and "capitalism". Thus, in the past 30 years, the economic reform and opening up in China have also been a constant process of ideological liberation.

The economic reform in China over the past 30 years can be described by the following three terms: "progressive", "opening up" and "spontaneous".

The progressive

The economic reform in China is no doubt progressive. This is different from the radical (or shock therapy) system reforms in the former Soviet Union and

Eastern European countries. The so-called progressive reform of the economic system refers to the type of reform that gradually introduces new factors (market factors) into the existing system on the premise that the old system is gradually reformed rather than being destroyed in a one step.

One of the reasons why China adopted the progressive type of economic reform is that there was no blueprint for an objective system for the Communist Party of China in the early stages of economic reform. In contrast to the radical approach, which has a holistic set of planned goals before reform, the economic reform in China, though market-oriented, didn't have any pre-designed blueprint. In the words of Deng Xiaoping, the economic reform in China takes the approach of "wading across the river by touching the stones". This indicates that economic reform in China proceeds step by step, while gradually modifying the reform direction. For example, when China introduced reform and opening up in 1978, there was no such thing as a proposal for China to develop a socialist market economy, and policy-makers merely believed that the introduction of market factors could overcome the most urgent problems at that time. The Third Plenary Session of the 12th Central Committee of the CPC, held in 1984, brought forward the establishment of a "socialist commodity economy". It was only in 1992, when the 14th Central Committee of the CPC was held, that the goal of economic reform was clearly put forward – that is, to establish a "socialist market economy". It can be seen that at the beginning of the reform and opening up, the desired goal of government was not a market economy. Instead, with the continuous deepening of reform and opening up, especially the constant growth of "economy out of the government system", the government came to realize that only gradually abandonment of the traditional planned economy could lead to a fundamental solution to the shortcomings of the planning system.

It needs to be noted that economists were not bullish about progressive economic reform in China. Western economists promoted "shock therapy" reform. That type of reform achieved success in South America; however, it also led to disastrous consequences in the Soviet Union and Eastern Europe. At the same time, China's progressive reform led to China gradually to becoming the fastest growing economy in the world.

The opening up

The economic reforms in China are generally associated with the gradual growth of private economy and foreign-funded enterprises outside the traditional system. Therefore, the economic reform in China is also a process of opening up to the outside – the economy outside the traditional system. This means that over quite a long period, two systems are allowed to coexist; this is known as the "two-track" system. The two-track system means not only a two-track price system in the usual sense, but also the coexistence of planning and market in the economy, as well as that of different ownership. In fact, it is this growing economy outside the traditional system and the differences in effectiveness shown in the collision of two economies that has promoted the system reform of the Chinese economy and eventually merged the two systems. It needs to be pointed out that, even now, we can still see the presence of a two-track banking system.

Spontaneous style

The economic system reform in China was not only a top-down process, but also a bottom-up process. Many measures of China's economic reform were not proposed by the central government, but rather by local governments and even ordinary people in a spontaneous way. Those measures had achieved positive results, and were subsequently approved by the central government as national policy to be popularized. In practice, this bottom-up process manifested itself in such forms as "first implemented but not announced", "implemented and then announced", and "first have a baby, and then get a marriage license".[2] Xiaogang Village, as discussed below, is the best example of spontaneous reform.

3.2 Rural economic reform

The 18 red fingerprints of Xiaogang villagers

There is a special collection in the Museum of the Chinese Revolution: an agreement printed with 18 red fingerprints. This first-class national heritage was created by the farmers in the first village to carry the economic reform in rural China – Xiaogang Village, located in Fengyang County of Anhui Province.

During the period of the Great Leap Forward, 60 Xiaogang Villagers starved to death, and six families died out completely. By the end of 1977, most families, large or small, had moved out of the village; anyone who was able to walk, man or woman, had been a beggar. "Only three thatched cottages, a head of farm cattle, a piece of rake, and a plow were left in the farm collective of the brigade", said Yan Junchang, captain of the production brigade at that time (all now over 70 years old), in an interview, with hands trembling in pain. Yan Junchang had the strongest sense of the commodity economy among all his fellows. In 1975, his family of seven members planted two *fen*[3] of ginger around his house, one *fen* of pepper and onion and 10 persimmon trees, and fed two pigs. This allowed them to obtain approximately 800–900 yuan annually, so they no longer needed to beg for food like other villagers. However, these kind of hard workers were then being criticized for "taking the capitalist road" and "being upstarts". Because of this, Yan Junchang was criticized three or four times by his brigade and commune, under the guise of "the rich need to be criticized, and the poor are proud of being poor". In fact, he was at best such an "upstart" who only wanted to avoid being a beggar.

In early 1978, the "system of production contract to groups" was introduced on an experimental basis in Fengyang County, and also in Anhui Province. Xiaogang villagers with full interests divided 20 households into four groups. Conflicts arose in groups after just a short period of time. One night, the village held a meeting. Some suggested that the system of production contract to groups was not proper, and that production and farming work should be contracted to a single family. They eventually came to three decisions: (1) the first batch of grain harvested in summer and fall would be handed over to the country and the farm collective, respectively, as public grain and shared reserves; (2) farming work would ostensibly be contracted to a group, but actually to a household; and (3) if the captain of the brigade were sent to prison due to the breach of law, then his family's farming work would be shouldered by the whole villagers, and his children raised by the villagers up to the age of 18. The heads of 18 households present swore to this and pressed their red fingerprints onto an agreement. For the ordinary people, it was clear enough: life or death is determined by fate, and there is no turning back.[4]

This "household responsibility system" sent shockwaves through the nation at that time. The Xiaogang villagers' 18 red fingerprints marked the start of a magnificent rural reform in China.

By 1979, when the "household responsibility system" had been implemented for two years, the per capita income of Xiaogang villagers had soared from 22 yuan to 400 yuan, and the grain output of the whole brigade had reached 132,000 *jin*,[5] which was equivalent to the sum of the 1966–1970 five-year grain output. The villagers, who had not submitted any grain to the state since 1956 – 23 years earlier – and had needed a grain subsidy from the government every year, were suddenly able to hand 25,000 *jin* of grain to the state.

Household responsibility system

At the birth of the "household responsibility system", some people censured the system for its violation of the "three levels and term-based" principle, and criticized it as being typical capitalism; others blamed it for its trait of opportunism. On May 31, 1980, Deng Xiaoping delivered an important speech about rural issues with other central leaders:[6]

> After the reform of rural economy, a number of suitable regions have carried the policy of contracting output quotas to households. They have achieved good effects and rapid change … in the Fengyang County mentioned in the song of Fengyang Flower Drum,[7] the overwhelming majority of farmers have implemented the household responsibility system, and it took just one year for the county to be out of poverty. Some comrades are concerned whether or not this practice will adversely affect the group, but I believe such worries are unnecessary.

Deng Xiaoping's speech played an important role in breaking rigid concepts, eliminating fear, and promoting and developing the household responsibility system marked by contracting farming work to households. In September 1980, the CPC Central Committee Document No. 75 initially expressed limited support for contracting farming work to households. In January 1982, the National Rural

Working Conference, led by the CPC Central Committee, officially affirmed the legitimacy of "contracting output quotas and farming work to households". In January 1983, a *Notice on the Current Rural Economic Policy*, issued by the CPC Central Committee, gave a high appraisal of it.

It needs to be noted that in the early years of implementation of the household responsibility system with "contracting output quotas and farming work to households" as the core, the contracting term was generally three years. While this did, to some extent, have a positive effect on agricultural production, the short term of land management adversely affected the enthusiasm of farmers who wanted to invest in the long term. Thus, in January 1984, the *Notice on Rural Work in 1984* from the CPC Central Committee decided that the land contract term should be extended from the original three years to 15 years. In 1993, the contract term was extended further, to 30 years.

The Property Law, passed in 2007, made some further stipulations regarding stabilizing the rural land contracting system. It pointed out that after the contracting term has expired, farmers can continue with the contract, which legally grants farmers rights for long-term and secured land use.

The village committee – the grassroots organization in rural China

On June 29, 1998, just after President Bill Clinton had visited the election of a village committee by farmers from Shanxi Province in China, the Village Committee Organization Law of People's Republic of China (Draft) was released publicly. Before the release of this draft law, most villages in China had carried out the direct election of village committees. On July 6, 1997, CNN broadcast to the world a report on China that gave a detailed description of the whole election process in two villages in Fujian Province. In the view of a CNN reporter, "China has such a democracy as many Western countries simply cannot imagine".

The village committee system in China came from the Constitution of China, promulgated in 1982, and then was specifically established and perfected by the Village Committee Organization Law (Trial), in 1987, and the Village Committee Organization Law (Revised Draft), in 1998. The main functions of the village committee system can be divided into three categories: autonomy, assistance in administration, and management of collective assets.

The autonomy function includes two parts: one is to create a system of villagers' autonomy – that is, establishing the village committee and setting its rules of conduct by a democratic electoral process; the other is the realization of the villagers' self-management, self-education, and self-service. Specific contents include handling the village's public affairs, providing public goods services, mediating civil disputes, reflecting villagers' opinions to township-level governments, and managing the village's collective properties. The township-level government is the most basic government organization in rural China. The function of assistance in administration includes helping in the township government's work, such as the collection of agricultural taxes, payment of government subsidies, and maintenance of the village's social law and order. The function of managing collective assets mainly involves contracting to the villagers for the use of collective land, and conducting business activities such as investment, leasing, joint venture, and partnership with regard to the village's collective land and other assets.

3.3 Urban economic reform

Compared with rural economic reform, the economic reform in urban areas, especially in state-owned enterprises, was a more complex and difficult process. In the traditional economic system, the rural economy was regarded as the economy on an institutional edge. There was no mandatory national planning for rural areas, and thus no assessment of plan implementation.[8] Therefore, rural economic reform did not deal with the core of China's traditional economic system. The major part of the traditional Chinese economy was in urban areas, where state-owned enterprises were the core. Prior to discussing the reform of state-owned enterprises, however, we will first explore the liberalization of the economy outside the government system.

Smash McDonald's?

The following dialogue is said to be true, a tale that is of great significance.[9]

> On a summer day in 1998, a newspaper reporter and a fruit hawker had a chat on Xiao Zhuang Road in Chaoyang District of Beijing.
>
> Pointing at a nearby McDonald's fast food restaurant, the hawker said bitterly: "McDonald's should be smashed!"
>
> The reporter asked in surprise: "Why?"
>
> HAWKER: "You see Americans are too clever. They come to China to earn money from the Chinese, and put the Chinese people's money into their pockets. Chinese people are so stupid!"
>
> REPORTER: "To be fair, Americans and Chinese are both making money from opening fast food restaurants. Americans invested to build a house and renovated it, and China provided a piece of land. Both sides can make money by dividing up profits. Since Americans have invested, of course, they are allowed to make money. If you pay money to build a restaurant or a beauty shop, will you have nothing in return?"
>
> HAWKER LAUGHED: "Of course not!"
>
> REPORTER: "Besides, this fast food restaurant hires over 20 girls and boys, and they earn more than 1,000 yuan each month. If it was smashed, would you offer them jobs?"
>
> HAWKER: "Where can I find a job for them? Even I am still out of work after being laid off. If there is a job available, will I be peddling the peach on the street?"
>
> REPORTER: "Yes, since there are so many laid-off workers right now, why do you have to smash McDonald's? When I ate at the restaurant just now, I saw two parents took their children for a job there, who are graduates from secondary school."

At this time, bystanders gathered a lot, all of whom were listening with relish.

REPORTER: "This McDonald's is very clean inside, and there is also air conditioning that makes people feel pretty cool so that it also offers a hangout for children and adults. You see it's full of people day and night. Haven't you taken your kids there?"

HAWKER NODDED: "For several times. My kids are always worrying me to take them there!"

REPORTER: "Also, the McDonald's on this street promotes the environment improvement. Surrounding little restaurants are renovated, and also keep their chair and table cleaner…"

ONLOOKERS LAUGHED: "If what you prepare is not sanitary, no one will eat at your restaurant."

REPORTER: "How could you say that the introduction of McDonald's shows we Chinese people silly? This is where we are smart."

Hawker was confused.

REPORTER: "In the late 1970s, China had no star hotels, and we even did not know what a star hotel was like. In the early 1980s, we borrowed money and built the Great Wall Sheraton Hotel and the Kunlun Hotel, and that money was borrowed from Americans. Each hotel cost about 1 billion dollars to be built. Well, it was a deal that we needed to pay off the debt within more than 10 years. Now 10 years later, the debt was paid off. These two hotels belong to us right now. This is called 'borrowing chickens to lay eggs'. Moreover, ever since the setup of the Great Wall Sheraton Hotel, we have trained a large number of talented people who can manage modern hotels. Now there are countless star hotels all over the country, most of which are managed by Chinese people themselves. Can you understand why we Chinese people are smart now? "

Hawker nodded.

REPORTER: "The food Chinese people cook is the best. Chinese people have opened countless Chinese restaurants in the United States, the number of which is many times more than that of McDonald opened in China."

People around nodded.

REPORTER: "If Americans are jealous of Chinese restaurants earning money, will they smash Chinese restaurants in the US, won't they?"

Bystanders laughed a lot. Resentment dissolved in laughter.

Opening the economy outside the traditional system

Over the past 30 years, China has been launching reform and opening up. This means that economic system reform and opening up are closely linked. While the "opening up" here is usually understood as "opening the door of China to the outside world", it also can be interpreted as "opening up the economy outside the traditional system". Here, the economy outside the traditional system contains not only foreign-funded enterprises, but also domestic private enterprises.

Since the reform and opening up, China's private enterprises and foreign-, Hong Kong-, Macao- and Taiwan-funded enterprises have witnessed extremely vigorous development. Their position in the Chinese economy has shifted from being an initial "supplement" to the socialist economy up being an "important component". Currently, they have actually become the major part of the Chinese economy (see the next section for relevant data). In this sense, the non-state-owned economy that is formally not within the system has now been fully integrated into the current system of the Chinese economy.

Opening up the economy outside the traditional system has contributed to the Chinese economy at least in the following ways. First, because China is a developing country, there exists a huge amount of labor that has not previously been used. The economy outside the traditional system has mobilized a large amount of Chinese surplus labor through investing in manufactories and service industries. This has contributed not only to GDP growth but also to employment, thus enriching people's livelihood.

Second, in comparison with the state-owned economy, the economy outside the traditional system provides stronger economic incentives. Their vitality puts pressure on the state-owned economy within the system. This pressure and the role model promote the further reform of state-owned enterprises. It can be said that if there were no economy outside the traditional system, the state-owned enterprise reform in China would not have progressed as it has. As shown previously, it is the growing economy outside the traditional system and the differences in efficiency that have promoted continuous reform within the traditional system, eventually materializing in the merger of the two systems.

Third, the development of the economy outside the traditional system has gradually weakened the traditional planning mechanisms, and driven the transition from a planned economy to a market economy. As noted in the first chapter, the economic system has two main aspects (i.e., operating mechanism and enterprise system) that need to be suitable to each other. Because of its ownership property, the state cannot demand that the economy outside the traditional system follows the central planning. Therefore, along with the development of the economy outside the traditional system, the planning, which acts as an allocation mechanism of economic resource, has gradually been weakened and eventually lost its role in resource allocation.

Fourth, the economy outside the traditional system – especially foreign enterprises – has advanced technology and management experience. When they invest in China, many foreign enterprises introduce advanced technology and at the same time also train the relevant employees, technical staff and managers in China. All these can help improving the economy in terms of technologies and individual skills.

Reform of state-owned enterprises

Rural economic reform and opening up the economy outside the traditional system formed the external environment for the economy within the traditional system (state-owned enterprises). It is this external environment that continuously deepens the reform in state-owned enterprise. There are four stages in the process of state-owned enterprise reform.[10]

The first stage (1978–1984): expansion of autonomy

The reform in this stage was mainly to mobilize firms' production enthusiasm through the expansion of enterprise autonomy and profit retention, among other measures. In this stage, China's planning mechanism still existed and continued to affect the allocation of social resources. This means that enterprises were still required to complete the national plan. Of course, the state encouraged the firms' production activities beyond what had been planned while the profits from these additional activities could be retained in proportion by the enterprises.

It needs to be stated that although there were as many as 12 operation rights of enterprises' autonomy, only about four rights were generally implemented.[11] Therefore, despite some achievements, there was still not too much improvement from the traditional system.

The second stage (1985–1993): separation of the operation right from ownership

This phase saw the reforms that separated the management and operation right of state-owned enterprises from the right of ownership. Such a separation was implemented mainly by the contract responsibility system, among others. The contract responsibility system has the following basic features: (1) set a target production (quantity of output, profit, etc.) in the contract; (2) ensure the delivery of the target to the state; (3) maintain the surplus beyond the target. The contracting system was implemented for two terms, each of three years: one was from the late 1987 till the end of 1990; the other was from early 1991 till late 1993.

Clearly, the contract responsibility system can be seen as following the household responsibility system in the rural area. In comparison with the expansion of enterprise autonomy, the separation of two rights – the operation right and the ownership right – marked a major leap forward of state-owned enterprise reform: it meant that state-owned enterprises were no longer run by the state. But the separation of the two rights only recognized the right to operate, and not the property right the enterprises should have as legal entities. Because of this, many problems from the old system were still not resolved. In practice, such a system generated, to a large extent, a variety of short-term behaviors of enterprises: in order to pursue immediate profits within the contract period, enterprises fought for equipment and assets, and recklessly granted bonuses.

The third stage (1994–1999): establishment of a modern enterprise system

The Company Law of the People's Republic of China, adopted in 1994, marked the state-owned enterprise reform entering a new stage of establishing a modern enterprise system with clear property rights. According to the company law, state-owned enterprises would be given not only the right not to operate but also the right to own property legally. The shareholding system, which had been considered highly capitalistic, was now seen as a model modern enterprise system to be popularized in China.

However, because the majority of shares (usually more than 50 percent) were still held by the government, even such a modern enterprise system still did not really resolve the problems of the traditional system, such as the dual functions of the government and enterprises, and the lack of an incentive mechanism, among others. That also meant that, in the competition with the economy outside the government system, state-owned joint-stock companies would obviously be at a disadvantage while at this time the economy outside the traditional system was witnessing vigorous development in China.

The fourth stage (1999–now): reconfiguration of the state-owned economy

Following the 15th National Communist Party Congress, new ideas about state-owned enterprise reform emerged. These innovative ideas were embodied in restructuring the state-owned economy in its strategic distribution. This strategy had the core of the so-called "managing the large well while easing the small ones". This also meant that the state-owned economy would gradually withdraw from competitive industries, while strengthening its status in industries related to national security and the economic lifeline.

The State-owned Assets Supervision and Administration Commission (SASAC), established in 2003, directly supervised 196 central enterprises on the behalf of investors of state-owned assets. The establishment of the SASAC has made the state-owned economy show such features as reflecting the investor's strategic plan while its operation is purely market-oriented. After nearly 30 years of exploration and practice, an efficient method of economic reform has finally been found for state-owned enterprises.

3.4 "Transitioning", "developing", and "large" – the environment of contemporary Chinese economy

We pointed out in the first chapter that economics is the study of the decision process of economic variables in certain economic environments. At the same time, we probed two major elements of the economic environment (i.e., the economic system and economic resources). After the earlier discussions about the economic reform in China, we can now return to our major concern: What is the environment of the contemporary Chinese economy? We believe that China's current economic environment can be summarized as "transitioning", "developing" and "large".

A market economy in transition

After 30 years of reform and opening up, the Chinese economy can basically be seen as a market economy, despite the fact that the status of a "market economy" in China has not been widely recognized by the international community.

First, China has essentially removed mandatory planning. The state has even removed the planning department – that is, the State Planning Commission – which has now been replaced by the current National Development and Reform Commission (NDRC).

Second, the state-owned economy, which is supposed to be the basis of planned economy, has reduced its proportion of the national economy. Tables 3.1–3.3 show the respective shares of the economy, with different types of ownership, in GDP, employment and investment.

It can be seen that in all three tables, the proportion of state-owned enterprises is decreasing year by year, apart from the investment in 2009.[12] In 2009, the proportion in industrial output was only about 8.33 percent, in employment was about 20.63 percent while in investment was about 31.03 percent. As noted earlier, the reconfiguration of the state-owned economy has made state-owned enterprises basically out of competitive industries, and has concentrated on those industries that are natural monopolies and related to national security and the economic lifeline. Table 3.4 presents those industries that are strictly controlled by the state.[13]

Third, commodity prices in China have basically been liberalized and determined by the market. Table 3.5 demonstrates such a situation. It can be seen that the prices for over 96 percent (calculated according to the proportion of transactions) of commodities have been determined by market. In terms of the material used for production, this percentage has reached 87.3 percent.

However, we have to admit that the degree of market orientation in China is still lower than that in developed economies: the state-owned economy still makes up a large proportion of the national economy; the shadow of the traditional planned economy can still be found in some industries (such as banking industries);[14] at the same time, the prices for some commodities (such as oil, etc.) are still not fully liberalized and are controlled by the state. All of this means that the market economy in China, unlike that of developed economies, is still in transition.

A developing economy

China is no doubt still a developing (or undeveloped) country. According to World Bank data (see Table 3.6), China's per capita income in 2010 was 4,260 US dollars, thus categorizing it as one of the middle income countries. If calculated by purchasing power parity, China's per capita income in 2010 was 7,570 US dollars. In both cases, these were lower than the world average. From the table we can also see that China's per capita income was less than 10 percent of that in the United States, and it was only 16 percent if calculated by purchasing power parity.

It needs to be stated that the characteristics of China as a developing country are also represented in such differences from developed countries as its industrial structure, relatively scarce capital and large surplus of labor, low level of human capital and technology, etc. Here, we only compare the industrial structure (see Table 3.7).

Table 3.1 Industrial output grouped by ownership (unit: 100 million yuan)

Years	2000	2002	2004	2006	2007	2009
National total	85,674	110,776	222,316	316,589	405,177	548,311
State-owned enterprises	20,156 (23.53)	17,271 (15.59)	23,519 (10.58)	30,728 (9.71)	36,387 (8.9)	45,648 (8.33)
Collective-owned enterprises	11,908 (13.90)	9619 (8.68)	9,819 (4.42)	9,175 (2.90)	10,170 (2.51)	9,587 (1.75)
Cooperative enterprises	2,897 (3.38)	3203 (2.89)	3,397 (1.53)	3,079 (0.97)	3,561 (0.88)	3,608 (0.66)
Joint-owned enterprises	901 (1.05)	942 (0.85)	1,033 (0.46)	1,306 (0.41)	1,583 (0.39)	1,296 (0.24)
Limited liability corporations	10,926 (12.75)	20,070 (18.12)	44,043 (19.81)	70,814 (22.37)	90,336 (22.30)	121,078 (22.08)
Share-holding corporations Ltd.	10,090 (11.78)	14,119 (12.75)	23,121 (10.40)	33,597 (10.61)	40,159 (9.91)	50,209 (9.16)
Private enterprises	5,220 (6.09)	12,951 (11.69)	49,705 (22.36)	67,240 (21.24)	94,023 (23.21)	162,026 (29.55)
Other domestic-funded enterprises	110 (0.13)	143 (0.13)	541 (0.24)	574 (0.18)	1,328 (0.33)	2,173 (0.40)
Enterprises with investment from Hong Kong, Macao and Taiwan	10,574 (12.34)	13,669 (12.34)	24,386 (10.97)	33,760 (10.66)	42,418 (10.47)	52,221 (9.52)
Foreign funded enterprises	12,890 (15.05)	18,790 (16.96)	42,751 (19.23)	66,317 (20.95)	85,211 (21.03)	100,466 (18.32)

Data from the National Bureau of Statistics of China (2007, 2010). Figures in brackets refer to the related percentage.

Table 3.2 Urban employment grouped by ownership (unit: 10,000 persons)

Year	2001	2003	2004	2006	2007	2009
Total employment	73,025	74,432	75,200	76,400	76,990	77,995
Subtotal employment in urban	23,940	25,639	26,476	28,310	29,350	31,120
State-owned enterprises	7,640 (31.91)	6,876 (26.82)	6,710 (25.34)	6,430 (22.71)	6,424 (21.89)	6,420 (20.63)
Collective-owned enterprises	1,291 (5.39)	1,000 (3.90)	897 (3.39)	764 (2.70)	718 (2.45)	618 (1.99)
Cooperative enterprises	153 (0.64)	173 (0.68)	192 (0.73)	178 (0.63)	170 (0.58)	160 (0.51)
Joint-owned enterprises	45 (0.19)	44 (0.17)	44 (0.17)	45 (0.16)	43 (0.15)	37 (0.12)
Limited liability corporations	841 (3.51)	1,261 (4.92)	1,436 (5.42)	1,920 (6.78)	2,075 (7.07)	2,433 (7.82)
Share-holding corporations, Ltd.	483 (2.02)	592 (2.31)	625 (2.36)	741 (2.62)	788 (2.68)	956 (3.07)
Private enterprises	1,527 (6.38)	2,545 (9.93)	2,994 (11.31)	3,954 (13.97)	4,581 (15.61)	5,544 (17.81)
Enterprises with investment from Hong Kong, Macao and Taiwan	326 (1.36)	409 (1.60)	470 (1.77)	611 (2.16)	680 (2.32)	721 (2.32)
Foreign funded enterprises	345 (1.44)	454 (1.77)	563 (2.13)	796 (2.81)	903 (3.08)	978 (3.14)
Self-employment economy	2,131 (8.90)	2,377 (9.27)	2,521 (9.52)	3,012 (10.64)	3,310 (11.28)	4,245 (13.64)

Data from the National Bureau of Statistics of China (2007, 2010). Figures in brackets refer to the related percentage.

Table 3.3 Investment in fixed assets grouped by ownership (unit: 100 million yuan)

Years	2000	2001	2003	2005	2007	2009
Total investment in fixed assets	32,918	37,213	55,567	88,774	137,324	224,599
State-owned enterprises	16,504 (50.14)	17,607 (47.31)	21,661 (38.98)	29,667 (33.42)	38,706 (28.19)	69,692 (31.03)
Collective-owned enterprises	4,801 (14.59)	5,279 (14.18)	8,009 (14.41)	11,970 (13.48)	4,637 (3.38)	8,483 (3.78)
Private enterprises	4,709 (14.31)	5,430 (14.59)	7,720 (13.89)	13,891 (15.65)	33,114 (24.11)	55,795 (24.84)
Joint-owned enterprises	95 (0.00)	95 (0.25)	188 (0.34)	230 (0.26)	608 (0.44)	666 (0.30)
Share-holding corporations	4,062 (12.34)	5,663 (15.22)	12,734 (22.92)	23,536 (26.51)	44,039 (32.07)	68,843 (30.65)
Foreign funded enterprises	1,313 (3.99)	1,415 (3.80)	2,534 (4.56)	4,657 (5.25)	7,355 (5.36)	8,396 (3.74)
Enterprises with investment from Hong Kong, Macao and Taiwan	1,293 (3.93)	1,583 (4.25)	2,375 (4.27)	3,767 (4.24)	5,999 (4.37)	7,092 (3.16)
Others	140 (0.42)	142 (0.38)	346 (0.62)	1,056 (1.19)	2,866 (2.09)	5,631 (2.51)

Data from the National Bureau of Statistics of China (2007, 2010). Figures in brackets refer to the related percentage.

Table 3.4 Percentage of state-owned enterprises in industries with a high level of state control

	Value added		Fixed assets	Employed personnel	Company numbers
	1998	2003	2003		
Manufacture of tobacco	97.4	98.6	98.9	93.9	81.9
Extraction of petroleum and natural gas	99.9	93.8	97.7	99.1	71.8
Production and supply of water	96.0	86.7	88.9	94.2	89.0
Production and supply of electric power	86.9	83.4	87.9	89.1	77.5
Mining of coal	84.6	81.4	92.2	82.4	32.3
Processing and supply of natural gas	92.7	77.5	88.6	89.7	65.7
Processing and supply of petroleum	83.8	77.3	85.6	61.8	17.4
Smelting and pressing of ferrous metals	78.1	63.6	77.1	63.2	11.1
Manufacture of transportation equipment	69.5	63.1	71.3	54.8	22.2
Smelting and pressing of Non-ferrous metals	57.2	46.8	64.8	55.6	14.3

From OECD (2006).

Table 3.5 Transaction proportion according to pricing method

	Percentage of total trading volume					
	1978	*1985*	*1991*	*1995*	*1999*	*2003*
Materials for production						
Market pricing	0	13	46	78	86	87.3
Price guided by state	0	23	18	6	4	2.7
State pricing	100	64	36	16	10	10.0
Retail goods						
Market pricing	3	69	69	89	95	96.1
Price guided by state	0	10	10	2	1	1.3
State pricing	97	21	21	9	4	2.6
Aggregate products						
Market pricing	6	40	58	79	83	96.5
Pricing guided by state	2	23	20	4	7	1.6
State pricing	93	37	22	17	9	1.9

Source: From OECD (2006).

Table 3.6 Comparison of per capita income in China and other economies in 2010

Countries and regions	Per capita income	Per capita income (PPP)
China	4,260	7,570
United States	47,140	47,020
Japan	42,150	34,790
Germany	43,330	38,170
UK	38,540	36,580
Korea	19,890	29,010
World average	9,097	11,058
Low-income countries and regions	510	1,246
Middle-income countries and regions	3,764	6,780
Lower-middle-income countries and regions	1,658	3,701
Upper-middle-income countries and regions	5,884	9,904
Middle-low-income countries and regions	3,304	5,991
High-income countries and regions	38,658	37,183
European Monetary Union	38,580	34,177

Data from the World Bank database: http://siteresources.worldbank.org/DATASTATISTICS/Resources/GNPC.pdf.

As shown in Table 3.7, in 2006 the employment percentage of primary industry in developed countries was below 5 percent. In the US and the UK, it was only about 1.5 percent and 1.3 percent respectively. The percentage in China was 42.6 percent – pretty much the same as in Thailand (42.1 percent). At the same time, the employment percentage of tertiary industry in developed countries was usually above 65 percent. In the US and the UK, these were 77.7

Table 3.7 Percentage employed, grouped into three types of industry

Country or area	Primary industry		Secondary industry		Tertiary industry	
	2000	2006	2000	2006	2000	2006
China	46.3	42.6	17.3	25.2	12.7	32.2
Israel	2.2	1.8	24.0	21.5	73.0	75.8
Japan	5.1	4.3	31.2	28.0	63.1	66.6
Korea, Rep.	10.6	7.7	28.1	26.3	61.2	65.9
Malaysia	18.4	14.6	32.2	30.3	49.5	55.1
Philippines	37.4	36.6	16.0	14.9	46.5	48.5
Thailand	48.5	42.1	17.9	20.6	33.5	37.0
Egypt	29.6	31.2	21.3	22.0	49.1	46.6
South Africa	15.6	8.5	24.2	25.6	59.4	65.6
Canada	3.3	2.6	22.5	22.0	74.1	75.3
Mexico	17.3	14.1	27.0	27.4	55.3	57.8
United States	2.6	1.5	23.2	20.8	74.3	77.7
Argentina	0.7	0.8	22.7	23.7	76.2	75.2
Brazil	18.5	19.3	21.2	21.4	59.1	59.1
Czech Republic	5.2	3.8	39.9	40.1	54.8	56.1
Germany	2.6	2.3	33.7	29.8	63.6	67.8
Italy	5.4	4.3	32.4	30.5	62.1	65.2
Poland	18.8	15.8	30.8	30.0	50.4	54.2
Russian Federation	14.5	10.0	28.4	29.3	57.1	60.7
Spain	6.7	4.8	31.2	29.7	62.2	65.5
Turkey	36.0	27.3	24.0	25.4	40.0	47.3
Ukraine	23.4	17.6	20.8	24.2	13.3	58.2
United Kingdom	1.5	1.3	25.2	22.0	73.0	76.4
Australia	5.0	3.5	21.8	21.2	73.3	75.0
New Zealand	8.7	7.1	23.2	22.3	67.6	70.1

Data from National Bureau of Statistics of China (2009).

percent and 76.4 percent, respectively. These high percentages of tertiary industry in developed countries are supported by modern service industries with high-tech content (such as the banking industry, etc.). Yet the percentage in China was only 32.2 percent, which was once again pretty much the same as that of developing countries like Thailand (37.0 percent).

A large economy

While China is still a developing economy, there is no doubt that it is a large economy. This status is clearly determined by its population. China has 9.6 million square kilometers of territory with a population of 1.3 billion, accounting for one-fifth of the world's total population. It is China's demographic advantage that gives the comprehensive national strength of China a high ranking in the world. In 2006, China's GDP was ranked fourth in the world. China was ranked third in import and export trades, second in power generation, and first in steel, coal, cement, grains and fruits.

The large economy of China has significant dual effects. On the one hand, a large economy has obvious advantages in attracting foreign direct investment because of the potential market. At present, China has already attracted more foreign investment than any other country. Still, with the rapid development and rise of its economy, China's influence on the world economy is gradually growing while at the same time the pressure on China continues to increase too. At this time, China's advantages as a large economy are likely to be perceived as "the threat from China", and opinions such as "China is exporting deflation to the world" are cropping up continuously. Related issues will be explored in the later chapters of this book.

Discussion and questions

1   What are the three main features of economic reform in China? Explain them.
2   What is the household responsibility system? Currently, how long is the land contracting period in rural China? What happens when the land contract period expires?
3   What functions does a village committee have? How is a village committee generated?
4   What do you understand by the "reform" and "opening up"? How are they linked?
5   Provide four major economic impacts of "opening up" in the past 30 years on the Chinese economy?
6   Which four stages have the state-owned enterprise reform in China gone through? What are their respective contents?
7   Explain three basic environment features of the contemporary Chinese economy.

Part II
Reading the brilliance

4 The data from China

What do they tell us?

In the previous chapters, we have given a preliminary presentation on the current economic environment in China. We have seen that the economic reforms in China have made the Chinese economy shift from the traditional planned economy to an economy with the market as its primary mechanism of resource allocation. In terms of ownership, a variety of forms coexists in China. In terms of economic development level, China remains as a developing country. In official documents, the contemporary Chinese economy is defined as a socialist market economy with Chinese characteristics.

It should be noted that the status of market economy in China has not been widely recognized in the international community.[1] This throws many obstacles in the way of China's full integration into the international community. An interesting question, then, is how is the economic operation of the contemporary Chinese economy different from a typical market economy as in developed countries? In other words, does the economic operation of the Chinese economy obey the rules and features of a typical market economy as in Western countries? In this chapter, we examine this problem from the perspective of macroeconomic data.

4.1 Data from the developed market economy

Three types of macroeconomic problems are often of concern in economics: the first is the output, represented by GDP or the growth rate of GDP; the second is the price, represented by inflation rate; and the third is employment, often represented by unemployment rate. In a typical market economy, how do these variables change? How do they interrelate with each other? Are there rules that can be found? If the empirical data tell us that these rules do exist, then an economic theory that is appropriate to the current economic environment is bound to be able to explain this phenomenon. In this section, we shall first reveal some rules and features related to the interaction of these macroeconomic data in developed countries. This will offer a basis for the comparison with current Chinese economy in the next section.

Economic growth in the business cycle

In Figure 4.1, we give the real GDP growth rate in the United States from 1961 to 2003. We can identify at least two phenomena from the figure. First, although

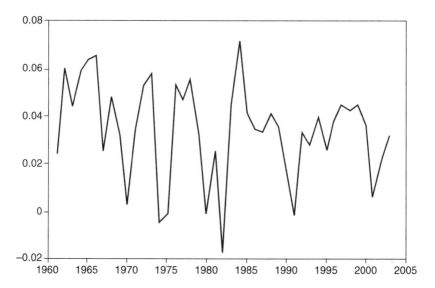

Figure 4.1 Real GDP growth rates in the United States, 1961–2003. Data from OECD (2004).

GDP fell at times, generally speaking the US economy was constantly growing (the average growth rate of GDP was 3.3 percent). Second, economic growth reflected a fluctuation in cycles. This cyclical fluctuation is called the "business cycle". Frequently a business cycle goes through a continuous process from recovery to prosperity, to recession and, last, to crisis. The business cycle phenomenon typical of the modern market economy is an important subject for economic study.

Unemployment in the business cycle: Okun's Law

Next, we will examine the fluctuations of unemployment in the business cycle. Figure 4.2 shows the relationship between unemployment and growth rate in the United States from 1961 to 2003. We find there is a negative correlation between the two – that is, higher GDP growth means a fall in unemployment. If N_t denotes the unemployment rate in period t, and g_t the real growth rate of GDP in that period, we find the following relationship from a simple regression:

$$N_t - N_{t-1} = -0.5(g_t - 2.25)$$

This equation shows that for a decline in unemployment to occur, economic growth must be higher than 2.25 percent.

The relationship between growth rate and unemployment rate is often called "Okun's Law", named after Arthur Okun, the economist who, in 1962, was the first to find this relationship. Although it might be an exaggeration to call such a

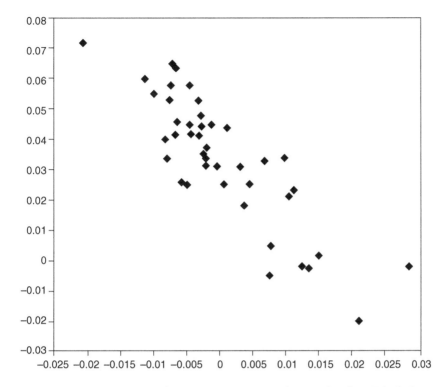

Figure 4.2 Growth rates and unemployment rate changes in the United States, 1961–2003. Data from OECD (2004).

relationship a "law", it does provide guidance for macroeconomic policies to reduce unemployment. At the same time, economic theory also needs to explain the relation.

Inflation rate in business cycle: Phillips curve

Is there a stable relationship between inflation and unemployment? What can empirical data tell us? Figure 4.3 presents the relationship between inflation rate and unemployment rate in the United States between 1961 and 2003. The figure seems to tell us that there is no apparent stable relationship between them.

However, careful examination of the scatters in Figure 4.3 seems to reveal three vague downward curves nearly parallel to each other. To explore this, we can organize the observed sample into three groups. Table 4.1 lists the three groups of sample intervals we want to examine. Figures 4.4, 4.5 and 4.6 show the relationship between inflation rate and unemployment rate in each of the three samples.

It is easy to find that, among the regrouped three samples, there is an obvious correlation between inflation rate and unemployment rate: when inflation rate

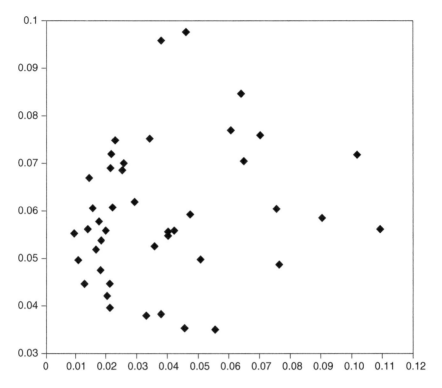

Figure 4.3 Inflation rates and unemployment rates in the United States, 1961–2003. Data from OECD (2004).

Table 4.1 Three samples of the relationship between inflation rate and unemployment rate

	Years	
Sample 1	1961–1969	1994–2003
Sample 2	1970–1973	1984–1993
Sample 3	1974–1983	

rises, unemployment rate falls, and vice versa. This analysis allows us to see that, prior to 1970, there was an inverse relationship between inflation and unemployment (see Figure 4.4). In fact, if we extend the sample interval from 1960 to the early 1950s, this inverse relationship still exists.[2] Such a relationship between inflation and unemployment is known as the "Phillips curve", which is named after the British economist A.W. Phillips, who discovered the inverse relationship. The discovery of this stable relationship was once regarded as a major victory of Keynesian economics, because not only can it be interpreted by

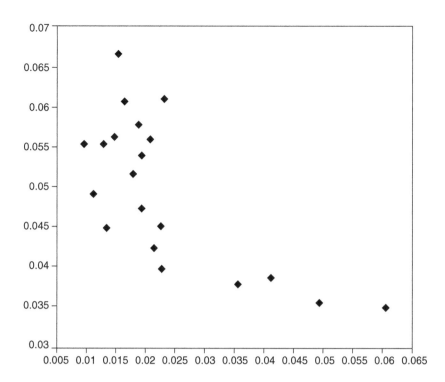

Figure 4.4 Inflation rates and unemployment rates in the United States: sample 1.

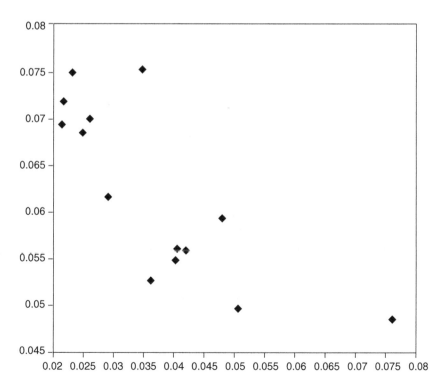

Figure 4.5 Inflation rates and unemployment rates in the United States: sample 2.

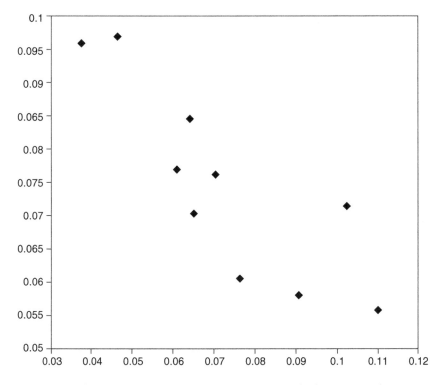

Figure 4.6 Inflation rates and unemployment rates in the United States: sample 3.

Keynesian economics, but it also paves the way for implementing Keynesian demand management policies.

Yet the Phillips curve seems to gradually move outwards after the 1970s. This movement reached its extreme in 1973. Actually, during the post-1973 decade, Western developed countries generally experienced so-called "stagflation" – that is, a state in which high unemployment and high inflation coexist. Despite the inverse relationship between inflation and unemployment still existing during this period (see Figure 4.6), relative to the situation before the 1970s both the unemployment rate and the inflation rate were higher. The emergence of stagflation made economists doubtful about the reality of the Phillips curve. This also influenced the dominating position of Keynesian economics in academics: traditional Keynesian theory could neither explain stagflation, nor identify an appropriate macroeconomic policy to deal with the stagflation. The occurrence of stagflation also led to the rise of modern neoclassical macroeconomics.[3]

After 1984, the Phillips curve shifts downwards. During the following decade, the substitution between unemployment and inflation stayed stable at the level of 1970–1973 (see Figure 4.5). By 1994, the Phillips curve had fallen to the level before the 1970s (see Figure 4.4). At this point, what was revealed was the coexistence of the low inflation rate and low unemployment rate.

We thus find that the inverse relationship between the inflation rate and the unemployment rate does exist, although this relationship is not always stable, indicating that the Phillips curve can be shifted.

4.2 Data from contemporary Chinese economy

The variety of rules related to macroeconomic variables we have discussed previously stem from the empirics of the market economy in Western developed countries. The contemporary Chinese economy is also assumed to be a market economy, though with some special characteristics. Is, then, the economic operation in contemporary Chinese economy in accordance with the rules as appearing in a typical market economy?

Economic growth in China

Regarding contemporary Chinese economy, we start from the late 1970s. Prior to this, economic reform had not begun. It was economic reform that made the Chinese economy different from the traditional planned economy. Figure 4.7 reveals the growth rate of the Chinese economy since 1979.

As shown in the figure, there have been periodical fluctuations in the growth rate of GDP in the Chinese economy, just as in the United States and other countries. Yet the average growth rate is much larger than that of the United States and other developed countries: in the past 30 years, the average growth rate of GDP in China has been 9.69 percent, while that of the United States and other

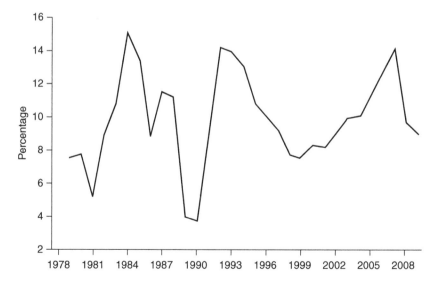

Figure 4.7 Real GDP growth rates in China, 1979–2009. Data from National Bureau of Statistics of China (2010).

Western developed countries has hovered around 2–3 percent. In fact, high economic growth has been the biggest bright spot in the Chinese economy since its reform and opening up. The interpretation of high economic growth in China will be given in the next chapter.

Okun's Law in China

Does Okun's Law hold true in China? Figure 4.8 depicts the link between the change in unemployment rate and the growth rate in China. In comparison with the US, depicted in Figure 4.2, we find that there is no clear relationship between the change in unemployment rate and the growth rate.

The Phillips curve in China

The Phillips curve does not seem to hold true in China, either. Figure 4.9 reveals the relationship between the inflation rate and the unemployment rate in China since 1979. As indicated, there is no obvious correlation between them.

Examination of our three major macroeconomic variables – growth rate, inflation rate and unemployment rate – allows us to reach the following two conclusions:

- Compared with the market economy in developed countries, the Chinese economy has significantly higher growth dynamics.

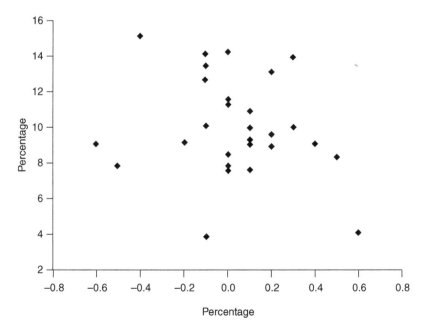

Figure 4.8 Growth rates and unemployment rate changes in China, 1979–2009. Data from National Bureau of Statistics of China (2010).

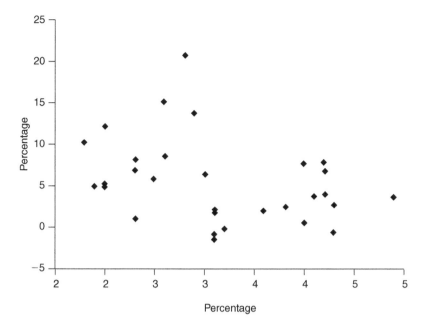

Figure 4.9 Inflation rates and unemployment rates in China, 1979–2009. Data from National Bureau of Statistics of China (2010).

- Correlations among the three major macroeconomic variables are evidently different from those of a developed market economy: neither the Phillips curve nor Okun's Law hold true in China.

So, is China a market economy?

4.3 Is China a market economy? – A perspective from macroeconomic data

We note that although the Chinese economy has maintained a significant high-growth tendency over the past three decades, it does not follow the same basic rules with regard to macroeconomic fluctuations as do developed market economies: neither the Phillips curve nor Okun's Law hold true in China. Does this difference mean that contemporary Chinese economy is not a market economy?

The lack of statistical data

As mentioned above, both the Phillips curve and Okun's Law deal with statistical data regarding the unemployment rate. Yet the unemployment rate in China cannot be computed correctly.

First, employment data in China are only collected for urban residents. Employment of the overwhelming majority of rural residents in the total population is not included in national statistics. This is largely due to the so-called *hukou* system in China. The *hukou* system is a system of household registration as requested by law in China. A household registration, or *hukou*, records a person officially as a resident of an area. The *hukou* has widely been used by local governments to regulate their residents and their welfare payments to those who have *hukou* in the local area. Such welfare may include retirement funds, unemployment funds, medical insurance and even education. An important property with regard to the *hukou* system in China is that the system distinguishes two types of *hukou*: agriculture *hukou* and non-agriculture *hukou*. A household that has agriculture *hukou* is assumed to be self-employed, since the household members are endowed with a piece of land for them to work. However, the land for each family in China is usually extremely limited. This indicates that there is an enormous surplus of labor in the rural areas of China. Economic reform and the emergence of a large amount of non-state-owned enterprises have allowed the labor surplus in rural areas to move into urban areas to search for a job. However, such migration does not allow them to change their *hukou*, and therefore not only do they not enjoy the same welfare as urban residents, but also their employment status is not considered by the local government.

Second, under the traditional system, the employment of urban residents was seen as a decision made by the government. This meant that the increase in employment was not considered to be due to the demands of production in an enterprise, but rather to distribution by the government. Although this distribution system created the false appearance of full employment for urban residents, it increased the burden on businesses and caused a lot of hidden unemployment. The economic reform of state-owned enterprises has to some extent exposed the hidden unemployment of the old system, but this exposure is a gradual process.

Third, if we want to describe the labor market status in China correctly, then the dual economy system assumed by Lewis (1954) for less developed countries might be followed. In the labor market of a less developed country, the supply of labor is infinite due to possible migration from rural areas.

All of these may explain why the Phillips curve and Okun's Law cannot hold true in China. In short, we are actually unable to obtain the correct statistics regarding unemployment rate.

The relationship between growth and inflation

If the statistics regarding unemployment rates cannot truly reflect the labor market status in China, then do we have another method to examine whether the economic operation follows the rules indicated by the Phillips curve and Okun's Law?

Note that Phillips curve indicates that there is an inverse relationship between inflation rate and unemployment, while Okun's Law expresses negative correlation between unemployment rate changes and growth rates.

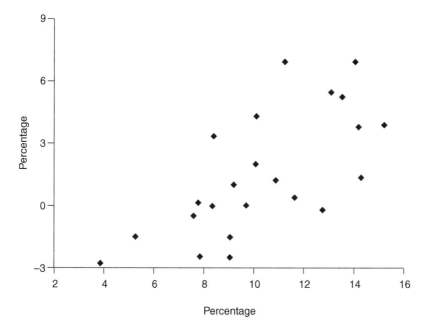

Figure 4.10 Inflation rate changes and growth rates in China, 1979–2009.

Evidently, these two rules also mean that there is a positive correlation between inflation rate changes and growth rates: a higher growth rate implies a higher inflation rate change.

Using the same data provided earlier, Figure 4.10 plots the relationship between inflation rate changes and growth rates since the economic reform. As indicated in the figure, there is a clear positive correlation between China's inflation rate changes and growth rates. We thus find that the variation of major macroeconomic variables in China follows the typical rules of a market economy.

Discussion and questions

1   If a rural citizen in China comes to a city searching for a job, but fails, then is he or she regarded as being unemployed in the statistics data from China? Why, or why not?
2   What is Okun's Law? Does it hold true in developed countries? Does it hold true in China?
3   What is the Phillips curve? Does it hold true in developed countries? Does it hold true in China?
4   What is stagflation? How does the emergence of stagflation affect the Phillips curve?

5   Given the economic relationships reflected in Okun's Law and the Phillips curve, how do you think growth and inflation interrelate with each other? Why?

6   Do you think the macroeconomic operation in contemporary Chinese economy obeys the basic business cycle rules as shown in developed market economies? Why, or why not?

5 The high growth in contemporary Chinese economy

Since the launch of economic reform and opening up, the most remarkable performance for the Chinese economy is its rapid growth. In the past 30 years, the average growth rate of GDP in China has been about 9.69 percent, while in developed countries it has been around only 2–3 percent. Figure 5.1 shows a comparison of growth rates between China and some developed countries over the same period.

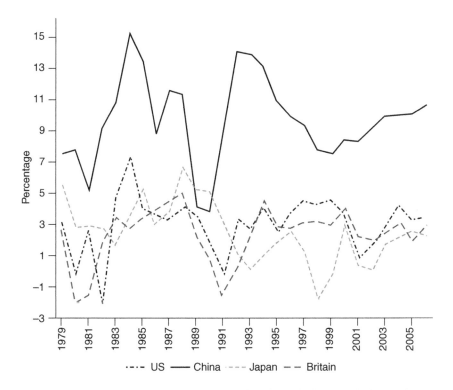

Figure 5.1 Growth rates of real GDP (%) in China, the United States, the UK and Japan, 1979–2006 (source: National Bureau of Statistics in China (2007)).

Why is the growth rate of Chinese economy so high? What is the momentum of the high growth in China? To what extent can the existing growth theory that has successfully explained the growth phenomenon in developed economies account for China's high economic growth? This chapter will discuss some of these issues.

5.1 Some facts about economic growth

A theory is supposed to be able to explain the facts in reality. Economics is no exception. What facts are there regarding economic growth? Are there differences in these facts between developed and developing economies (including China)? Can economic theories explain these differences?

Convergence hypothesis

One of the facts about economic growth is the so-called "convergence". Figure 5.2 plots the average growth rates of GDP per capita from 1950 to 1992 against the levels of GDP per capita in 1950 for OECD countries. As we can see from the figure, GDP per capita in 1950 correlates somewhat negatively with the growth rate of GDP per capita. While this negative correlation is not perfect, we may still find that the backward countries, reflected by lower per capita GDP in 1950, grew faster compared to the countries with higher per capita GDP. The higher growth in these backward countries helps them converge towards the rich countries.

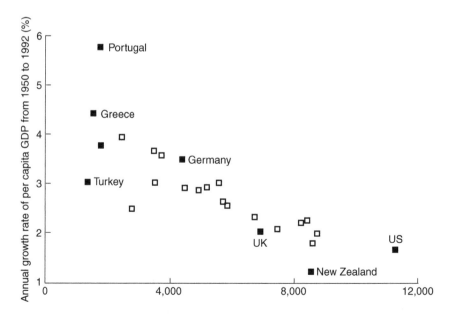

Figure 5.2 Convergence in the OECD countries (source: Blanchard (2000, Chapter 10)).

Let us now expand observations to a worldwide scope. Figure 5.3 again describes the average growth rates of per capita GDP from 1960 to 1992 against per capita GDP in 1960 – but here we have extend the sample to 97 countries, including some of the poorest countries in Asia, Africa and Latin America. The so-called convergence hypothesis does not exist in this wider range. Overall, the relatively poor countries in 1960 did not necessarily grow faster.

The preceding discussion on the convergence hypothesis indicates the following:

- First, poor countries might grow faster so that they can catch up with rich countries. This also means that the high growth of the Chinese economy over the past 30 years is not the exception.
- Second, convergence is not universal, or does not exist worldwide. This also means that a poor country who wants to be on a path of convergence must meet some criteria. Therefore, the so-called convergence should be termed conditional convergence.

Explanation of convergence

We note that when economists explain economic growth, they rely on a single, unified model. That model is called the neoclassical growth model.[1] It is no exaggeration to say that the neoclassical growth model has been regarded by economists as a "holy scripture" when dealing with the issues of economic growth and convergence.

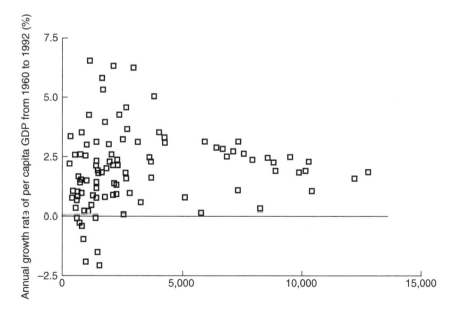

Figure 5.3 Convergence in the worldwide economy (source: Blanchard (2000, Chapter 10)).

For conditional convergence, economists have their own interpretation, relying on the neoclassical growth model.[2] First, countries with similar political and economic systems should have a similar savings rates, depreciation rates, and parameters related to technology. These are the important parameters as specified in the model. Therefore, the similarities with regard to the parameters indicate that the countries with similar political and economic systems should have a similar steady state with regard to per capita GDP so that convergence eventually occurs among them. During the convergent process – that is, the process in which the countries with lower per capita GDP move to their steady states – their growth rates are naturally higher before they reach the steady state. Second, as the OECD countries are basically identical in their political and economic systems, convergence is more likely to occur among these countries. Third, those poor countries in Africa, Asia and Latin America that do not get on to the convergence path have a steady state in per capita GDP that is lower than that of OECD countries because of their differences regarding political and economic systems, which determine the differences in savings rates, depreciation rates and technology among them.

The rise of the Chinese economy, however, seems to go against this conjecture. China's political and economic systems are different from those of the existing OECD countries in many ways. Despite the market-oriented reform of its economic system over the past 30 years, China, as a transitional economy, has still inherited the legacy of its past planned economy. There exist obvious differences between China and OECD countries in terms of political systems. The rise of the Chinese economy appears to show the world an alternative mode of economic growth, which suffices to capture the interest of scholars in growth and development.

While the reasons for convergence are not completely clear, some are still for sure. First, stability of the social environment is a prerequisite for a poor country to join the ranks of convergence and realize rapid economic growth. Some of the poorest countries in Asia, Africa and Latin America have unstable social environments, military coups and frequent social disturbances, which hamper their economic growth. Clearly, China's rapid economic growth has also benefited from its stable social and political environment since reform and opening up. This is in striking contrast with the frequent political movements, such as the Great Leap Forward and the Great Cultural Revolution, that occurred before the reform and opening up. Second, in terms of the economic system, a market economy or the transition to a market-oriented economy is another necessary condition for the economy to be included in the ranks of converging countries. The high economic growth in China over the past 30 years undoubtedly benefits from the economic reform with a market orientation.

Some facts about growth in China over the past 30 years

The preceding discussion on the convergence hypothesis is only one of the basic (though perhaps the most important) facts about economic growth.[3] Here we shall also discuss some other growth facts that are special to China (and perhaps also to other less developed countries). We note that these facts cannot be expressed by neoclassical growth theory, and therefore become a challenge to the theory of economic growth with regard to less developed economies.

First, as a developing country, there exists a large (even infinite) amount of surplus labor in the rural areas of China. The launch of reform and opening up makes it possible for the rural surplus labor to enter the cities for searching jobs. This indicates that the high growth in China over the past 30 years has been accompanied by the presence of huge (or even unlimited) surplus supply in its labor market.

Second, over the past 30 years, the product market in China has experienced a transition from shortage of supply to the situation of oversupply. The excess capacity is significant for many industries in China and thus has been a matter of serious concern. Figure 5.4 shows the rate of capacity utilization in China since 1978. As can be seen from the figure, capacity utilization has been declining since 1994.

The other direct evidence on the excessive capacity is that the growth rate of investment in China has been significantly larger than that of GDP since the reform and opening up. For example, the average annual growth rate of GDP was 9.4 percent from 1979 to 2003, while the growth rate of investment was 11.5 percent. Since investment creates capacity, the fact that growth rate of investment is higher than that of GDP means that the increase in capacity is higher than the increase in GDP. Therefore if investment is continuously higher, excessive capacity in the product market will become more and more significant.[4]

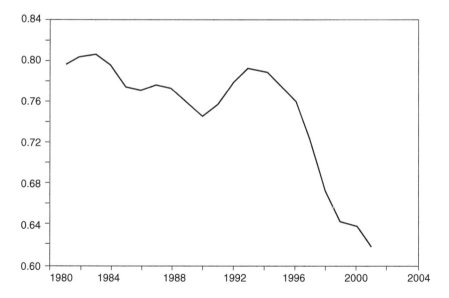

Figure 5.4 Capacity utilization rate in China, 1979–2001. Data from Gong and Yang (2002).

The duality of excess (excessive supply in the labor market and excessive capacity in the product market) indicates that over the past 30 years the higher growth in China has been realized in a disequilibrium economy in terms of excessive supply.

Third, technological progress has not been the major driving force of economic growth in China. Though there are many modern industries in China that appear to be connected to advanced technologies, the core technology is often imported. This indicates that the value added by the production process in China is often in low proportion even in those products that are related to modern technologies. On the other hand, the labor-intensive production mode is the major production method underlying the Chinese economy to a large extent. It is also the major comparative advantage that China has as it enters the international market.

Due to the special growth factors in China over the past 30 years, the interpretation of higher economic growth in China requires us to answer the following three questions:

- Why has the Chinese economy had such a high rate of economic growth over the past 30 years?
- How has China's high growth been made possible in an economy in which both the labor and product markets are excessively supplied?
- How can China's high economic growth be achieved by the mode of production without obvious technological progress?

It seems unlikely that these three questions can be answered simultaneously by following the usual logics of economics. Excess supplies in labor and product markets often imply economic recession or crisis, thus indicating low economic growth. On the other hand, without technological progress, which is often the major driving force of economic growth in developed economies, it is hard to imagine that the economy can grow fast. Therefore, interpretation of high economic growth in China is indeed a theoretical challenge.

5.2 The interpretation of China's high growth

Some viewpoints on the high growth in China

Many well-known foreign economists have provided their explanations for China's high economic growth. For example:

- China's high economic growth should be attributed to the fact that "foreign-funded enterprises have played a dominant role, rather than technological advances" (Gilboy, 2007);
- "The main reason for China's high economic growth is its successful use of foreign investment and export expansion" (Hale and Hale, 2007);
- "Moderate, progressive reform and a strong government are fundamental to China's economic growth" (Barro, 2007);

- "China's rapid development is achieved mainly by undervaluing its currency so as to promote the export of low-cost manufacturing industries" (Miller, 2007);
- "The government still controls most of the country's financial resources and allocates them effectively, which is the principal cause of economic growth" (Wotezeer, 2007).

To a certain degree, these "foreign viewpoints" offer some insights, in a variety of ways, into the high growth in China, but do not grasp the essence because of their insufficient understanding of what is really happening in China. On the other hand, they also cannot answer the aforementioned three questions – and especially the latter two, which are related to the special growth factors with regard to China.

Investment as a key driving force in China's economic growth

The so-called growth refers to the growth of GDP, the gross output produced domestically. In a market economy, there are always two distinct forces – demand and supply – in determining output. Given supply (or production capacity), GDP is determined by demand; however, if GDP determined by the demand is too close to the given supply, inflation might arise. This indicates that supply only provides the *possibility* of economic growth, while growth must be realized through demand. Therefore, the explanation of the high growth in China must consider both the demand and supply sides of the Chinese economy.

Let us first examine demand. Figures 5.5 and 5.6 respectively describe the comparison of two major demands in China – consumption and investment –

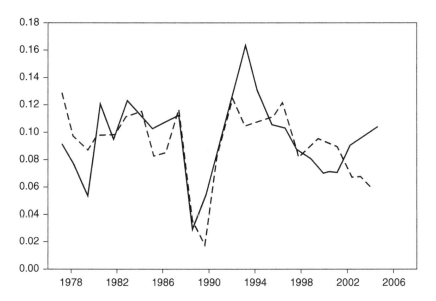

Figure 5.5 Growth rates of consumption (dashed line) and GDP (solid line). Data from National Bureau of Statistics of China (2004).

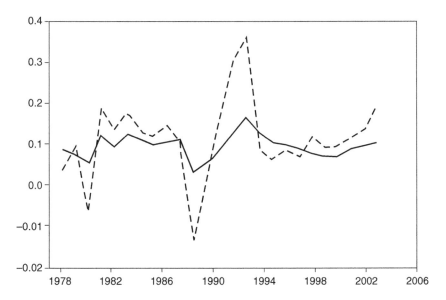

Figure 5.6 Growth rates of investment (dashed line) and GDP (solid line). Data from National Bureau of Statistics of China (2004).

with the growth rate of GDP over the past 30 years. In Figure 5.5, although the growth rate of consumption is very close to that of GDP in terms of its level (but, on average, still less than that of GDP), the volatility of consumption is not entirely consistent with that of GDP. At the same time, as shown in Figure 5.6, even though the growth rate of investment is not very close to that of GDP (on average, significantly higher than that of GDP) and the volatility is greater than that of GDP, the direction of volatility is essentially in accord with that of GDP. This seems to suggest that the growth and volatility of GDP arise mainly from that of investment. This conclusion can be evidenced further from Figure 5.7, where the proportion of consumption over GDP is declining while the proportion of investment is rising.

It should be noted that the demand created by investment not only includes the investment itself, but also generates other demands such as consumption demand. In Keynesian economics, there is a so-called multiplier theory according to which the total demand generated by an investment is often equal to the multiplier of that investment. Appendix A of this book provides a detailed discussion on how an investment, once carried, will generate a sequence of other demands.

Next, we turn to supply. Supply (or production capacity) essentially comprises three elements: labor, capital and technology. If we ignore technology for the moment, the supplies of labor and capital must be such as to meet the needs of economic growth. As a less developed country, China has sufficient surplus labor, although the average quality of labor is not high. The existence of surplus

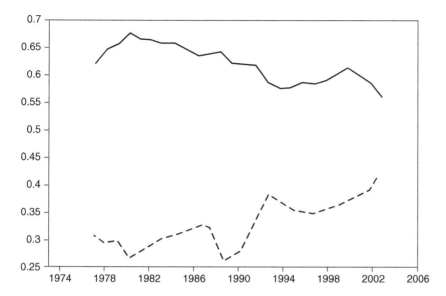

Figure 5.7 Proportions of consumption (solid line) and investment (dashed line) over GDP. Data from National Bureau of Statistics of China (2004).

labor in China does not pose constraints to the rapid economic growth of China. As for capital stock, this is accumulated through investment, but an upsurge in investment has been a major feature of the contemporary Chinese economy over the past 30 years.

Thus, the high growth in China has been primarily driven by the high growth in investment over the past 30 years. Investment not only stimulates the demand through the multiplier, but also enhances the production capacity by building new production lines, plant and buildings. For plant and buildings to work, more labor needs to be attracted into the cities – and the existence of huge amounts of surplus labor in China means that the labor supply is not a constraint.

It should be noted that this investment-driven interpretation of high growth in China can be independent of whether technological progress is significant or not. It is also consistent with the existence of huge amounts of surplus labor. As discussed earlier, it is the huge surplus of labor that makes the investment-related resource (labor) cheap and thus stimulates high investment; it also means there is plenty of labor available to work in the plants and buildings driven by the new investment. However, that interpretation still needs to answer why investment in China is so high, given that the economy has experienced excess capacity for most of the past 30 years.

Why is investment so high?

Now we will turn to the reasons why there have been such high investments in China over the past 30 years.

First, the stable social environment in China creates a favorable investment environment for investors (whether at home or abroad). Since the reform and opening up, the focus of the Chinese government has been transferred from the past class struggle to economic construction. While the Chinese leadership has changed repeatedly, the guideline of reform and opening up has not altered. Chinese society has experienced no major unrest, which is in sharp contrast to the frequent occurrence of political movements in the past, such as the Cultural Revolution. The stable social environment of China is completely different from the recurrent wars, coups and turmoil of some developing countries in Asia, Africa and Latin America. Clearly, the stable social environment provides one of the prerequisites for China to join the ranks of convergence.

Second, China is a populous country with a vast territory. When a big country like China begins to join the ranks of convergence, its advantage in size will attract investors (especially foreign investors) to the country. China has become one of the largest countries in the world to attract foreign direct investment. The advantage in being big is reflected in its huge market potential of its economic development. A wise entrepreneur will not easily give up the business opportunities brought by this huge, growing market.

Last but not least, many investment-related resources are very cheap in China. These resources include not only cheap labor and land, but also the financial resources. Since the reform and opening up, surplus rural labor has been allowed to work in cities, placing enormous pressure on the cities' employment market. At the same time, due to the system reform of state-owned enterprises, large numbers of workers in the cities have been laid off. As a result, wages, particularly of low-skilled workers, have not increased appropriately despite the rapid economic growth and the increase in labor productivity.

The provision of land resources in China is usually determined by local governments. Under the motivation of local development, local governments often launch a variety of preferential policies to attract investment. Among them is the establishment of economic zones, through which very cheap land is provided. Further, the government establishes an extremely relaxed financial environment for investors through the workings of the state-owned commercial banking system. In this way, not only are the financial resources in China more accessible, but costs are relatively low as well (see Table 1.1 in Chapter 1 for details).

It follows that over the past 30 years, the high growth in China has not only benefited from the stability of the social environment and the constant policy of reform and opening up; its advantages regarding investment-related resources and the opportunity to become a large economy have also played an important role. The resource advantage is not just because China is a developing country (making the provision of cheap labor possible); it also benefits from the fact that it is a country in transition (making the provision of affordable financial and land resources possible). The depreciation of RMB implemented by China, to some extent, makes the resource advantage more prominent.

5.3 Can existing growth theories explain the high growth in China?[6]

Can neoclassical growth theory explain the high growth in China?

This section discusses economic growth in China from a more academic perspective. The so-called growth refers to the growth of GDP. Two theoretical frameworks can be distinguished as to how GDP is determined: the first is the neoclassical framework, the second the Keynesian framework. The former believes that GDP is determined by supply (through production function), and the latter holds that GDP is determined by demand.

Economists commonly use neoclassical theory to study economic growth. As pointed out earlier, the neoclassical growth model has to some extent been regarded as a "holy scripture" when talking about economic growth. However, the neoclassical growth model can hardly explain the growth factors in China, even though it may explain many growth phenomena in OECD countries. Due to its way of determining output through production function, this theory implies an important assumption – namely, market clearing in both the labor and product markets. In other words, unemployment and excessive capacity are not significantly important in modeling economic growth. This may not generate problems when explaining the growth phenomenon in developed countries, but does bring difficulties when interpreting economic growth in less developed countries such as China.

As discussed earlier, disequilibrium in terms of excess supply is a prominent feature in both labor and product markets in China. They are not only the two growth facts that can be observed, but are also significantly important in formulating the growth mode of contemporary Chinese economy. As stated above, it is the huge surplus of labor that makes the investment-related resource (labor) cheap and thus stimulates high investment; it also means there is plenty of labor available to work in the plants and buildings driven by the new investment. On the other hand, it is the high investment (which serves as a major driving force of high economic growth) that creates huge excessive capacity in the product market.

Next, in the neoclassical growth model, technological progress is the only major driving force of growth in per capita GDP. However, the growth mode in China does not necessarily rely on technological progress. The major driving force in China is investment: as long as investment is high, growth will be high regardless of technological progress, which does exist to some extent.

Determination of investment is also not treated well in the neoclassical growth model: it is simply assumed that it is equal to saving. In other words, there is no independent investment function in the model. This method of investment determination is insufficient to explain why investment is high in China: a simple saving ratio does not provide enough information about how investment is determined.

Requests for modeling economic growth and dynamics in China

Ignoring the demand side of the economy may only be one kind of simplification whose effect is to enable us to get rid of the complexity when supply and demand are both taken into account. However, it cannot in itself exclude those models of economic growth in which supply and demand are both included. As shown earlier, given supply (or production capacity), GDP is determined by demand – but if the demand-determined GDP is too close to the given supply, inflation might arise. Therefore, supply only provides the *possibility* of economic growth while growth must be realized through demand. An explanation of the high growth in China cannot ignore the demand side of the economy.

An appropriate model to explain high economic growth in China should have the following properties:

- The theoretical model should include not only the supply but also the demand sides of the economy.
- Investment plays a key role in the model for creating not only demand but also supply, and therefore the behavior function of investment must be independently and carefully studied.
- Disequilibria in terms of excessive supply should be reflected in the model for both labor and product markets.

Thus, a model with these properties can be summarized as a model of disequilibrium growth (or dynamics) in which investment plays a key role in creating both demand and supply.

Returning to the classical approach of Harrod

The essence of Keynesian economics is its method of output determination – that is, output is determined by demand. This is consistent with the norm of the Chinese economy and, perhaps, that of many other less developed economies. Yet Keynesian economics traditionally only considers the demand (while ignoring the supply) side of the economy. This has meant the traditional Keynesian models (such as IS-LM and AS-AD models) cannot be used to study the growth phenomenon, since without an increase in the ability to supply, growth cannot be realized.

Introduction of the supply side of an economy into a Keynesian demand-determined economy can be traced back to Harrod's contribution in 1939. Indeed, Harrod's "Essay in Dynamic Theory" (Harrod, 1939) was a pioneering work in studying economic dynamics. Before this, there had been no systematic research on dynamic economics (including growth and cycles). Moreover, the investment in Harrod's model plays a significant role not only in creating demand and supply, but also as a driving force in growth and dynamics. Disequilibria are also dominant for both labor and product markets in Harrod's economy. All these seem to be consistent with the requirements for modeling the Chinese economy, as discussed earlier.[7]

However, over time Harrod's theory has gradually faded from people's memory: not only do textbooks not introduce it, but also neoclassical economics has replaced Harrod's theory in academia, to become a sacred theory when studying economic growth. The following might explain why Harrod's theory is now ignored. By introducing the supply side, Harrod's analysis can naturally be regarded as complementary to Keynes's static analysis on the demand side of the economy while generating dynamics. But the dynamics are unfortunately unstable. Indeed, the purpose of Harrod (1939) is only to explore some instability puzzles inherent in his model, such as the knife-edge puzzle and the puzzle of unbalanced growth, when we discuss economic dynamics. Therefore, to some extent, Harrod's contribution is more likely to motivate economists to resolve his puzzles.

The existence of Harrod's instability puzzles essentially means that there is a destabilizing mechanism in the economy.[8] Therefore, there are logically two approaches to Harrod's instability puzzles. One is simply to change the model. This is what Solow (1956) had done by ignoring the demand side, which established the standard neoclassical growth model. The other is to introduce some stabilizing mechanism into Harrod's model while leaving the basic structure unchanged. The stabilization mechanism in the economy may include price, wage and government stabilization policies, among others, none of which is introduced in the seminal paper of Harrod (1939).[9] This model usually has very rich empirical results for both developed and less developed economies. However, due to introduction of these stabilization mechanisms, it is difficult to say that it is still the growth model as defined academically.

Yet Harrod entitled his seminal paper "An Essay in Dynamic Theory". In modern economics, the so-called dynamics can refer either to growth or to business cycles. This seems to suggest that Harrod may not confine his economic dynamics to the growth issue. It was Solow who later restricted Harrod's dynamic problem to the growth field. According to Solow (1956: 66), Harrod

> consistently studies long-run problems with the usual short-run tools. One usually thinks of the long run as the domain of the neoclassical analysis, the land of margin. Instead Harrod and Domar talk of the long run in terms of multiplier, the accelerator, "the" capital coefficient.

By this restriction, Solow resolved Harrod's puzzle within the neoclassical framework that ignored the demand side of an economy.

However, when complexity is not a problem, adding the demand side into the economy only with the supply side should always enrich economic analysis, whether in the short run or the long run. On the other hand, the distinction between short term and long term is very ambiguous. For a particular period t, say 2010, we are not clear whether it is in the short run or in the long run. Perhaps a more reasonable treatment is to follow a rule similar to Calvo's price setting mechanism (Calvo, 1983). In a particular period t, some firms are in the long run (or in the medium run) so that they can change facilities and technology (or they can change prices), others are in the short run so they can alter nothing except the output. If we consider the short run and long run (or medium run) in this way, there is again no reason to exclude the demand side from the model economy. Finally, ignoring the demand side of the economy will make the model less suitable for studying the growth and development in less developed economies where disequilibria are more apparent, especially for the labor market (Lewis, 1954).

The model presented in Appendix D, whose theoretical preparation is given in Appendices A–C, is a macro-dynamic model for contemporary Chinese economy. It is hardly regarded as a growth model for China in the usual sense; rather, it is a dynamic model in the sense of Harrod (1939).

Discussion and considerations

1 What is the convergence hypothesis? Does this hypothesis hold everywhere in the world? If not, why does this hypothesis not hold for some countries?
2 How do economists explain the convergence hypothesis? What do you think of this explanation?
3 What are the three basic factors in China's economic growth?
4 Discuss the role of investment in China's economic growth. Is the high economic growth in China driven by high growth in investment? Why, or why not?
5 Why has the growth in investment been so high in China over the past 30 years?
6 Can neoclassical growth theory account for China's high economic growth? If so, why? Can Keynesian theory explain economic growth in China? If so, why?
7 To your knowledge, what can you tell us about Harrod's classical approach to economic dynamics? Is it still viable?

6 The financial system in contemporary Chinese economy

As noted in Chapter 3 of this book: transitioning, developing and a large economy are the three major characteristics of contemporary Chinese economy. Here, the transition property is more reflected in China's financial system, which will be the focus of this chapter.

6.1 The commercial banking system in China

Like other industries, China's commercial banking system has undergone a fundamental restructuring since the reform and opening up.

People's Bank of China (PBC)

The People's Bank of China (PBC) is the central bank of China, responsible for implementing China's monetary policy. Prior to the reform and opening up, however, the PBC was not only a central bank. After the founding of New China, a mono-bank system with the PBC as the sole bank came into being under the planned economic system. In this mono-bank system, the PBC actually played a dual role. First, being the central bank of China, it was charged with issuing the Chinese Yuan, with its unlimited credit. Second, as a commercial bank monopolized by the state, it exercised the functions of absorbing deposits and providing loans in accordance with the plan. As a matter of fact, the PBC held almost all the financial assets of China before the reform and opening up, and was often referred to as the "cash, credit and settlement center" in China.

Subsequent to the reform and opening up, the functions of the PBC as a commercial bank began to be gradually weakened. The Agricultural Bank of China (ABC) resumed in 1979, breaking the traditional mono bank system. Following this, the other three major state-owned commercial banks, the Industrial and Commercial Bank of China (ICBC), the Bank of China (BOC) and the China Construction Bank (CCB), were also gradually established. This led to the PBC breaking away from its function as a commercial bank. In 1984, the government decided that the PBC should specialize in exercising the function of a central bank, with its major commercial business (such as absorbing deposits and providing loans) taken over by the four state-owned commercial banks. In 1994, the government once again confirmed the identity of the PBC as a central bank. Since then, the PBC has no longer made loans directly to enterprises; monetary policy with demand management as its main objective was introduced at the same time.

The commercial banks in contemporary Chinese economy

Prior to 1984, the four state-owned commercial banks in China were separated, in their banking business, with regard to their clients; mixed businesses were not allowed. For example, the Industrial and Commercial Bank of China (ICBC) focused on making loans to industrial and commercial businesses, the Agricultural Bank of China (ABC) was mainly responsible for offering loans for the rural and agricultural development, the Bank of China (BOC) specialized in dealing in foreign exchange and trade, and the China Construction Bank (CCB) was charged with providing loans primarily for infrastructure investment. As a result, all the banks were pure monopolies with regard to their own business areas. After 1984, the separation was broken down and competition was introduced among the four banks. However, it was not until 1987, when a number of joint-stock commercial banks and city commercial banks were established, that competition among the banks really began. At the same time, foreign-owned banks, which initially were only allowed to establish representative offices in China, were permitted to start conducting RMB business.

By the end of 2008, financial institutions in China's banking sector had a total of 5,636 legal entities, including five policy banks, five large commercial banks, 12 joint-stock commercial banks, 136 city commercial banks, 22 rural commercial banks, 163 farm cooperative banks, 22 urban credit cooperatives, 4,965 rural credit cooperatives, one postal savings bank, four financial asset management companies, 32 foreign-run financial institutions, 54 trust companies, 84 enterprise groups and financial companies, 12 financial leasing companies, three currency brokers, nine auto finance companies, 91 village and town banks, six finance companies, and 10 rural finance unions.[1]

Despite the fact that the number of banking institutions has increased greatly, the degree to which China's banking sector is monopolized remains high, with the four major state-owned commercial banks still holding the majority of the market share. In 2008, the total deposits of four major state-owned banks accounted for 53.6 percent of total deposits, 45.5 percent of total loans and 51 percent of total assets.[2] In this sense, China's four state-owned commercial banks can be considered representative of the whole banking sector in China.

The institutional features and the reform of commercial banks in China

It should be noted that for the variety of commercial banks in China, including the five large commercial banks, 12 joint-stock commercial banks and 136 city commercial banks, among others, the state has been the major shareholder. Even if the ownership of China's commercial banks has gone through a series of reforms, there is no substantive change to the feature that the state holds the majority.

As mentioned in Chapter 1, China's state-owned commercial banks have injected a lot of money into the rapidly growing Chinese economy. In many cases, loans from state-owned commercial banks are easily available and very cheap. Indeed, for a long period of time (1997–2003; see Figure 1.1) the growth rate of China's money supply (via loan creation) was usually higher than that of the nominal GDP by up to 5–10 percentage points. The lending behavior of state-owned commercial banks was usually arranged by the government program (for further discussion, see Chapter 7). While this may have helped China to recover from its economic recession, it also inevitably resulted in huge non-performing assets. In China, the non-performing assets of state-owned commercial banks were once as great as approximately to one-third of their total assets. Such a high proportion of non-performing assets led many foreign economists to make a bold prediction: China's financial system would collapse.

The huge non-performing assets from the commercial banks of China left the Chinese government with no option but to reform its state-owned commercial banking system. In 2004, reform was introduced on a trial basis into the Bank of Communications (BOCOM), and was subsequently officially promoted in the whole banking sector.

The reform of Chinese state-owned commercial banks was aimed at transforming wholly state-funded commercial banks into joint-stock commercial banks in line with the rules of market economy, and letting them be listed at home and abroad. What was different from the reform of state-owned enterprises was that the reform of state-owned commercial banks introduced strategic partners. These strategic partners are usually well-known international financial groups. They should be big shareholders of commercial banks in China, and hence directly involved in the daily management and operation of banks. The four state-owned commercial banks have completed the shareholding reform by now, and have succeeded in going public at home and abroad. The reform of commercial banks in China has strengthened China's commercial banks. On the other hand, the commercial banks in Western countries have been weakened due to the recent financial crisis, which indeed disrupted the rankings of market capitalization of the global banks. Currently, the ICBC, CCB and BOC are the top three in rankings of the global banks in terms of market capitalization, with BOCOM ranked 10th.[3]

Yet there is no denying that the institutional reform of China's commercial banks did not change their most fundamental feature: the state is still the biggest shareholder. To some extent, the so-called reform effectively refers to the fact that wholly state-owned banks have been transformed into joint-stock commercial banks with a dominant state share. This implies that the state's impact on commercial banks actually has not weakened: in spite of the seeming establishment of modern corporate governance, the chairmen and CEOs of those banks are all state-appointed officials, with a certain administrative ranking, such as vice-ministerial, etc. It follows that China's banking officials are usually appointed usually because of their identity as government officials. Thus, achievements in their political careers are still considered an important factor. This institutional feature of commercial banks in China also determines the unique feature of China's monetary policy (see Chapter 7 for further discussion).

6.2 China's capital market

New China's first stock: Feilo Acoustics

On November 14, 1986, Deng Xiaoping met a delegation of senior executives from some of the largest US companies and investment banks, led by John J. Phelan Jr, the Chairman and CEO of the Board of the New York Stock Exchange (NYSE) in Beijing. At that time, Mr Phelan brought Deng Xiaoping two special gifts — security samples of American Stock Exchange Securities and the emblem of the NYSE. At that time, stock was regarded by China as typical of a capitalist society. Mr Phelan was not sure whether Deng would be able to accept these two gifts, which made him very uneasy before the meeting.

However, Mr Phelan worried too much. Deng was not only glad to accept his gifts, but also presented him with stock of the Shanghai Feilo Acoustics Company with a denomination of 50 yuan – the first stock certificate in the history of the People's Republic of China. This share certificate of the Shanghai Feilo Acoustics Company became the first owned by a foreigner, and Mr Phelan became the first foreign shareholder of China's listed companies. The original stock certificate held by Mr Phelan is now permanently displayed in the show-case of the NYSE. Through many years of dividend distribution this original stock has grown into 3,183 shares, and its market capitalization has hit a maximum value of 107,600 yuan – a rate of return of 2,152-fold!

The development of China's capital market

China's capital market has experienced bumpy development, however. The same is true even for the Shanghai Feilo Acoustics Company. Before its inaugural cere-mony, a company must go through an essential procedure — licensing by the Administration of Industry and Commerce. Little did the Shanghai Feilo Acoustics Company expect that it would run into trouble. The staff in the Administration of Industry and Commerce asked in a puzzled tone: "What is your ownership?" Qin Qibin (then Chairman of Shanghai Feilo Acoustics Company) replied: "A joint-stock system." The staff said: "A joint-stock system? There is no joint-stock system in the ownership of the country!" At that point in time, there were only three options on the registration forms of the Administration of Industry and Commerce: state-owned, collective-owned and private. Qin thought that his company was cer-tainly neither state-owned nor private, so he registered his company as collective-owned. What he didn't expect was that this "collective-owned" nature would incur trouble with the first distribution of dividends later on.

At the beginning of 1986, the company distributed the dividends for the first time, with 35 yuan per share agreed unanimously by all shareholders of the company. Such a dividend distribution brought the officers from the Administration of Audit Unit. The officer from the Audit Unit said rudely: "You are dividing state-owned property!" Qin argued: "Our factory is not wholly state-owned." The staff replied: "Collective-owned companies also belong to the country!" The Audit Unit maintained that there was no such thing as the claim that collective-owned enterprises distribute dividends. Profits retained by collective-owned enterprises are often called reserved funds and public welfare funds, which cannot be distributed to the individual. Thus, Qin had to make a self-criticism report, and was fined.

Whether China's capital market needed to be established was still a hot subject for debate at that time. A capital market was widely regarded as being unique to capitalism. Even in 1993, when the discussion draft of the Securities Act was submitted for the first time to the National People's Congress Standing Committee for deliberation, some members simply ignored it, saying: "I do not know what the 'Securities Act' is. Is it something typical of socialist or capitalist? If it is something typical of socialist, I agree with you; if not, I am determined not to vote."

However, the practice of reform once again broke through the barriers of theory. In the mid-1980s, there was already a number of businesses in China that offered shares. Deng Xiaoping not only met Mr Phelan, the Chairman of the Board of NYSE in 1986, but also presented him with stock of the Shanghai Feilo Acoustics Company, which was a remarkable signal to the world that China was to develop the capital market. In 1992, the most critical year of China's reform and opening up, Deng Xiaoping once again threw his weight behind the development of a capital market in his speech of his Southern tour:

> Are things like securities and the stock market good or not? Are there any dangers with them? Are these things unique to capitalism that socialism cannot use? Watching is allowed, but we need to firmly try them. We can carry it out a year or two on a trial. If it's okay, go on with it; if not, correct it. We can call off them either quickly or slowly, even leave a little tail. There is nothing to be afraid of. We will not make mistakes as long as this attitude is adhered to.[4]

Deng's determination on the issue of developing a capital market in China made it impossible for the Chinese capital market to be nipped in the bud.

By the end of 2008, the number of listed companies in China had reached 1,625, with total assets of 48.7 trillion yuan.[5]

Share structure reform: China's capital market continues to improve

Yet the overall size of China's capital market is still small, with a lower proportion of direct financing. From 2001 to 2009, the ratios of direct financing and loan financing were, respectively, 9.50 percent, 4.11 percent, 2.97 percent, 4.49 percent, 2.05 percent, 8.38 percent, 21.95 percent, 21.36 percent and 24.22 percent.[6] The ratio is relatively low, but still gradually rising. Also, the capital market in China was improving anyway.

In fact, a large proportion of listed companies cannot be traded in China's stock market. By 2005, that proportion was about two-thirds. The most prominent feature of China's stock market is reflected in the so-called distinction between non-tradable and tradable shares. Such a distinction is an institutional arrangement made by the government when the Chinese stock market was initially established. Non-tradable shares essentially belong to the state – and the proportion of non-tradable shares is generally more than 50 percent, which ensures state control of listed companies. Such an institutional arrangement, however, has led to the problems that have made the development of China's capital market a bumpy journey.

First, because the state's control of listed companies cannot be reversed, the original state-owned enterprises (including the four major state-owned commercial banks), although having been transformed into joint-stock companies, have left the administrative relationship and personnel appointment system unchanged. This indicates that the traditional drawbacks unique to state-owned enterprises have not been eliminated.

Second, since the shares of the controlling shareholder cannot be traded, their interests will not be influenced by the ups and downs of stock prices. This leads to a lack of incentives by which companies could be managed well in order to facilitate the appreciation of the stocks.

Third, when the state is the de facto controlling shareholder and its representatives (chairmen and CEO) cannot hold many shares, listed companies often have no incentive to distribute dividends to their shareholders. Investors can make a profit only by speculating on fluctuations in stock prices, which triggers a high turnover in China's stock market. Table 6.1 presents a comparison of the turnover between China's stock markets and major stock markets in the world.

Table 6.1 Turnover in the world's major stock markets (%)

Year	Shanghai	Shenzhen	New York	London	Tokyo	Hong Kong
2000	504.07	396.47	87.7	69.3	58.8	60.9
2001	216.67	189.97	86.9	83.8	60	43.9
2002	208.74	200.65	94.8	97.3	67.9	37.9
2003	268.58	216.97	89.5	106.6	82.6	51.7
2004	308.31	311.78	89.8	116.6	97.1	57.7
2005	290.7	350.64	99.1	110.1	115.3	50.3
2006	564.5	671.34	134.3	124.8	125.8	62.1
2007	953.16	1,062.0	167.1	154.2	138.4	94.1
2008	401.6	503.45	192.7	98.7	128.5	77.7

The data for Shanghai and Shenzhen indicate the turnover of a share, and come from the Editorial Board of China Statistical Yearbook of the Securities and Futures (2010), while the other data can be found at the website of the World Federation of Exchanges (www.world-exchanges.org/statistics).

Table 6.2 The percentage of tradable shares over total shares, 2004–2010

Year	The total share capital (100 million shares)	Tradable shares (100 million shares)	Percentage (%)
2004	7,149.43	2,577.18	36.05
2005	7,629.51	2,914.77	38.20
2006	14,897.57	5,637.78	37.84
2007	22,416.85	10,331.52	46.09
2008	24,522.85	12,578.91	51.29
2009	26,162.85	19,759.53	75.53
2010	26,994.82	20,731.82	76.80

Data are available at the website of China Securities Regulatory Commission (www.csrc.gov.cn/pub/newsite/sjtj/).

China initiated the share structure reform in 2005. It was basically completed in 2007. In the aftermath of the share structure reform, all the new issued shares of listed companies are assumed to be tradable. This at least implies that the shares of new listed companies will no longer be divided into tradable and non-tradable. With regard to the original non-tradable shares, although they cannot flow into the market immediately, the state sets different datelines for when they can be traded. In recent years there has been a gradual increase in the proportion of tradable shares among total shares (see Table 6.2).

6.3 China's foreign exchange market

The exchange rate of the Chinese yuan (RMB), which has sent shock waves through the world, is set in the China Foreign Exchange Trading Center. This is located at No. 15, Zhongshan North Road in the Shanghai Bund of China. Yet there was no such thing as a foreign exchange market in China before the reform and opening up.

The earlier administrative control of foreign exchange

Over recent years, China has implemented a fixed exchange rate system pegged to the US dollar. This means that the PBC (People's Bank of China) maintains the exchange rate target against the dollar while the exchange rate of the RMB against other currencies is calculated automatically by market exchange rates between dollars and other currencies. Figure 6.1 reveals what has happened to the exchange rate of the RMB against the US dollar since 1981.

As illustrated in Figure 6.1, over the past 30 years, the exchange rate of the RMB (that is, the price of US dollars in terms of RMB) has experienced a significant change, implying that the PBC is continuously adjusting the exchange rate target of the RMB. In 1981, the exchange rate of the RMB against the US dollar was 1.70. There is no doubt that the RMB was overvalued at that time. After 1981, the RMB began to devaluate (i.e., the exchange rate of the RMB

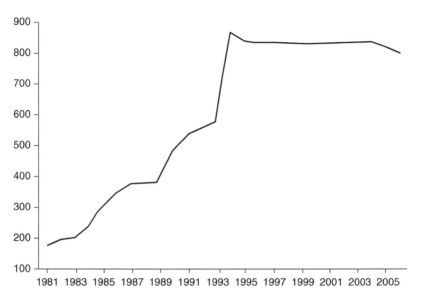

Figure 6.1 Exchange rate of the RMB in 1979–2006. Data from National Bureau of Statistics of China (2007).

increased). By 1994, the exchange rate had risen to 8.44. Since 1995, the RMB
exchange rate has gradually stabilized. Since 2005, the RMB has been facing the
pressure of appreciation.

There are two ways of maintaining an exchange rate target: one is market-
based, the other is administrative. The so-called market-based method refers to
the fact that the central bank maintains its exchange rate target through trading
foreign currencies in the foreign exchange market. The administrative method
implies that a country directly sets a legal transaction price of the foreign
exchange (i.e., the exchange rate) by its authority.

Here, we should remark that if the exchange rate is targeted at a level that is
below what is should be in the market without the trades from the central bank
(or in order to make the domestic currency deliberately appreciate), that target
cannot be maintained by the central bank through the market-based method. As
might be imagined, if the domestic currency is deliberately caused to appreciate,
the central bank will have to continuously use its reserves of foreign exchange to
buy the domestic currency (or to make the demand for domestic currency deliberately increase) in the foreign exchange market in order to maintain the higher
market value of its domestic currency. Although a central bank may have an
unlimited supply of domestic currency, its foreign exchange reserves are limited
regardless. Over time, the central bank's foreign exchange reserves will be
depleted, and thus a financial crisis will be triggered. Conversely, when the
exchange rate is targeted at a level that is higher than the market value with no
government trading (or the domestic currency is deliberately devaluated), the

central bank, to maintain that target, generally needs to use its own currency to buy foreign currency. It's clear that such a target can be maintained sustainably.

Thus, at the beginning of the economic reform when the PBC set the exchange rate target to deliberately cause the RMB to appreciate, a variety of administrative means had to be used. The government not only set a legal price of foreign exchange by its authority, but also controlled the use of foreign exchange. Indeed, for a long period of time China had adopted a system to strictly control the use of foreign exchange in its economy. All foreign exchange earned by the households and enterprises in China had to be sold to the state banks in accordance with related provisions. Every use of foreign currency had to be approved by the monetary authorities, and the currency then had to be purchased from the state banks.

Regulation of foreign exchange led directly to serious distortions in the prices for foreign exchange, and a lot of black market transactions. For instance, there was a special currency of the RMB known as the "foreign exchange coupon". This special currency could only be obtained by trading foreign currencies according to the official exchange rate. With this special currency of the RMB, people could go to particular shops (where regular RMB was not allowed to be used) to purchase special goods.

The dual pricing system of the exchange rate

The overvaluation of the RMB and its accompanying administrative regulation of foreign exchange caused inconspicuous growth in China's foreign exchange reserves for a long time (see Table 6.3). This made the foreign exchange reserves

Table 6.3 China's foreign exchange reserves, 1978–2010

Year	Foreign exchange reserves (100 million US dollars)	Year	Foreign exchange reserves (100 million US dollars)
1978	1.67	1994	516.20
1979	8.40	1995	735.97
1980	−12.96	1996	1,050.29
1981	27.08	1997	1,398.90
1982	69.86	1998	1,449.59
1983	89.01	1999	1,546.75
1984	82.20	2000	1,655.74
1985	26.44	2001	2,121.65
1986	20.72	2002	2,864.07
1987	29.23	2003	4,032.51
1988	33.72	2004	6,099.32
1989	55.50	2005	8,188.72
1990	110.93	2006	10,663.40
1991	217.12	2007	15,282.49
1992	194.43	2008	19,460.30
1993	211.99	2009	23,991.52

Data for 2009 are from the website of the Bank of China (www.pbc.gov.cn/); other data come from Editorial Board of Almanac of China's Finance and Banking (2009, 2010).

(mainly US dollars and other international currencies) scarce resources, which could lead to a direct impact on the economic security (related discussions will be given in Chapter 10).

The system reform of foreign exchange in China began in the late 1970s. To encourage local authorities and enterprises to actively engage in foreign trade, China introduced the retention system of foreign currencies in 1979. This meant that the state conducted the unified management of foreign currencies to ensure their rational use, but gave a certain percentage of foreign currencies to enterprises as retention. Enterprises earning foreign currencies had certain autonomy of the retained foreign currencies, and could participate in the dispensation of retained foreign currencies among enterprises. The so-called dispensation refers to the fact that the retained foreign currencies could be traded to the enterprises badly in need of them, and its purchasing price might not be in accordance with the official exchange rate. This indeed created a dual pricing system of foreign exchange. At the same time, it also created the earlier market for trading foreign currencies.

Clearly, the price of foreign exchange formed in the market for dispensing foreign currencies provides useful information for setting a reasonable and market-based price of foreign exchange. Thus, between 1979 and 1993, the official exchange rate was continually moving closer to the market exchange rate. With the economic growth, the market for dispensing foreign currencies was also growing in size. By the end of 1993, 80 percent of foreign exchanges in China were traded in the market track.[7] At the same time, the official exchange rate had come very close to that formed in the dispensing market. Eventually, in 1994, the government abolished its official exchange rate while integrating the variety of dispensing markets scattered in various regions across the country into a united auction market of foreign exchange. That resulted in the formation of a unified exchange rate. At the same time, the government canceled the retention system for enterprises and allowed them to begin to participate in free transactions of foreign currencies. This essentially opened the current account of the RMB exchange with regard to foreign exchange.

The China Foreign Exchange Trading Center in Shanghai

There is no doubt that the exchange rate formed around 1994 was based on the market in a certain sense. With the continuous development of the Chinese economy, however, the status of the RMB in the international community has been greatly enhanced, so we have all reason to believe that the exchange rate formed after 1994 is relatively higher (or the RMB has been depreciated). As analyzed earlier, the central bank can maintain the exchange rate targeted to devaluate its home currency through market interventions. To be specific, the PBC could utilize its unlimited supplies of the RMB to buy foreign currencies through bidding in the foreign exchange market.

The foreign exchange market in China, officially called the China Foreign Exchange Trading Center, is located in Shanghai. The center is a type of exchange market that adopts a membership system. After examination and approval by the PBC, all the commercial banks and other financial organizations, which can legally trade foreign exchange in China, can become members of this center. Whether from trade surplus, foreign direct investment or so-called "hot money", foreign currencies that flow into China are first allocated into the foreign exchange account by these members, and then bought or sold by a member of the China Foreign Exchange Trade Center. The RMB exchange rate, which nowadays attracts so much attention from the world, results really from the members' competitive bidding in the Center. In this sense, the statement that the exchange rate of RMB is formed on the basis of demand–supply equilibrium in the market can be really cogent.

But there is one special super-member among all the members of the China Foreign Exchange Trading Center. This is the PBC, the People's Bank of China. Like all other members, the PBC is allowed to purchase foreign currencies. The reason it can be called the special super-member is because the PBC has an unlimited supply of RMB and therefore it can bid highest for foreign currencies. This makes the PBC often the last buyer, and indeed it actually buys most foreign currencies flowing into China. The $3,000 billion of China's foreign exchange reserves include all the accumulated foreign currencies purchased by PBC.

Nevertheless, we still need to say that the special super-member is still one of many members in the center. Since China no longer requires the compulsory settlement of foreign currencies today, the reason why the PBC purchases most of the foreign currencies is simply because it can bid the highest!

Thus we can see the following:

1   The continuing climb in China's exchange reserves has been accumulated by purchase from the PBC using its infinite supply of RMB at the market named the China Foreign Exchange Trading Center.
2   If the PBC does not carry out this type of transactions, RMB will appreciate.

This market behavior of the PBC not only produces a significant influence on China's macroeconomic dynamics, but also leads to heated controversy between China and the US about the RMB exchange rate. The related discussion will be given in Chapter 10.

Discussion and questions

1   Describe the banking system in China before the economic reform and opening up. Do you think, under such a system, a financial crisis regarding the banking industry is likely to happen? If so, why?
2   Describe briefly the reform of the state-owned commercial bank system in China which started in 2004.
3   "China's major commercial banks have been listed in the stock markets in China and abroad (including the US), and their market value has been

ranked among the highest in the world. So they are no longer state-owned commercial banks." Do you agree with this view? Why, or why not?

4   What is a tradable share? What is a non-tradable share? Explain briefly the share structure reform in China.

5   At the beginning of the economic reform and opening up, was the RMB devaluated or did it appreciate? From 1994 to 2005, was the RMB devaluated or did it appreciate? How about now?

6   "RMB exchange rate is determined by market equilibrium. Therefore, there is no sense of whether the RMB is devaluated or not." Do you agree with this view? Why, or why not?

7   If a central bank wants to maintain a target exchange rate, do you think the target should be devaluation or appreciation of the domestic currency? Why?

8   How are foreign exchange reserves accumulated in China?

7 Economic fluctuations in contemporary Chinese economy

The Chinese economy has experienced the prosperity of high growth since 1978. Yet its high growth has also been accompanied by cyclic fluctuations. What are the features of cyclic fluctuations in contemporary Chinese economy? How does the government manage the economic fluctuations? How they are different from those of developed countries? These will be the topics discussed in this chapter.

7.1 Understanding economic fluctuation

Stabilizing and destabilizing mechanism

In economics, there are basically two approaches to studying business cycles (or economic fluctuations). One approach is to regard business cycles as being caused by exogenous shocks. In this view, the observed recurrent and irregular fluctuations are generated by repeated stochastic impulses to the economy. Historically, this can be traced back to Frisch (1933) and Slutsky (1937). Recent business cycle theories in mainstream economics, such as real business cycle (RBC) theory, are often based on this view.

The other approach is to regard business cycles as systematic, deterministic and self-generating recurrent cycles inherent to the underlying economy. This endogenous approach to business cycles is often found in the literature related to Keynesian economics, non-linear dynamics and disequilibrium economics.

Whether business cycles are exogenous or endogenous depends on whether there are some destabilizing mechanisms in the economy. Many economists believe that by price variation, an economy can be stabilized. While the price variation can be regarded as a stabilizing mechanism, there may also be other mechanisms that destabilize the economy. An important example is the investment mechanism, as explored by Harrod (1939, 1948).

The destabilizing mechanism of investment results from the dual rules of investment in creating both demand and supply (or capacity). For example, when there is a certain degree of overheating in the economy, investment will increase to meet the increased demand (or insufficiency in capacity). Yet investment not only increases capacity, but also generates the aggregate demand. Since investment has multiplier effect in generating demand, for the economy as a whole the increased demand brought by the same investment will be larger than the increased capacity. This will overheat the economy and thus impel firms to invest more. On the other hand, if there is excessive capacity, firms will reduce their investment. Yet the reduction in investment will reduce the aggregate demand too. The reduction in aggregate demand will be larger than the reduction in capacity, and therefore excess capacity will be increased. Harrod calls this a "knife-edge problem".[1]

It should be noted that the knife-edge with regard to investment is only one type of destabilizing mechanism. There could be many other destabilizing mechanisms – for instance, Minsky's financial instability.[2] The coexistence of stabilizing and destabilizing mechanisms along with external shocks brings about business cycles, as we have observed in the economy. Whether the cycles can be dampenedd or self-corrected depends on the interaction of the two forces: the stabilizing and destabilizing mechanisms. This way of understanding business cycles has important implications for macroeconomic policy.

Demand management policies

If the force from the destabilizing mechanism is larger than that from the stabilizing mechanism, then the business cycle (perhaps initiated by some external shocks) cannot be dampened or self-corrected. In this case, counter-cyclic policies from the government are essential for the economy to be stabilized. In this sense, government policy can also be understood as a stabilizing mechanism.

The theory of counter-cyclic policy from the government springs from *The General Theory of Employment, Interest, and Money*, written by John Maynard Keynes.[3] It is often called "demand management" policy.

Reducing unemployment and inflation is what the government should pursue. Any responsible government should not allow either of them to deteriorate. However, according to the Phillips curve, as discussed in Chapter 4, there is a substitution between unemployment and inflation, indicating that they will not deteriorate simultaneously under normal circumstances. At the same time, a combination of unemployment and inflation (a specific location on the Phillips curve) is entirely dependent on the aggregate demand of the society (see Figure 7.1).

As may be imagined, the economy basically moves up and down along the Phillips curve, and its position on the curve hinges on aggregate demand. If the aggregate demand is relatively low, there will be lower output, less inflationary pressure, and higher unemployment. In business cycles, this is a known as a recession and is represented by point A in Figure 7.1. Conversely, if there is excessive demand, there will be higher output, larger inflationary pressure, and lower unemployment, shown by point B. The Phillips curve thus provides a basis for a government to conduct its counter-cyclic policy of demand management.

For example, if the economy is in recession (i.e. at point A), unemployment is serious, with less inflationary pressure. We know that this results from a lack of aggregate demand. At this point, sound macroeconomic policy should stimulate (or increase) the aggregate demand so that the economy can move up along

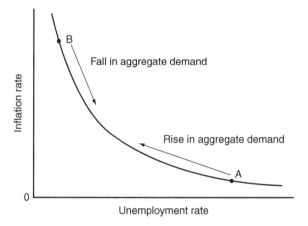

Figure 7.1 The Phillips curve.

the Phillips curve. On the other hand, when the economy is at point B, suitable macroeconomic policy will reduce aggregate demand, shifting the economy down along the Phillips curve. Thus, a Keynesian macroeconomic policy aiming at regulating aggregate demand (or adjusting the balance between aggregate demand and aggregate supply) is often known as a demand management policy.

According to such a goal of adjusting aggregate demand, there are two types of macroeconomic policy: expansionary and constrictive. Expansionary macro-economic policies are aimed at stimulating aggregate demand, and constrictive macroeconomic policies are at reducing aggregate demand. At the same time, macroeconomic policies, being expansionary or constrictive, can be executed by either the government or the central bank. The former is called fiscal policy while the latter is referred to as monetary policy. Since in developed countries governments and central banks are often independent, fiscal and monetary policies can also be executed separately.

Monetary policy

Monetary policy refers to the measures taken by the central bank to adjust aggregate demand. There are several instruments of monetary policy, such as open market operation, discount rate and required reserve ratio, for adjusting aggregate demand. To carry out an expansionary monetary policy, the central bank may purchase bonds in the open market, lowering the discount rate and reducing the required reserve ratio. The opposite is true for constrictive monetary policy.

In the process of implementing its monetary policy, the central bank often sets an intermediate target in accordance with the general economic situation and tries to realize it using various instruments of monetary policy, such as open market operation, among others. The achievement of this intermediate target, of course, is for the ultimate target of monetary policy, such as an appropriate level of aggregate demand.

In developed countries, the intermediate target of monetary policy has been shifted from the past money supply to the current interest rate. Such a shift reflects the institutional transformation of financial intermediaries, which further leads to the money supply changing from exogenous to endogenous. The so-called exogenous money supply indicates that the money supply in the economy is targeted by the central bank, which uses a variety of instruments of monetary policy to achieve the target. An endogenous money supply exists in financial institutions which the central bank does not target, and thus wants to influence the money supply; the money supply is determined by the demand for money from the underlying economy. As noted above, an endogenous money supply does not mean that the central bank can do nothing about the money supply. In effect, it still can easily influence the cost of the money supply (i.e., interest rate), and thus affect the whole economy. For this reason, the interest rate naturally becomes the intermediate target of monetary policy.

Fiscal policy

Fiscal policy is executed by a government that utilizes income and expenditure to affect the economy. Expansionary fiscal policy refers to government behavior that increases spending or reduces taxes (or both) in order to stimulate aggregate demand. Therefore it is used when the economy is in recession. Constrictive fiscal policy means the opposite.

As for Keynes himself, he preferred fiscal policy. Compared to monetary policy, fiscal policy can have an immediate effect, because government spending can increase aggregate demand directly. Monetary policy initially requires a decline in interest rates, thus stimulating private investment. Yet the government cannot directly control private investment, which depends on market response. This immediate effect also leads to fiscal policy being preferred by many governments, despite different attitudes held by economists.

Expansionary fiscal policy usually means increases in government spending. This in turn relates to how to use government spending. In reality, expansionary fiscal policy usually provides a good opportunity for the government to increase investment in infrastructure. During the deflationary period starting in 1997, the Chinese government did not hesitate to adopt an expansionary fiscal policy. From 1997 until 2002, the Chinese government issued more than 200 billion RMB of treasury bonds per year, most of them used for infrastructure investment. There is no doubt that the implementation of expansionary fiscal policy since 1997 has made an indelible contribution towards China's complete removal from the shadow of deflation in 2003. Meanwhile, the large number of infrastructure built due to the investment financed by treasury bonds will surely offer a solid foundation for long-term economic growth in China.[4]

In fiscal policy, what people are concerned about is the issue of debt. Whether cutting tax or increasing spending, expansionary fiscal policy will incur a deficit.

7.2 Market and administrative instruments – the way the Chinese government manages economic fluctuations

The three decades of reform and opening up in China have led to the Chinese economy being transformed from a traditional planned economy into a socialist market economy with Chinese characteristics. But compared with the Western developed economies, China has its own individuality: it is not just a transitioning economy, but also a developing economy. This has caused economic operation in China to be different from that in developed countries. At the same time, it has given rise to some unique features for the government in managing its macro-economy. In this section, we shall first review briefly how the Chinese government manages economic fluctuations. This brief review will be followed by some case studies and academic evaluation.

How the Chinese government managing its macro economy?

First, in China the method of managing economic fluctuation is different from that of developed countries in terms of organizational and administrative structure. In developed countries, the central banks are generally independent from governments, so their monetary policy can be designed and implemented independently. This is even more prominent among the euro-zone countries. But the People's Bank of China (PBC), the central bank in China, is not independent in administration; it is administrated by the State Council. Managing the macro-economy in China has been seen as a systematic project which is under the unified leadership of the State Council, and is jointly organized by the National Development and Reform Commission (NDRC), the Ministry of Finance and the PBC.

Second, in terms of the choice of targets, the macro-management in China is not only to reduce economic fluctuations and maintain price stability, but also to promote economic growth. It should be noted that these two goals are mutually contradictory in many cases. As stated in Chapter 3, inflation rate and economic growth are positively correlated: higher growth often leads to higher inflation. It is in such a contradictory target system that China's macro-management tries to maintain an unsteady balance. Besides, China's macro-management basically ignores the problem of unemployment due to the existence of a dual economic structure in China.

Third, the external environment for China's macro-management is not the same as that for developed countries. China's capital market is not completely open. At the same time, China's exchange rate system can basically be viewed as a fixed (or manageable floating, after 2005) exchange regime. Though such a system allows China effectively to stay away from financial crises (including the 1997 Asian financial crisis and the recent 2007 financial crisis), it has brought some complications to its monetary policy. We discuss this further in the next section of this chapter.

Fourth, China's macro-management often includes an adjustment in industrial structure. This means that the Chinese government will usually refine macroeconomic issues with regard to individual industries. Due to the development, transformation and imperfection in its market economy, the industrial structure in China often needs adjustment. In many cases, it is the imbalance and continuous adjustment of industrial structure in China that has caused its macroeconomic fluctuations. Because of this, China's macro-management cannot be separated from adjustment of industrial structure, or intervention from NDRC. The following case studies show exactly how specific measures are taken by the government for individual industries.

Finally, and most importantly, instruments in China's macro-management are often diverse. Perhaps we may call those instruments (such as open market operations, etc.) often adopted in Western countries "market instruments", because they often appear to be market behavior (buying and selling) by the government. However, in addition to using those market instruments, China also frequently uses some special instruments, which may be called "administrative instruments". These instruments often appear as restrictions and regulations that are set up according to the current state of the economy. Clearly, these administrative instruments are a legacy from the planned economy era. The followed two case studies also refer to the application of administrative instruments.

Case study 1: regulation of the steel industry[5]

From 2002 to 2005, the steel industry in China witnessed rapid growth in investment, with an annual growth rate of more than 30 percent and, at its peak, even exceeding 100 percent. In the meantime, China's steel production had an annual growth rate of more than 20 percent, and was ranked the first in the world for nine consecutive years. In 2004, the total steel output in China was approximately equal to the total sum of that from Japan, the United States and Russia, which were ranked second, third and fourth in the world, respectively.[6] In addition, there was a large number of firms engaged in steel production – more than 8,000 – while the number of companies involved in steel sales was said to exceed 200,000.

The overheated investment in the steel industry was largely due to various large-scale infrastructure constructions kick-started during the deflationary period (1997–2003) which brought the expansionary fiscal policies. It was also due to the expectation of rapid development in the real estate industry following housing reform. This led to a surge in demand for various steel products, and thus boosted the soaring of steel price. In 2002, the composite price index of domestic steel was 74.65; by 2004, the index had risen to 120 or more.

The rapid rise in steel prices triggered investment enthusiasm for the steel industry from many enterprises (including private enterprises), which actually created many problems. First, the steel industry is capital-intensive, with relatively higher technical requirements and, potentially, levels of pollution that may affect the environment. As a result, smaller private enterprises are not well suited to investment in the steel industry. Second, according to the outlook from national economic programming (set up by NDCR), a large number of high-tech, lightly polluting and large-sized steel plants were already in the pipeline. This would lead to excessive capacity in the steel industry.[7]

In response to the overheated investment in the steel industry, the government took a series of measures. In April 2004, the State Council decided that the capital proportion of investment projects for steel industry would be raised from 25 percent, to 40 percent or more. Coordinating with this, the PBC also launched guidance, in a timely manner, to commercial banks in order to limit loans to investment in the steel industry.

Second, on July 20, 2005 the NDRC formally promulgated the Development Policy of the Steel Industry. This policy covers a range of administrative measures to raise the access threshold for new enterprises to enter to the steel industry. For example, the examination and approval of new enterprises was strictly limited; a series of stringent technical standards was also provided. Indeed, the policy, in principle, no longer advocates the establishment of new iron and steel enterprises. For existing iron and steel enterprises to conduct trans-regional investment in iron and steel projects, there is also a clear threshold: enterprises should have an ordinary steel output of over five million tonnes for the previous year, or a special steel output of 0.5 million tonnes. For foreign-owned steel companies who look to enter the Chinese market, the policy provides that they must have independent intellectual property rights, with the previous year's ordinary steel output of up to more than 10 million tonnes or a special steel output over 1 million tonnes; at the same time, their investment can only be by way of transforming and relocating existing domestic iron and steel enterprises, with newly established operations forbidden. This regulation dashed the hope of many large overseas conglomerates who wanted to enter the Chinese iron and steel industry immediately.

In 2006, when the Development Policy was issued for the second year, China's steel investment began to decrease.

Case study 2: regulation of the real estate industry

In 1998, China started its market-oriented reform in the housing supply system. This reform released the housing demand from residents and stimulated housing construction and supply. In 1998–2008, residential investment in China had an average annual growth rate of up to 17.2 percent, and investment in urban real estate reached an average annual growth rate of 27.6 percent. The real estate industry had become a pillar industry of China's economy, and played a significant role in China's economic growth. Yet the market-oriented reform of China's real estate industry was also accompanied by a large swing in housing prices. During 1998–2003, house prices rose only slightly; however, towards the end of 2003 housing prices began to soar.

Excessively high housing prices pose a great threat to economic and financial security, thereby leaving residents facing heavy financial pressure when making house purchases, and even exacerbating public discontent. To solve such problems, the State Council has issued a series of guiding principles and specific measures since 2005. As in the case of the steel industry, the measures started with commercial loans. Regulations state that for the non-first-time buyer, the minimum down-payment ratio of loans rises to 40 percent, and loan interest rates are discriminatory. Additional taxes are also levied on house sales according to the period of house ownership. Clearly, these measures are used to drive down speculative demand for real estate.

In addition to these monetary and fiscal measures, there are also some administrative controls, which are typical of China, highlighting China's institutional features. For historical reasons, China has many state-owned enterprises that have been reconstructed into giant, industry-leading "central enterprises".[8] After restructuring and reforming, these "central enterprises" usually carry huge financial strength. Yet many of them are also major players in the real estate industry, even if their main business may not originally have been related to real estate. Due to their huge financial resources and capabilities, these "central enterprises" had become the so-called "rulers of the real estate industry". Their frequent purchases of land had, to a large extent, exacerbated the speculation in the real estate market, thus arousing public criticism. In March 2010, an instruction by the State Council and the State-owned Assets Supervision and Administration Commission (SASAC) ordered 78 central enterprises to exit the real estate industry.

Even these measures are still not enough. Recently, the central government added the target of stabilizing housing prices to the performance evaluation system of local government. In China's political system, the major officers of local government are often appointed by the central government, which establishes a performance evaluation system for regulating and examining the local officers. Such a system often includes several targets, such as GDP growth, environment protection and public opinion, among others. The political promotion of a local officer largely depends on the achievement of these targets. Including stabilizing housing price in the performance evaluation system of local governments reflects the determination of central government to control housing prices. As a result, many local governments have launch varieties of sales orders. For example, on February 16, 2011, the municipal government of Beijing launched the sales order that:

- those who have no Beijing *Hukou* and have not paid taxes to the municipal government of Beijing for five consecutive years will not be allowed to buy a house in Beijing;
- those who have Beijing *Hukou* and who own only one house can buy, at maximum, one additional house in Beijing;
- those who have no Beijing *Hukou* but have paid taxes to the municipal government of Beijing for five consecutive years will be allowed to have, at maximum, one house in Beijing.

Such a sale order is a typical example of an administrative instrument used by the Chinese government to manage its economy.

Time inconsistency: the problem of administrative instruments

On a beach frequently struck by floods, the government erected a warning sign, clearly stating that no buildings were allowed. But a couple with luck in mind set up their own "beach house". When floods approach, should the government offer help to them as per "good wishes"?

The preceding classic case was given, in their award-winning papers, by Kydland and Prescott, laureates of the 2004 Nobel Prize in Economics. They concluded that, in the short term, "to act as per the will" seems to be beneficial since it is "the best policy in the current circumstance"; however, it often has the opposite effect in the long run – that is, there is a so-called "time inconsistency". For the case above, if the government offers a helping hand, more opportunists will follow the example of the couple in building on the beach. This way, there is no point at all in setting up the warning sign by the government.

The administrative instrument often indicates a change in the rule of doing business, or setting up a new standard by destroying the old. For a transitional economy, there are reasons for using administrative force to perfect institutions and regulations. Nevertheless, the frequent use of administrative instruments will result in time inconsistency, and thus hurt the economy in the long run. With the progress in perfecting institutions and regulations, we expect that the Chinese government will less rely on administrative instruments for its macroeconomic management.

7.3 Monetary policy in China

In this section, we shall focus on China's monetary policy. As stated in the preceding chapter, the institutional ground for China's monetary policy is established on the state-owned commercial banking system. Although the majority of commercial banks fall into joint-stock banks and have gone public at home or abroad, state-owned shares still dominate. This means that the state has an important administrative influence on commercial banks. For instance, the chairmen and CEOs are often appointed by the government. Such an institutional property means that China's monetary policy is tinctured with many traditional shadows of planning, both administration and regulatory.

A system of conflicting objectives

In accordance with the Banking Law of the People's Republic of China, promulgated in 1995, the goal of monetary policy is defined as: "to maintain the stability of currency value of the RMB and thus promote economic growth". In light of this objective, monetary policy is not used directly to promote economic growth, but to create a favorable financial environment for economic growth by stabilizing the currency value of the RMB. In practice, however, "the promotion of economic growth" still becomes another hidden direct goal of monetary policy in a certain sense.

The so-called "stability of currency value of the RMB" basically carries a double meaning: first, it is about the stability of the exchange rate; second, it refers to the stability of domestic prices (i.e., maintaining a lower inflation rate). In the case of the goal of stabilizing the exchange rate, China has long been running a fixed exchange regime – that is, the PBC manages to maintain a target (or target zone) exchange rate in the foreign exchange market by selling or buying foreign currencies. As the target exchange rate is set to make the RMB depreciate, the task of stabilizing the exchange rate is relatively easy to achieve (see discussion in Chapter 6 and also in Chapter 10). Here, we will examine the task of stabilizing domestic prices.

We know that the Phillips curve and Okun's Law in China are not significant. We also know that this might be due to the dual structure of contemporary Chinese economy. In the dual economy, the labor supply can be seen as infinite. At the same time, China's unemployment statistics are only taken from urban residents, making it impossible to gain access to accurate unemployment statistics. But the insignificance caused by the dual structure does not mean that we can deny the positive relationship between inflation rate and economic growth reflected in the Phillips curve and Okun's Law. In fact, as depicted in Chapter 4, over the past 30 years there has been a significant positive correlation between the inflation and growth rates in China.

The discussion above implies that promoting economic growth and stabilizing domestic prices are essentially two mutually contradictory goals. Therefore, China's monetary policy can be seen as striking a balance between these contradictory targets. In practice, the strong desire to promote economic growth is embodied in the fact that the amount of China's money supply has been high for a long period of time, at approximately 20 percent, which is much larger than the growth rate of nominal GDP (see Table 1.1 and Figure 1.1). The current so-called issue of excessive liquidity may be more or less due to China's monetary policy featuring the two conflicting objectives.

Intermediate targets

We already know that in implementing monetary policy, the central bank may generally draw up an intermediate target of monetary policy based on the current situation of the economy, and try to achieve this target by using various instruments of monetary policy. Of course, the purpose of achieving the intermediate target is to attain the ultimate goal of monetary policy, such as a stable price level (and a higher rate of economic growth, as in China). At present, the developed economies in Western countries commonly consider the interest rate to be their intermediate target of monetary policy, which is dictated by the transformation of the money supply from exogenous to endogenous.

However, China has long practiced a planned economy, while state-owned commercial banks still dominate the current banking system. Hence, China's money supply is still largely exogenous, implying that it can still be controlled by the central bank. In addition, the impact of interest rate on investment does not seem significant in that there is an abundance of investment opportunities in China and many enterprises remain under soft budget constraints. For these reasons, the intermediate target of monetary policy in China is inevitably money supply rather than interest rates. This can be evidenced by the fact that each year the government sets a target money supply, M1 and M2, and uses it as an indicator to reflect the intention of monetary policy.

Credit schemes and administrative instruments

As stated above, each year the Chinese government sets a target growth rate of money supply, M1 and M2, as the intermediate target of monetary policy. At the same time, the government may use a variety of monetary instruments to achieve this target.

In developed countries, the tools of monetary policy are generally divided into open market operations, adjustment of the discount rate, and required reserve ratio. The required reserve ratio is generally considered to be the most powerful instrument, which can suddenly change the reserves available for lending in the whole banking system. Consequently, the central bank will not easily adopt this instrument under normal circumstances. In China, though, this instrument is often invoked. For example, China's required reserve ratio was adjusted six times in the first six months of 2008 alone.

The main instrument of monetary policy in China, however, is the credit scheme and the related administrative measures for completing the scheme. Such a scheme is not seen in developed countries, and is a legacy of China's previous planned economy. Furthermore, it is also inseparable from the state-owned commercial banking system in contemporary Chinese economy.

When the target money supply is set, the State will construct a series of annual credit plans as the main instrument to achieve this target. In the annual credit plans, a certain credit line is assigned to a state-owned commercial bank. Sometimes credit lines will be refined according to different provinces and industries. It should be noted that in many cases the credit plan may only be "indicative", so that state-owned commercial banks may have a certain degree of freedom in their credit supply. However, the government can use administrative measures (named as "window guidance") to implement the credit plan at certain times, especially when the economy is in a serious condition, such as in high inflation or deflation. In this case, the credit plan becomes "mandatory".[9] When the economy is pressured by higher inflation, "loan inhibition" is often applied in accordance with the plan. On the other hand, if the economy is in deflation, a "forced loan supply" might be enforced. For example, the monetary policy implemented in 2004 can be understood as a "loan inhibition" imposed on some industries, such as the steel industry (discussed above). Prior to this, when the economy is in deflation, all state-owned commercial banks are forced to take the initiative to search for the right lender to complete the loan schemes issued by their higher leadership. This process is known as a "forced loan supply".

In addition to "loan inhibition" and "forced loan supply", the state-owned commercial banks are also sometimes required to provide policy loans to help state-owned enterprises that are in financial trouble. There is no doubt that such a transmission mechanism of the loan supply will inevitably generate huge non-performing assets. As mentioned in Chapter 6, the non-performing assets of state-owned commercial banks in China once hit approximately one-third of their total assets. Such huge non-performing assets left the government with no option but to reform the state-owned commercial banking system. We note that since the reform of commercial banking system, the "policy loan" and "forced loan supply" processes have been greatly reduced.[10]

Finally, regulation of interest rates is another important form of administrative instrument. In China, various lending and deposit rates for commercial banks are still largely controlled by the state. To be specific, the state will set a benchmark interest rate, and the interest rates effectively charged by commercial banks are required to be within a certain range of this benchmark rate.

All these show that China's monetary policy is still tinctured with many traditional shadows of planning, administrative and regulatory. To a large extent, this is certainly related to the institutional basis of the monetary system – that is, the state-owned commercial bank system.

International reserves and issuance of high-powered money

As mentioned in Chapter 6, the PBC accumulates international reserves by bidding for US dollars in the foreign exchange market of China. Without doubt, such a purchase artificially raises the value of the US dollar relative to the Chinese RMB, thus causing the RMB to depreciate. At the same time, such a purchase also brings problems to China's monetary policy.

When the PBC uses RMB to buy dollars, the foreign exchange reserves in China are increased. Yet the monetary base (or high-powered money) is also injected into the economy, and thus immediately increases the liquidity of the economy.[11] In recent years, this has become the main channel of issuing a monetary base. Table 7.1 compares the structure of the monetary base between China and the United States.

It can be seen that the monetary base in the US is mainly in the form of purchasing government bonds, which accounts for approximately 90 percent. The monetary base in China, however, is dominated by the funds outstanding for purchasing foreign exchange. As a matter of fact, the funds outstanding for purchasing foreign exchange have surpassed the total monetary base since 2005. For instance, the funds outstanding for foreign exchange were equal to 122.9 percent of the total monetary base in 2007. Such huge funds create a problem of excessive liquidity, which means the PBC has to issue central bank's bills to withdraw the monetary base in circulation. In 2007, central bank bills amounted to 33.9 percent of the total monetary base.

What must be emphasized here is that the central bank's bills issued by the PBC are different from treasury bills or bonds issued by the Ministry of Finance.

Table 7.1 Structure of the monetary base (%) in China and the US

	China				United States	
	Re-lending to financial institutions	Purchasing foreign exchange	Net right to government	Central Bank's bills	Treasury bills	Re-lending to financial institutions
1996	54.4	35.7	1.1	0	88.02	0.04
1997	47.2	41.2	0.4	0	89.10	0.03
1998	25.4	55.8	−2.1	0	87.57	0.07
1999	24.1	48.8	−1.5	0	91.07	0.10
2000	47.7	39.8	−5.1	0	90.95	0.03
2001	43.7	43.7	−4.2	0	91.48	0.01
2002	38.1	49.4	−4.0	−3.3	92.32	0.01
2003	34.6	64.1	−10.8	−5.8	92.53	0.01
2004	31.5	84.4	−10.6	−18.8	93.33	0.01
2005	39.7	104.3	−10.5	−31.5	94.21	0.01
2006	36.2	114.9	−12.0	−38.2	94.41	0.02
2007	20.5	122.9	−7.1	−33.9	90.56	0.55

The data in the table are available from the websites of the PBC (www.pbc.gov.cn/) and the Federal Reserve (www.federalreserve.gov/).

The bills issued by the PBC are not used for economic development and government spending, and its role is only in withdrawing the base money in circulation. This is a completely financial innovation.

7.4 "Deflationary expansion" – the recent business cycle in China

"Deflationary expansion" – a new terminology in economics

A recent business cycle in China began in 1990, when the economy bottomed out with an annual growth rate of 3.8 percent – the lowest in the past 30 years. The economy started to recover in 1991, then peaked at a super-high growth rate for three consecutive years, with a growth rate of 12 percent or more. This unconventional growth was accompanied by a high inflation rate of more than 13 percent for three consecutive years, starting at the beginning of 1993. Subsequently, the economy began to fall into a deflationary period (see panels (a) and (b) in Figure 7.2). In this business cycle, one of the most obvious features is that

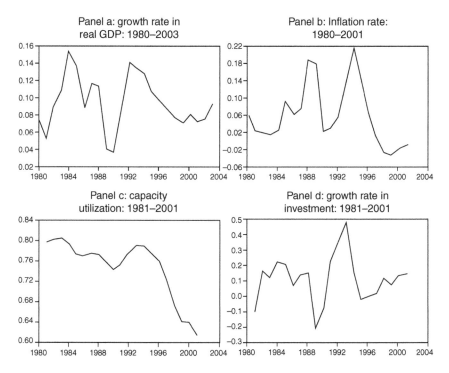

Figure 7.2 Key macroeconomic variables in recent business cycles of China. The rates of inflation, GDP growth and investment growth come from the National Bureau of Statistics (2004); the rate of equipment utilization is calculated by Gong and Yang (2002).

even when the economy has been in deflation, the growth rate of the Chinese economy has still hit about 8 percent, as opposed to other countries in the world today.

This high growth accompanied by deflation leaves many economists confused. According to Okun's Law and the Phillips curve, economic growth and inflation are positively correlated, so the coexistence of high growth and deflation is not supposed to occur. Chinese economists have coined a new terminology for this phenomenon: "deflationary expansion". Many Chinese economists have tried to explain the mystery of "deflationary expansion". Some foreign economists have even suspected the reliability of the official statistics published.[12] This indicates that economists, especially Chinese economists, have a duty to offer a reasonable explanation for "deflationary expansion". This is the main task of this section.

Supply shock – a standard interpretation from economics

According to economic theory, "deflationary expansion" may come from a positive supply shock, such as a rise in labor productivity. This can be explained by the so-called aggregate supply and aggregate demand (AS–AD) model.

The AS–AD model is composed of two basic curves: the aggregate supply curve and the aggregate demand curve (see Figure 7.3). Here, the aggregate demand (AD) curve is a downward-sloping curve, which reflects the society's aggregate demand for the output at a given price: the higher the price level, the lower the aggregate demand.[13] The aggregate supply (AS) curve is upward-sloping, suggesting how the price is determined at a given level of aggregate output (which itself is determined by aggregate demand). The aggregate supply

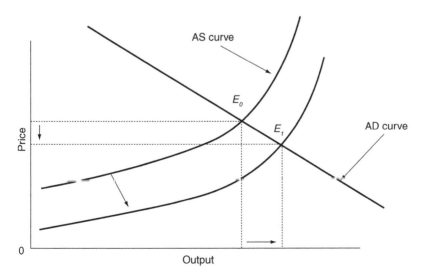

Figure 7.3 Aggregate Supply–Aggregate Demand (AS–AD) model.

curve is consistent with the principles embodied in Phillips curve and Okun's Law: the higher the aggregate output (or economic growth rate), the higher the price level (or inflation rate) will be.

As shown in Figure 7.3, when there is a positive supply shock, other things being equal (i.e., given AD curve), the aggregate supply curve will shift to the right and therefore the output will rise and the price will fall, so the coexistence of high growth and low inflation (or "deflationary expansion") becomes possible. Indeed, most foreign economists hold this view,[14] and this standpoint is also shared by some Chinese economists.[15] If we look at the Chinese economy around 1997–2003, during which period deflationary expansion occurred, we can see some positive supply shocks, as described below.

First, the reform of state-owned enterprises (SOEs) in China entered a new stage at that time: state-owned enterprises were allowed to lay off workers. Laying off workers can reduce the burden for SOEs and improve their labor productivity, thus leaving more margin for enterprises to lower prices in order to facilitate competition. Laying off employees also implies an increase in unemployment in urban areas, which is further worsened by a large quantity of surplus rural labor flowing into cities. A severe unemployment problem in cities will obviously affect workers' wages – an important factor in determining prices. Here, we would like to emphasize that laying off of workers was completely the result of institutional reform, and nothing to do with whether the economy was booming or not. For this reason, unemployment and economic growth can coexist simultaneously, as evidenced by related data. For instance, China's registered unemployment rate was 3.1 percent during 1997–2000, while it hit 3.6 percent in 2001. Note that here the registered unemployment rate excludes laid-off workers from its calculation. Taking into account the laid-off workers, the urban unemployment rate was 7.8 percent in 2000.[16]

Another phenomenon of supply shocks is related to the value of the Chinese RMB. In the aftermath of the 1997 Asian financial crisis, the currencies across countries depreciated one after another, while the US dollar gained strength in value. China pursues a fixed exchange rate system pegged to the US dollar; therefore, the RMB began to appreciate, too. This also meant a decline in prices of imported products, thereby resulting in a positive supply shock.

Excessive investment – another explanation for "deflationary expansion"

The interpretation of "deflationary expansion" of the Chinese economy can also be given from another perspective – namely, the dynamics of economic fluctuations: the "deflationary expansion" of the Chinese economy may be rooted in excessive investment for previous years, starting in 1993.[17] Over-investment creates excessive demand prior to the establishment of production capacity, thereby accelerating inflation. At the same time, there will be an obvious increase in capacity upon its completion. So, when the government adopts an anti-inflation policy through demand management, aggregate demand will fall, with production capacity in excess, thereby resulting in deflation. Such an interpretation seemingly dovetails with the volatility of key macroeconomic variables of China in recent years. For the growth rate of investment (which creates production capacity) and capacity utilization, see panels (c) and (d) in Figure 7.2.

The viewpoint of over-investment (or over-shock) may offer us an insight into deflation occurring in the recent business cycle in China, but the idea itself cannot by itself explain why the Chinese economy has still maintained a high growth rate against the background of deflation. If the fluctuations in the economy itself hover around a higher growth rate (or a higher steady state of growth rate), the phenomenon of "deflationary expansion" is likely to occur. This inference accords with the fact that the growth rate of the Chinese economy was about 8 percent during deflationary period, which was not only significantly lower than that for previous years but also less than the average annual growth rate of 9.69 percent over the past 30 years. For this reason, when we use over-investment to interpret "deflationary expansion", we still need to explain why China has maintained a high economic growth over the past 30 years. And that has already been examined in the previous chapter.

Gong and Lin (2007, 2008) have provided a more detailed analysis on the view of over-investment by building a dynamic macroeconomic model consistent with contemporary Chinese economy. The model is provided in Appendix D.

It should be noted that the over-investment perspective also reveals a very important policy implication: to prevent the Chinese economy from being entrapped in deflation in the future, it is necessary now to prevent the excessive growth in currency and investment that may bring an unnecessary shock to the economy.

Discussion and questions

1 Explain what is meant by business cycles. Are business cycles exogenous or endogenous? Under what conditions is counter-cyclic macroeconomic policy necessary for the economy to be stabilized?
2 Why can Keynes's macroeconomic policies be interpreted as a demand management policy? What are their goal and basic principle?
3 Distinguish between the ultimate target, the intermediate target and the instruments of monetary policy.
4 Why can fiscal policy achieve effects fast and directly compared with monetary policy? In the period of 1997–2002, the Chinese government implemented an expansionary fiscal policy. Discuss the background and feasibility of implementing this policy. Provide an analysis of the short-term and long-term effects of this policy, based on Chinese economy.
5 What characteristics does macro-management in China have compared with those in developed countries? Why does China's macro-management strike a balance in a system of contradictory targets?
6 What is "window guidance"? What is "forced loan supply"? What is "loan inhibition"? What are "central bank's bills"? Explain why the PBC issues the central bank's bills.

7   Is the intermediate target of monetary policy in China different from that of developed countries? What is the significant difference in monetary instruments between China and developed countries? Does this difference have anything to do with the institution of the banking sector in China?

8   What is "deflationary expansion"? How do you explain it?

9   "To prevent the Chinese economy from being entrapped in deflation in the future, it is necessary now to prevent the excessive growth in money supply and investment that may bring unnecessary shock to the economy." Explain why this passage is economically sensible.

Part III
Challenges in the future

8 Transformation to the second stage of economic development

We have provided an interpretation of China's economic growth and volatility over the past three decades since the reform and opening up. From this chapter onwards, we will try to envisage the Chinese economy in the future. Our primary task is to explore the possibility of and conditions necessary for China to sustain its current high growth. To do this, we will first examine the quality issue involving economic growth in China over the past three decades. We then will discuss the challenges that China will have to face in the future, and present an extremely important theme: that China will enter, and has perhaps already entered, its second stage of economic development. This theme will run through the rest of the book.

8.1 The quality of high growth in contemporary Chinese economy

The growth mode over the past 30 years

We already know that over the past 30 years the high economic growth in China has been pulled by demand, especially investment demand. Investment not only boosts demand, but also accumulates capital and thus creates capacity. The stable political environment along with abundant and cheap investment resources has led to the high growth of investment in China. At the same time, economic fluctuations in China also stem from fluctuations in investment while China's macro-management has largely been focused on adjusting investment. All these indicate that over the past 30 years, the mode of economic growth in China can be regarded as an investment-driven growth mode.

It needs to be stated that such a growth mode depends on the premise that there is a huge amount of surplus labor in the economy. Investment often means building factories, which need labor to function. China's dual economy makes this possible. Because of this, such a growth mode is typical of developing countries, and thus unable to be explained by neoclassical growth theory.

But what might the quality of such a growth mode be? What consequences will arise? Is it sustainable? Can developing countries rely only on this mode to catch up with developed countries?

A fictional dialogue

Perhaps the following fictional dialogue may help us to get some insights into the quality problems with regard to the high growth in contemporary Chinese economy.

A: Hey! How are you doing these days?
B: Ha, I've been too busy. I am building a steel plant (Ha! Steel again).
A: What? Do you have the ability to build a steel plant?
B: Why not?
A: But that is high-tech!
B: It is no big deal. We can use traditional ways to produce steel.
A: Where did you build that plant?
B: In Jinshan, a development zone where land is extremely cheap.
A: Where are your workers from?
B: This is too easy. There are so many surplus workers out there.
A: You have to hire some engineers.
B: No need for too many, since we use the traditional method for steelmaking.
A: Money? Where is the money from?
B: It does not need too much money, most of which is loans from banks.
A: I still feel a little weird. Do you think it will work out?
B: Why not? You can see the steel price rising all the time.
A: But if it does not work out, that means you will owe a lot of money.
B: No big deal, just repudiate! They would not kill me.

Despite the fiction of this dialogue, it may help us to imagine the problems that could be ahead with the investment-driven growth mode in China.

Low technological content

Such a growth mode in itself does not require the advancement of technology and human capital. As long as investment is higher, growth will be also higher, regardless of whether the production means of the factories built through investment are high technology or not.

We should first clarify that so-called low-technological content here does not refer to the structure of the products produced in China, but to the means of production (or the method of producing certain type of products). Many products produced in China can be regarded as high-tech products; China even produces some aerospace products. Yet, in many cases the core components of these products are often imported. Production in China of these high-tech products often appears to involve the final stage of production – that is, assembly. This indicates that the additional value (resulting from production in China) is often low relative to the total value of these products.

Of course, some core components (especially those of military products) may be produced domestically, but this is costly. For instance, in order to make a single qualified high-precision core component in China, a large amount of labor and materials is required in the effort to meet the required level of precision, whereas in the US and other developed countries that component can be mass-produced by a production line with artificial intelligence.

Therefore, regardless of whether the products produced are high-tech or low-tech, the production activities carried out in China are themselves often low-tech in nature. This is further reflected by the low labor productivity, and thus low wages and low per capita income for the economy as a whole. Here are some other data that reflect the low-tech production activity in China. In 2005, the energy that China consumed in producing one unit of GDP (measured in US dollars) was about 1.36 times that of India, 2.07 times that of Brazil, four times that of the United States and eight times that of Japan.[1] In 2004, the electricity that China consumed in producing one unit of GDP (measured in US dollars) was 2.6 times the world average, and 3.52 times that of OECD countries.[2]

The major reason for the low-technology production methods in China is the low resource cost of investment. As pointed out in Chapter 5, the resource cost of investment includes the costs of land, of labor and of financial resources such as loans, among others. If the resource cost of investment is low, there is no need for high quality investment. This implies that even if the investment leads to an exceedingly backward means of production, there will still be a profit margin.

The low-technology production methods in China also result from the lack of initiative among Chinese enterprises to conduct research and development (R&D) by themselves, and even the innovative ability to absorb and assimilate new technologies. Such a lack is partially due to cheap investment resources,[3] but is largely because of the institutional properties and related policy in contemporary Chinese economy that do not provide enough incentives for R&D and for human capital development. We will return to this issue in Chapter 9.

The growing rich–poor gap

Although the high growth in China is unparalleled in Asia and even in the world, the rich–poor gap is also growing. According to the estimates of domestic scholars, between the late 1970s and 2005, China's Gini coefficient increased from about 0.3 to 0.45.[4] From the perspective of functional income distribution, such a gap between the rich and the poor can, to a large extent, be reflected by the continuously decline in the proportion of wage income over total income. This is demonstrated in Figure 8.1.

Such a widened gap between the poor and rich (or the decline in the proportion of wage income to total income) is again attributed to the investment-driven growth mode that is established on the premise of surplus labor. If labor is in excess supply, workers will have no strength to bargain with their employers once they get into the labor market. The low-technology production methods, as just discussed, also indicate that production activities in the economy do not generate enough demand for high quality workers with a high human capital level and thus higher wage demands.

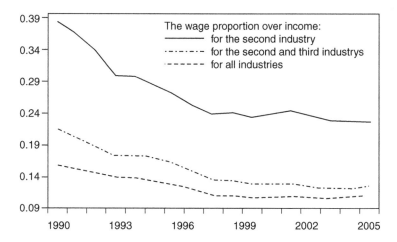

Figure 8.1 The proportion of wage income over total income: ——, second industry;
– - –, second and the third industries; – –, all industries. It should be noted
that the numbers regarding wages are not necessarily correct here, since many
types of wage are not included due to the difficulty in collecting data.
However, what is important is the trend: one can still see the trend of decline
of wages over the income. Figure reproduced from Gong and Yang (2010a).

Environmental damage

The high growth in China over the past 30 years has also brought a lot of
environmental changes, which may not be beneficial to the economy as a
whole. Investments such as construction of buildings, plant, highways, rail-
ways, airport and power stations, etc., often involve restructuring the existing
environment. Such a restructure might be environmentally friendly but could
also be environmentally damaging, depending on the technology that it
adopts.

Generally, environmentally friendly production methods are often high-
technology in content, while those that do not have high-technology content
not only have low energy efficiency but are also environmentally damaging. In
fact, it is true to say that over the past 30 years China has created and accumulated a large number of resources (fixed assets) through investment while
destroying a large number of alternative resources – the natural resources of
our environment. A more detailed discussion on this issue is given in Gong
(2008: Chapter 11).

All in all, although the high economic growth in China over the past 30 years
has been remarkable and important, it has not provided the country with the corresponding technological progress and improvement in human capital. The fruits
of growth have not been shared equally by its citizens. Meanwhile, such a mode
of growth has also led to environmental issues. In short, the quality of China's
economic growth over the past 30 years has not been high.

Perhaps such a growth mode has certain rationality in the early stages of economic development, since it has liberated a large amount of surplus labor after all. Yet, could such growth mode be sustainable in the future?

8.2 The sustainability of the existing growth mode in China

High growth is still possible

We already know that when a less developed country gets onto the path of convergence, the economy is likely to maintain high growth for quite a long period, and eventually to become convergent with developed countries. Of course, not all of the less developed countries can get onto the path of convergence. China's stable political and social environment, the continuous transformation toward a market-oriented economy and the rapid economic growth that has achieved over the past 30 years indicates that China is now on the path of convergence.

However, compared to developed countries, the level of per capita GDP in China is still not high; there is still, to some degree, a dual structure; surplus rural labors still exist; income distribution remains poor; development levels among different regions are still unbalanced; the technological content involved in production is still not high; and the human capital level is generally still low. All in all, China is still a developing country at present. This non-optimal state means that the Chinese economy still has huge space for development. The existence of such a huge space means that continuous high growth in China will still be possible in the future.

However, does the tremendous potential for high growth in China mean that the high growth can be naturally achieved by itself in the future? Is the current growth mode in China sustainable? To answer these questions, we need to discuss the future challenges faced by the Chinese economy.

Pressures from the international community

We pointed out in Chapter 3 that one of the three major characteristics of the Chinese economy is that it is a large country, with its population accounting for one-fifth of the world's population. In the early stages of economic development such a large country will have many advantages, such as in attracting more foreign direct investment. However, with the rise and rapid development of the Chinese economy, China's influence on the world is gradually increasing while pressure on China from the international community is also rising. The advantage as a large country could be perceived as "the threat from China", "China exporting deflation to the world", and other hostile expressions.

Let us first look at Figure 8.2, where the growth rate of exports since 1991 is presented. It can be seen that the growth rate of exports is usually at a high level, often at 20 percent and peaking at 60 percent, though that high level has declined since 2003. Recently, the growth rate in real exports even became negative due

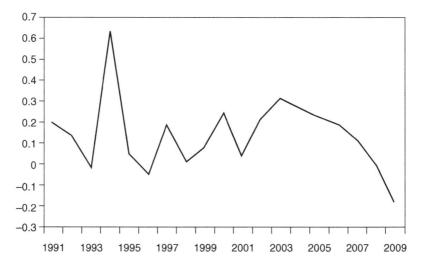

Figure 8.2 Growth rates of exports since 1991 in China. Here, the export is the real
export of product; the export of services is not included. Data from National
Bureau of Statistics of China (2010).

to the financial crisis occurring in 2008. On average, the growth rate of exports
was about 14.06 percent between 1991 and 2009.

Figure 8.2 has already told us that the future environment of international
trade will become less and less conducive to China participating in the international community with the current pattern of trade. The growth rate of developed
countries is much smaller than that of China. This implies that the expansion of
their market size is smaller than China's economic growth. If China were a small
country, there would be less pressure for China to keep exporting to developed
countries at high speed. However, China is a large country: its GDP has been
recently ranked as second in the world. We cannot expect China to continue to
export its output at 14 percent or more to developed economies whose market
expansion is only about 2 percent or 3 percent. From the viewpoint of trade
balance, China's future exports should also be growing at the rate of 2 percent or
3 percent. Otherwise, trade friction will be frequent.

One of the reactions of international community regarding the rapid rise of
China's export and trade surplus was the request that China appreciate the RMB.
In response to this request, China, on July 21, 2005, launched a reform of the
RMB exchange regime from the previous fixed exchange regime to the current
manageable floating exchange regime. This initiated the process of gradual
appreciation of the RMB. There is further discussion on the RMB exchange
regime in Chapter 10.

Another pressure from international community is their concern regarding the
increase in energy consumption from China. This increase is largely due to
China's high economic growth: a larger economy often leads to larger energy

demands. This is sometimes regarded as the culprit in the rise of oil prices in the world market. Further discussion on this issue can be found in Gong (2008: Chapter 11).

Pressure from the domestic economy

One of the properties of the current investment-driven growth model is that investment growth is larger than GDP growth. However, such a tendency cannot be sustainable. Investment creates capacity. Investment growth larger than output (GDP) growth indicates that the growth in capacity is larger than that in output. This will lead to excessive capacity. From this point of view, investment growth cannot always be larger than GDP growth. Otherwise, it only means blind investments, duplicated investments and non-performing assets created by investment firms.

The most important pressure on the Chinese economy in the future will perhaps be the labor market status in China. If there is not a sufficient increase in labor productivity, rural surplus labor will gradually be depleted. Over the past 30 years, the average growth rate of labor productivity in China has been about 4–6 percent per year. Yet we must stress that the increase in labor productivity in China has resulted mostly from economic reform, such as allowing extra workers to be laid off. The increase in labor productivity caused only by technological progress (such as adopting a new production mode, etc.) will obviously be much less.

In order to give a brief idea of the status of the future labor market in China, we may make some simple calculations. Suppose that the increase in labor productivity caused by technological progress is about 4 percent. If the GDP growth rate stands at 8 percent, then total annual employment will grow by 4 percent. Five years later, the employment demand will be $(1+0.04)^5 = 1.21$ times as much as it is now; seven years later it will be 1.31 times higher. Although further research might be needed on this issue, we can already see that there will be no surplus labor left in China in the foreseeable future.[5]

We thus find that although the Chinese economy has realized high growth over the past 30 years and there is still a huge space for high growth in the future, high future growth cannot be achieved naturally by itself. Indeed, from both the supply (i.e., labor supply) and demand (i.e., export demand and investment demand) points of view, the current growth mode in China – that is, the growth mode with investment as a main driving force but lacking technological progress (or improvement in labor productivity) – will not be sustainable. The contemporary growth mode in China must be transformed!

8.3 Transformation to the second stage of economic development

We have seen that the growth mode of the current Chinese economy must be transformed in order to sustain high growth. We will continue to follow the demand–supply approach to discuss growth transformation.

Growth transformation from the demand-side perspective

Of the major three components (i.e., export, investment and consumption) in the demand side of the Chinese economy, export growth will, with the increase in size of the Chinese economy, have to be faced with a restriction. From the perspective of balanced development, China's export growth rate in the future should reasonably be around 3 percent – not the past 14 percent. In addition, investment growth cannot be continuously higher than GDP growth, as it has been previously. On the one hand, this will aggravate overcapacity in China; on the other, investment costs such as labor, among others, will no longer be cheap. Thus, of the three major components, consumer demand will be the only option for promoting sustained high economic growth.

The historical data from OECD countries that have experienced convergence seem to suggest a similar transformation in the demand structure. In Figures 8.3 and 8.4, the horizontal axis represents the real per capita GDP measured in US dollars. This can be seen as a country's development level. The vertical axis reflects consumption (in Figure 8.3) or investment (in Figure 8.4) over GDP against different levels of per capita GDP measured by the horizontal axis.[6]

The figures seem to suggest the following transformation in the demand structure. When a country is lagging behind its economic development level, the proportion of consumption over GDP is high while the proportion of investment is small. However, with economic development, the investment–GDP ratio will begin to climb, while the consumption share of GDP declines. Such a trend will remain until a certain level of economic development is achieved. When the economy develops to that level (measured in per capita GDP), the trends are reversed: the consumption–GDP ratio will start to rise while the investment–GDP proportion declines.[7]

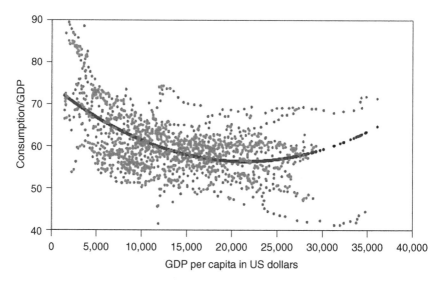

Figure 8.3 Transformation of consumption over GDP: OECD countries, 1950–2004.

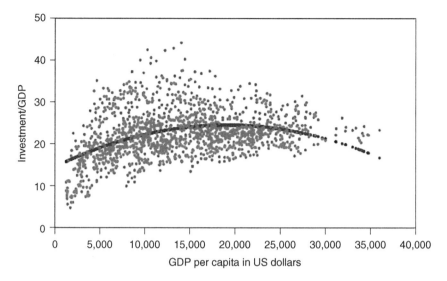

Figure 8.4 Transformation of investment over GDP: OECD countries, 1950–2004.

However, there are still many obstacles to China's stimulation of increased consumption. First, income distribution in China is still deteriorating. According to economic theory and large empirical evidence, the marginal propensity to consume for the poorer is generally larger than that for the richer. This indicates that the more unequal the income distribution, the smaller the average propensity to consume for society as a whole. Therefore, if the deterioration of income distribution cannot be stopped, stimulation of consumption in China will be difficult.

Second, the current health care and social security systems in China are not well established. This means that most families (especially those poor families) lack a sense of security about their future. Since most families prefer to maintain a stable living standard (reflected by their consumption), they will save more money to prepare for the future if the future is not secured. Thus, without good social security and health insurance, there will be greater difficulty in stimulating domestic consumption.

Growth transformation from the supply-side perspective

The main symbol of the fact that developing countries lag behind developed countries is the difference in their per capita GDP (or output). Yet the differences in per capita output can be separated into the following two factors:

* Human resources have not been fully utilized; that is to say, there is generally a large amount of surplus labor in developing countries under the dual economic structure.

- Among hired workers, productivity is low compared with developed economies.

According to these two differences, a developing country must experience the following two stages (or processes) in order to catch up with developed countries (see Figure 8.5):

- a process to absorb its surplus labor;
- a process to improve its labor productivity.

Clearly, China's investment-driven mode of economic growth over the past 30 years can be understood as a process to absorb surplus labor. As mentioned earlier, such a growth mode requires the existence of huge amounts of labor as its major premise. Although China still has surplus labor today, this will become depleted some day if there is no significant improvement in labor productivity – and, as noted earlier, that day seems to be not far distant.

Thus, from the supply perspective, the sustenance of current high growth in China must rely on the significant improvement in labor productivity for society as a whole.

How can labor productivity be improved?

We have seen that in the foreseeable future, such an investment-driven growth mode in China must be transformed. From the demand perspective, this indicates that consumption must be stimulated. From the supply perspective, it relies on the progress of labor productivity. It is relatively easy to understand stimulating consumption, but how can we understand improving labor productivity for society as a whole?

To have a better understanding, there is a need to look at the following Cobb-Dauglass production function:

$$Y = AK^{1-\alpha}L^{\alpha} \tag{8.1}$$

where Y is the output the economic society can produce, K is the fixed assets (or capital stock) created by firms' investment, L is the labor employed in production, and A is referred to technology in a general sense. We remark that in economics literature, the meaning of technology A can be very extensive. It can be expressed as knowledge capital – that is, a country's knowledge stock, such as

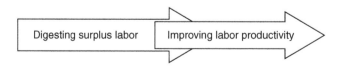

Figure 8.5 Catch-up process of developing countries.

academic papers, monographs, design and patents. According to Romer (1990), knowledge capital determines, to a large extent, the production methods (or technology) that a country utilizes in its economic activities. Its stock accumulation results from research and development (R&D) activities. Technology A can also refer to the quality of labor – that is, the so-called human capital.[8] Accumulation of human capital usually originates from education and health inputs.

Dividing both sides of equation (8.1) by L, we obtain

$$\frac{Y}{L} = A\left(\frac{K}{L}\right)^{1-\alpha} \tag{8.2}$$

Equation (8.2) indicates that the labor productivity Y/L depends on two factors: the capital–labor ratio K/L, and technology A.

It should be noted that production with a high capital–labor ratio K/L is often in capital-intensive industries such as steel, among other heavy industries. China's heavy industrialization has already been completed, and China's steel output has ranked first in the world for 10 consecutive years, having exceeded the British and American steel outputs long ago. The dream of the Great Leap Forward has already been realized! However, production with a higher capital–output ratio often requires higher investment, which we already know is unsustainable. Thus, the only choice for improving labor productivity is to increase the technology A.

Therefore, the call for improving labor productivity does not mean developing a capital-intensive mode of production. In effect, as far as the production mode and industry selection are concerned, the traditional division between labor-intensive and capital-intensive no longer holds. At the very least, we ought to add in a technology-intensive (or knowledge-intensive) mode as well.

The world economy today has entered a brand new era – an era of knowledge-intensive economy. Knowledge-intensive economy has replaced capital-intensive economy as a major direction of economic development. In a knowledge-intensive economy, workers with a high level of human capital are the major input to the economy. The economy must be characterized by a high level of per capita output, but this high level of per capita output does not need to be capital-intensive – i.e., have high levels of possession of capital (fixed assets) per capita. The high level of per capita output results from advanced knowledge (or technology) and highly-qualified workers who can create and master the knowledge.

The two major challenges in the second stage of economic development

The past 30 years in China can be regarded as the first stage of economic development. That stage has two apparent properties: the first is the existence of a huge surplus of labor; the second is that the economy is small (in terms of GDP and purchasing power, among others, rather than its population), so its influence in the world economy is negligible. These two properties no longer seem to exist currently, or will not in the near future in China. There is no doubt that China has now entered the second stage of economic development, or is about to do so.

Compared to the first stage, the second stage of economic development has exactly opposing properties: a huge surplus of labor no longer exists, while the economy becomes larger so that its influence on the world is no longer negligible. Following these two properties, China has two major challenges (or tasks) to be achieved in its second stage of economic development:

- internally, the economic growth mode needs to be transformed;
- externally, the RMB needs to be internalized.

Achievement of these two tasks is vital in order for China to catch up with developed economies, but also extremely difficult.

Let us discuss the first challenge. Initially, the improvement in resource allocation is reflected by utilizing surplus labor and thus is largely a matter of Keynesian demand management. As long as investment is high and the surplus labor can be allowed to move freely among the economy looking jobs, the growth can be high. However, when there is no longer a huge surplus of labor, improvement in resource allocation is mainly reflected by upgrading the quality of the resource (e.g., labor, etc.) that is no longer in surplus, and this requires that the advantages of market economy be unleashed completely – especially the advantage with regard to incentive. Due to a variety of market imperfections, the most important advantage of a market economy is not in allocating the existing resource. That advantage can partially be complemented by Keynesian demand management. The most important advantage of a market economy, compared to a planned economy, is that it provides a strong incentive to innovate under the pressure of competition. This will be the key to China sustaining its high economic growth and eventually catching up with developed countries in the future. Reform should be extended not only to the economic sector (composed of general enterprises), but also to the educational and research sectors, and even to the governance sector. In today's China, these sectors have not yet been touched by reform.

As the largest developing country, China sees its overall economic scale ranked second in the world. This indicates that many pressures might be imposed on China by the international community, as the Chinese economy is now beginning to influence the world economy. However, the RMB, the currency issued by China, has not been internationalized. This brings huge risks to the Chinese economy. While the RMB acts as a non-international currency, China must pay for a wide array of imports and international indebtedness with currencies of other countries (or international currencies). Since a large proportion of China's import demand is fixed, such as oil, iron ore and other non-substitutable strategic resources, while its exports are constantly affected by the demand from overseas markets (or cannot be controlled by China itself), China's international payments will always be in peril in the absence of adequate international currency reserves. This can be regarded as the internal pressure of RMB internationalization.

There are, however, still external pressures on RMB internationalization. The so-called external pressure does not refer to the pressure from the international community for China to internationalize the RMB. Perhaps, in their own interests, developed countries that issue international currencies may not want the RMB to be internationalized. The external pressure refers to their frequent criticism regarding China's accumulation of international currency via this exchange rate policy. But the only way for China to give up accumulating reserves of international currencies is to allow the RMB itself to be an international currency. Again RMB internalization is not an easy task. There is further discussion of this issue in Chapter 10.

Discussion and questions

1 Briefly describe the growth mode of the Chinese economy over the past 30 years. Why might this growth mode imply low technological progress, increasing the gap between rich and poor, as well as environmental damage?
2 After 30 years of high growth, do you think China still has room for high growth in the future? Why, or why not?
3 Can investment growth always be larger than GDP? What type of problems might occur if investment growth is always larger than GDP growth?
4 How do you expect the surplus labor levels in China to change? What might the impact on the current growth mode in China be if surplus labor were no longer to exist?
5 How do you expect the export growth in China to change? Do you think China will continue to be able to export products at a rate of 14 percent or more, as in the past?
6 Why is consumption stimulation important in China's growth transformation? What obstacles may exist regarding consumption stimulation in China?
7 What two processes (stages) do less developed countries need to complete to catch up with developed countries? Which process do you think China is currently in?
8 Provide a brief discussion of how labor productivity can be improved by relying on the Cobb-Dauglass production function. What is the implication for China transforming its growth mode?
9 Discuss briefly the topic of growth transformation in China, relying on both demand and supply perspectives.
10 What are the two major tasks for China in the second stage of economic development? Do you think these two tasks will be easily achieved?

9 Technological progress and human capital development

As shown in the last chapter, even though there is still a huge space for high growth in China, this does not mean that high growth will automatically be achieved by itself. In order to maintain the high growth in China, its growth mode must be transformed: the future growth mode in China must be transformed gradually from demand-pull growth (mainly pulled by investment demand) into the supply-driven growth mode prominently marked by technological progress.

Yet, what is the technology? How does it progress? And what are the factors affecting technological progress? How do advances in technology change our economy? What role does the government play in technological progress? These points will be discussed in this chapter.

9.1 Technology and its progress

In economics, technology can be defined basically in two ways: one is to interpret the technology as being directly related to human capital; the other is to see technology as knowledge capital. Here, we will first discuss human capital.

Human capital and its investment

In economics literature, which has a history of 200–300 years, there is no shortage of elaboration of ideas on human capital, for which many renowned economists have provided their own thoughts. The modern theory of human capital stems from the late 1950s and early 1960s, and investigates the basic characteristics of human capital, its formation process, and costs and benefits incurred by investment in human capital.[1] As with the emergence of other new economic theories, human capital theory, once it emerged, attracted much interest and expanded beyond the traditional area of economics. It has now become a powerful tool to solve the difficulties encountered in economics.

Human capital can be defined from the perspective of individuals or society. From an individual point of view, human capital takes the form of the knowledge, skills, abilities and health of individuals; from the perspective of society, human capital refers to the population quality in a country or a region.

Despite the fact that human resources (or labor) in a country are given exogenously, human capital is endogenous. As far as individuals are concerned, human capital is not an individual's genius, but rather is acquired by investment in people, mainly in the form of education. Investment in human capital is of great significance to human capital accumulation, and therefore the theory of investment in human capital is the core of human capital theory. Next, we will give a brief overview on the costs and benefits of human capital investment.

The investment costs of human capital can be divided into two categories. The first is direct costs – that is, the costs actually incurred in investment in human capital, such as the costs to the government (e.g. education expenditure in the government budget) and the costs borne by students themselves. The second is the opportunity cost – that is, current income given up for the future return from investment in human capital. It needs to be noted that not all investment in human capital will have opportunity costs. There is no opportunity cost in investing in preschool, elementary school, and junior high school education.

The social benefits from investing in human capital fall into several categories. Human capital is a factor of production that can directly increase productivity. A well-trained mechanic, for instance, has higher efficiency in repairing engines than those workers without training. This is the direct benefit of human capital.

The role of human capital is, however, more reflected in its indirect benefit. A well-educated individual may be more adaptable, more receptive to new knowledge, and more able to adjust in response to a new environment. This indirect benefit of human capital could make the society more likely to succeed in withstanding a variety of possible external shocks. A country with a higher quality of population will undoubtedly have stronger competitiveness in the world today, with the continuous progress in science and technology.

In addition to the economic benefits, human capital also benefits society in terms of it becoming more harmonious and more equal in income distribution. The income distribution in a country often depends on its demographic structure. The demographic structure in less developed countries usually takes on a pyramidal shape (see Figure 9.1). Most of the population, with a low level of human capital, is located at the bottom of the pyramid. Those people who do not receive a good education are engaged only in low-skilled jobs, or are simply unemployed. They have poor adaptability to the market economy, which leaves them more likely to be jobless. Yet if a country has a higher stock of human capital, its demographic structure will be more elliptical in shape. The majority of the population will have a good education, many of them being professionals – lawyers, doctors, accountants, engineers, etc. These people constitute the middle-income class in society. Clearly, such a demographic structure means that income distribution is more equal, thus making society more harmonious and stable.

It should be noted that the social benefits that we have just discussed are not same as the gain to the individual (or family) that carries the investment in human capital. To individuals, the return from investing in human capital can simply be reflected by increased future income. Numerous studies have shown

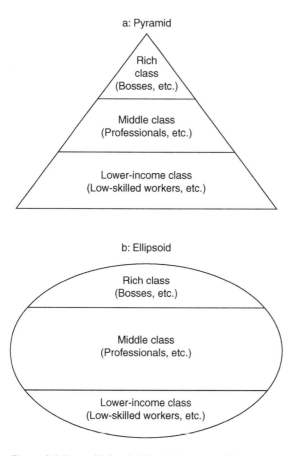

Figure 9.1 Pyramidal and elliptical demographic structures.

that the rate of return on investing in human capital is generally far greater than that on investing in physical capital.[2] However, investment in human capital is a long-term investment and also has high degree of risk and uncertainty, regardless of its high rate of return in general. Investment by parents in human capital for their children generates a return only after their children have grown up and entered the labor market. This delayed input–output relationship will obviously affect the enthusiasm of households (especially poor families) for investing in human capital. At the same time, returns on investing in human capital can be influenced by personal character, opportunity, health and other factors, with great uncertainty. These return properties (uncertainty and the long-term nature) will have a great impact on financing investment in human capital. In general, banks and other private organizations are not willing to provide the loans associated with education. This means that without government support, the children from poor families may have more difficulty in gaining a good education than those from wealthy families.

Knowledge capital

Another explanation for technology is to regard technology as knowledge capital. According to Romer (1990), the technological level of a country can be measured by its stock of knowledge. Specifically, the technology can be expressed as a variety of academic papers, books, monographs, designs and patents. The knowledge capital is assumed to be accumulated by investment in research and development (R&D).

Technology as a knowledge product has the following properties. First, the technology might be a commodity (e.g., a patent), but it could also be a non-commodity (say, a published paper). A technology, if not taken as a commodity, could be seen as "public goods", because everyone is able to get it at a very low cost. Technology as public goods must conform to two conditions: it must be non-rivalry, which means that others can repeatedly use it when it is already being used by a company or individual; and it must be non-excludable, that is to say the owner cannot prohibit others from using it. Obviously, most public facilities (such as parks, roads and street, etc.) are public goods.

For knowledge, all theories and ideas are non-rivalry goods: knowledge can be shared by all others. It is this non-competitive nature that makes some key technologies able to greatly improve the productivity of the whole society once they become public goods. Yet, technology is different from general public goods in that it is partially exclusive. As mentioned earlier, published papers and books can be deemed public goods due to their nature being non-rivalry. However, many technologies are kept strictly confidential by owners, or protected through a patent application. These types of technologies are exclusive.

It needs to be pointed out that non-rivalry technologies are often those of basic theories. In accordance with international practice, basic theories cannot apply for patent protection. While we cannot deny the importance of basic theories, the process from basic theories to the formation of real productivity still needs a myriad of applied research, and the result of applied research is usually exclusive. This exclusiveness of applied technologies restricts the promotion and application of technological achievements, thereby affecting the rapid growth of economy to some extent. However, this exclusiveness is necessary because it offers the incentive for research in applied technologies.

Innovation

Knowledge capital, whether it is basic or applied research, cannot itself turn into a productive force, since it only takes the form of the stock of a variety of papers, monographs, designs and patents. There must be a process in which knowledge is turned into productivity. In economics, this process is named innovation. Innovation is carried out by entrepreneurs, while the stock of knowledge capital only provides a resource so entrepreneurs can innovate. As Schumpeter pointed out, if there is no innovation, knowledge capital is useless (Schumpeter, 1934: 88).

Schumpeter offered a brilliant exposition on innovation. In his view, innovation falls into five categories: new products, new production methods, development of new markets, utilization of new raw material, and restructuring of industrial sectors (Schumpeter, 1934: 66). On this basis, modern economists classified innovation into two categories: process innovation and product innovation.[3] Hence, we can see that innovation plays an important role in promoting technical progress and transforming the mode of economic growth.

It should be noted that, in the current literature with regard to modeling technological progress, research and development are often assumed to be carried out independently by individual researchers (or institutes). There is assumed to be a market in the economy for trading new knowledge (patents), the result of R&D, and therefore all new knowledge is assumed to be transformed into a production force once these are created. This way of treating innovation might be too simple. Despite much research being carried out independently by individual researchers (or institutes) who are not a part of a production firm,[4] a large amount of research, especially applied research, is firm-specific and therefore carried out by a firm's research department. The new knowledge from a firm's specific research is often simply secured by the firm itself. Patents are not applied for, and are therefore not on the market for sale. Sometimes this new knowledge is not even immediately transformed into production. Only when existing products are no longer selling well does innovation then take place which transforms the knowledge generated from a firm's previous specific research into new products.

We can see, then, how technology progresses. Technological progress requires, first, high quality human capital. Given high quality human capital, knowledge can be created and accumulated. Next, there is an innovation process, carried out by entrepreneurs, to transform the knowledge capital into production. This is how a new production mode emerges. The emergence of a new production mode also indicates the destruction of old ones. This is what Schumpeter named "creative destruction". Thus, the so-called transformation of the growth mode is somehow related to Schumpeter's process of creative destruction.[5]

What type of economy, as defined by its institution and government behavior, can accumulate human capital and knowledge capital more quickly while firms have a strong incentive to carry out their specific applied research and innovation? Is the Chinese economy such an economy? If not, what can the Chinese government do to improve technological progress?

9.2 What can the government do towards technological progress?

The functions of government when the market fails

Our discussion begins with the functions of the government. In effect, this is also the issue that economists have long been debating.

The functions of government can be reflected in many aspects. For instance, the government should protect the country against foreign invasion and safeguard its citizens. In terms of the economic functions of government, however, its primary task is to establish and maintain the order of economic activities. This order should be conducive to the efficiency of economic activities, and safeguard the fairness and impartiality of economic activities. There is not much controversy between economists regarding the government's functions. What kind of economic order, then, will be propitious to the effectiveness, fairness and impartiality of economic activities?

As pointed out in Chapter 1, the order of economic activities basically falls into two types: one is market-oriented, while the second is planned. In a market-oriented economy, the government generally does not directly take part in economic activities, and its main role is to maintain market order. In planned economy, however, the government is directly involved in all aspects of economic activity, such as pricing, producing and distributing products.

Historical experience has taught us that market-oriented economy has advantages in enhancing the effectiveness of resource allocation and increasing the initiative for personal participation in economic activities. But does the success of market-oriented economy mean that the market is omnipotent? Could it solve any problem of resource allocation? Clearly, if the market is omnipotent, then the function of government should only be to maintain the market order.

Although there have been theories of market omnipotence in the history of economics, the vast majority of modern economists will not agree with this. According to economic theories, the market might be a failure:

- when economic activity has external effects;
- when monopoly occurs;
- when it is out of order and its self-correction (via price mechanism, etc.) slows down;
- when information is asymmetric or imperfect so that there is a big risk and uncertainty in economic activities.

It follows that when a market failure occurs, the corresponding function of government is to repair the market failure. According to a variety of market failures, this function in reality might be in the form of:

- formulating regulations for supervising and preventing monopolies;
- macroeconomic management via fiscal and monetary policy;
- subsidizing (or even participating directly in) economic activities of special areas (such as education, etc.)

Financial support

Now we turn back to the question of what can be done by government in promoting technological progress. We have seen that there are three basic conditions for technological progress: the faster accumulation of human capital, the faster accumulation of knowledge (including basic knowledge, applied knowledge and firm-specific knowledge) capital, and a strong incentive in the economy for innovation.

Our previous discussions have shown that human capital has a wide external effect: investing in human capital not only brings benefits to individuals, but also has an external effect on society. At the same time, it is a long-term investment and its return is influenced by personality, opportunity, health and other factors. All these indicate that investing in human capital is risky and uncertain, and therefore banks and other private organizations are unwilling to provide loans for education. The return properties (a long lag-time, uncertainty and risk) of investment in human capital will evidently affect the enthusiasm for families (especially those poor families) to invest in their children. In other words, without support from the government, the market itself will not warrant the fast accumulation and adequate supply of human capital.

A similar argument is also applied to knowledge capital. Much knowledge, especially basic knowledge, is public goods, indicating that the return is purely social. Usually, investment (or R&D) in knowledge (if not firm-specific) is carried out by universities and research academies supported by the state. Thus, without financial support from government, knowledge (especially non-firm-specific knowledge) cannot be accumulated faster. Market failure is again unavoidable.

Institutional arrangement

In addition to financial support, the institutional arrangement is also an important guarantee for technological progress. If the institution is not arranged appropriately for universities, schools, research academies and enterprises, technological progress will still be difficult even if the financial support from government is large.

In many cases, the government, because of its necessary financial support, has the power to determine the institution and the method of operation of universities, schools and research academies. Even in developed countries, many universities, schools and research academies are public or state-owned. The objective of proper institutional arrangement in this case is to avoid the problems (such as bureaucracy, lack of incentives and high transaction costs) that occur in traditional planned and state-owned economies.[6] This will warrant that allocated resources from government are used efficiently.

Technological progress is also, indeed ultimately, determined by firms' behaviour: the high quality people graduating from universities and schools are employed by the firms; the basic knowledge produced from universities and research academies is demanded by the firms that carry out applied research to generate firm-specific knowledge; it is also the firms that carry out the innovation to transform the knowledge (including firm-specific knowledge or the knowledge from purchased patents) into a productive force and thus promote technological progress by creative destruction.

Incentive is again the key component of the institution for firms. The proper institutional arrangement is to maintain a strong incentive to carry out firm-specific research and innovation. In this respect, the market economy has an obvious advantage over the traditional planned and state-owned economies. Yet that advantage is because of the competition from markets. If a market is monopolized, the incentive for carrying out innovation and also the firm's specific research will be diminished. As pointed out earlier, a monopoly is one kind of market failure, and therefore must be restricted in the institutional arrangement by the government.

9.3 Prospects and challenges: technological progress in China

The financial status of the Chinese government

Promotion of technological progress requires that the government spends money on education and scientific research. Spending must be compensated. When government spending is greater than its tax revenue, a budget deficit occurs. The accumulation of a budget deficit generates a debt problem for the government.

After World War II, the governments in OECD countries often opted to issue bonds to promote economic growth and stabilize the domestic economy. However, this generates a high level of debt. Now, debt has reached more than 60 percent of GDP for most OECD countries. Figure 9.2 shows the ratio of debt to GDP in several major OECD countries between 1970 and 2000.

The presence of such a large debt has become a serious problem for governments in developed countries due to its role in the economy. For instance, the Treaty on European Union (also called the Maastricht Treaty), signed by the EU countries, requires the budget deficit from the government to be no more than 3 percent.

The debt from the central government of China is not serious. The ratio of debt to GDP in China is less than 20 percent,[7] which is far lower than the 60–200 percent levels of developed countries.[8] Another reason that we need not worry about the debt in China is that China is still in high growth. Indeed, the higher the growth rate is, the bigger the space is for the government to issue bonds without causing problems.[9] From that perspective, the root cause of the debt plaguing developed countries is that their economic growth rate is no longer high.

The healthy financial status of the Chinese government provides the opportunity and prospect for China to accumulate human capital and knowledge capital rapidly via sufficient financial support from the Chinese government.

Institutional reform in education and research sectors

Sufficient financial support from the government is only one of the requirements for fast accumulation of human capital and knowledge capital, and thus for rapid technological progress. Institution is another prerequisite.

The economic reform that started 30 years ago has not touched the education and research sectors in China. Universities, schools and research academies still

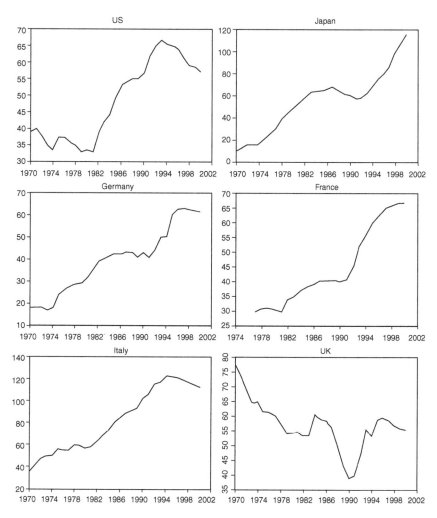

Figure 9.2 Debt–GDP ratios of some developed countries, 1970–2000. Reproduced from
Gong *et al.* (2001).

behave in the way of the past. Perhaps there are some reasons for the lack of
institutional reform: universities (among others) are not a firm; they are not
allowed to go bankrupt; they cannot exist without government support; a soft
budget seems to be unavoidable for universities (among others); even in
developed countries, many successful and famous universities are public (or
state-owned).

However, government support and state-ownership can exist in a variety of
forms. There are many institutional differences between universities in China
and public universities in Western countries. The quality of human capital and

knowledge capital generated from universities in China is generally behind that of universities in Western countries. One of the evidences to support this argument is that those who are awarded a PhD degree from a Western university generally have a higher market value than do those whose PhD comes from a university in China. Institution could be a factor in this difference, in addition to financial support.

It should be noted that institutional reform in education and research sectors is now of wide concern in China. We would expect that such reform will begin in the near future.

Institutional barrier to innovation and firm-specific research

An institutional barrier to technological progress in China may also exist in large enterprises, mainly the state-owned enterprises (SOEs). As pointed out in Chapter 3, the fourth stage of reform, which started in 1999, is to redistribute the state-owned economy with the core idea of "managing the large ones well while easing the small ones". Under this strategic consideration, the state-owned economy has been gradually withdrawing from competitive industries, while strengthening its status in industries related to national security and the economic lifeline.

Recently, under the protection of the state and with the other favorable conditions (such as easily obtained loans from banks, etc.) given by the state, many SOEs in China have become giants. Some of them have even re-accessed some attractive and competitive industries, such as the real estate industry. Due to their giant size and their wide connections with government and financial intermediaries (which are often again state-owned), they often easily achieve a monopoly of power once they have gained access to a new business field. In other words, their growing into a giant corporation is not because of their technological progress, but because of their power as a monopoly and their special connection to the government. Given such favorable conditions with no competition, they have no strong incentive to conduct firm-specific research and carry out innovation.

Due to competition from the market, small and medium-sized enterprises (SMEs) usually have the incentive to carry out innovation and firm-specific research – but their financial status often does not allow them to do so. Research often requires the employment of top scientists to work in well-equipped laboratories. For SMEs, this might be a burden. We thus identify the dilemma caused by the institution in China: those large companies that have the ability to carry out applied research and innovation do not have the incentive to do so, while SMEs may have the incentive to carry out research but they cannot afford to do so.

Evidences also seem to support our judgments. In Figures 9.3 and 9.4, we show the numbers of researchers per million and the numbers of patents per 10,000 inhabitants in China compared to other countries. As we can see, both numbers are much smaller in China compared to the US and Japan, among other developed countries.

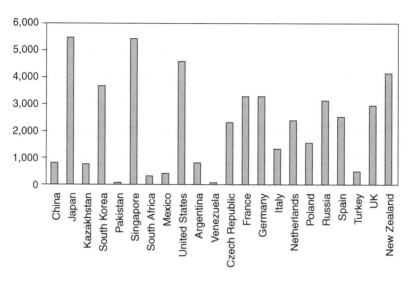

Figure 9.3 Number of researchers per million inhabitants (by country). Data from National Bureau of Statistics in China (2010).

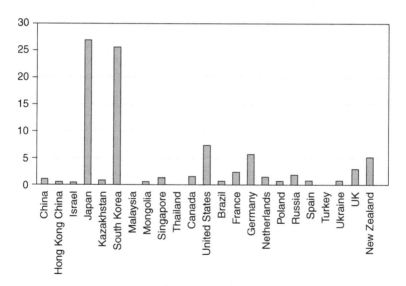

Figure 9.4 Number of patents registered per 10,000 inhabitants (by country). Data from National Bureau of Statistics in China (2010).

It should be noted that the investment in R&D by the government in China cannot be said to be smaller than in developed countries. According to the data from Huggins, Izushi, Davis and Luo (2008), Beijing is the area that has the largest R&D investment in China. Yet most of this investment is from the government, amounting to $1,008 per capita – while corporation investment is only about $403 per capita. The number of patents registered per million inhabitants is about 586. This is in sharp contrast to those developed countries where government investment in R&D is usually much smaller than corporation investment. For instance, in Tokyo, where R&D investment from government is about $180, but from corporations is about $927, the number of patents registered per million inhabitants has reached 2,277. Such a huge gap reflects two problems, as discussed previously: one is the inefficiency of governmental R&D expenditure (mainly by universities and research academies), and the other is the lack of R&D incentive from enterprises. Both are due to the institutional properties in China.

Human capital development: the top priority of the future Chinese economy

Before ending this chapter, we would like to stress once again the role of human capital in promoting technological progress and the transformation of the growth mode.

Our discussion begins with the relationship between human capital and knowledge capital. The understanding, mastery, application and creation of knowledge capital all rely on human capital. No matter how large the stock of knowledge capital, how many patents and designs are available, all of this is wasted unless it is understood and applied by people. Without this, knowledge would never be transformed into productive forces. On the other hand, even when there is not too much knowledge capital, we can create and absorb advanced knowledge to serve the economy as long as we have enough human capital. Thus, technological progress lies mainly in the improvement of human capital. Human capital is an essential precondition for the proliferation of new knowledge and technologies. Other things being equal, the greater the stock of human capital, the faster and the more widely new knowledge and technologies will spread.

More importantly, human capital is both exclusive and rivalry. This means that human capital cannot be used simultaneously by many, and that its owner can prohibit its use by the others. On the contrary, knowledge is non-rivalry and partly non-exclusive – it can be transmitted and spilled over. The spill-over of knowledge capital further explains the scarcity and importance of human capital for developing countries in order for them to catch up with developed countries in terms of technology.

Human capital is particularly important for transforming the growth model of the Chinese economy due to its adaptability. A well-educated individual can be more adaptable to new environments, more receptive to new knowledge and new skills, and know more about how to adjust to different situations. For example, graduate students with a degree in mathematics or physics can quickly turn to IT jobs after a certain degree of short-term training, if they cannot find a suitable job using their own degree subject. The transformation of the economic growth mode in China indicates the adjustment of industrial structure within the whole country, the change in the type of jobs, and the process of urbanization and industrialization. Therefore, a country that has a higher quality of population can be more adaptable to this continuously changing economy, thus making it easier to achieve the transformation of economic growth.

The successful transformation of the growth mode in China will first rely either on China's population quality, or on the level to which human capital can be comprehensively boosted. Yet the development of human capital in China dependts not only on government expenditure on education, which can be regarded as a supply of human capital, but also on the demand for human capital, which is more important in a market economy.

Indeed, the major obstacle to China's human capital development is perhaps the lack of demand for human capital. The current social environment and economic growth mode in China do not generate enough demand for high quality professionals. This has caused a conundrum in the very recent Chinese economy: on one side there is a shortage in the supply of low-skilled labor in some cities of the eastern coast area, so these workers' wages have increased significantly; on the other side, many college students and even graduate students can have difficulty in finding a professional job, so their wages are closer to those of low-skilled workers.

Discussion and questions

1   What is technology? In economics, which two methods are mainly used to explain the technology?

2   Analyze the costs and the benefits (including social benefits) of investing in human capital. What are the features of the return for individual families who invest in human capital? What do these features tell us?

3   What is knowledge capital? Is knowledge capital public goods? How can knowledge capital be accumulated?

4   What is firm-specific research? What is innovation? Explain the relationships among human capital, knowledge capital and innovation.

5   What is market failure? Under what circumstances will market failure occur? What are the functions of government when the market fails?

6   In addition to sufficient financial support, do you think an institution system is important for the governments in developing countries to promote technological progress? Why?

7   Compare the debt problems of China and developed countries. It is argued that "the higher the growth rate is, the more likely it is that bonds will be issued without causing a debt problem." Why is this?

8   Compare the efficiency of resources allocated to R&D research between China and developed countries. What might the institutional barriers be against China speeding up its technological progress? Why?

9   Discuss the role of human capital, by comparing it to knowledge capital, in transforming the growth mode in China.

10 It is argued that "since many college students and even graduate students in China may have difficulty in finding a professional job, it must be true that the supply of human capital in China is already enough." Evaluate this argument.

10 Reform of the exchange regime and RMB internationalization

In this chapter we shall discuss the second task in the second stage of economic development in China, as mentioned in Chapter 8, which is RMB internationalization. This topic is also related to the RMB exchange rate. The discussion in Chapter 6 and 7 seems to suggest that the current exchange regime adopted by China has the following properties:

1   It is designed for accumulating foreign exchanges (usually those of international currency) by following some standard.
2   It can either be a fixed exchange regime or a manageable floating exchange regime, but not a floating exchange regime.
3   The central bank interferes in the foreign exchange market (set within its own territory) often by buying (rather than selling) international currencies for the purpose of accumulating them.

Such an exchange regime might be called an accumulation-oriented exchange regime (AOER).

It should be noted that such an exchange regime may also imply the depreciation of domestic currency. Since the central bank has an unlimited supply of domestic currency, buying international currencies is always possible through bidding up their price. Therefore the domestic currency under this exchange regime is depreciated, comparing with if there were no such bidding up from the central bank. If China were a small economy, that exchange regime would not cause difficulty for China and the world. Yet as the Chinese economy becomes larger, that exchange regime is triggering more and more criticism from the international community while also bringing more and more danger to the Chinese economy itself.

The global economic imbalance has become a pervasive phenomenon. This is particularly prominent between China and the United States. For instance, China has continuously maintained a surplus in international trade, leading China's foreign exchange reserves to hit almost $3 trillion – the world's largest pool of international reserves (data from March 2010); the United States, on the other hand, has maintained a continuous trade deficit. Such a huge imbalance triggers many analyses, and some scholars have even attributed the financial crisis directly to this worldwide imbalance. In their view, the huge currency reserves accumulated by countries with a large trade surplus flowed back to the United States in "a reach for yields". This triggered the economic bubble in the United States, and thus resulted in the financial crisis in the global economy (Bernanke, 2008).

There is no doubt that the de facto criticism of China's big trade surplus and huge exchange reserves is directly against the accumulation-oriented exchange regime (AOER) as currently implemented by China.[1] However, such an exchange regime is not peculiar to China, and is actually a common phenomenon in developing countries (related data will be given later). Why, then, do China and other developing countries choose AOER? Is there any way to resolve the dispute regarding the RMB exchange rate?

We note that the economics profession has not provided a convincing explanation as to why developing countries prefer to choose an AOER. The preference, starting from Friedman (1953), by economists is often for a floating exchange regime: a floating exchange regime could promote the balance of payments via market force; it could also stabilize the domestic price by isolating external shocks; moreover, in the case of opening capital markets, it allows the independence of monetary policy. Yet we also note that the situation for developing countries is often excluded from related studies that include not only Friedman (1953), but also the Mundell-Flaming model, and the recent Redux model initiated by Obstfeld and Rogoff (1995).

This chapter examines why China and other developing countries choose an accumulation-oriented exchange regime (AOER). Our main argument is that the choice of an AOER by China, as well as other developing countries, is a natural response to the current asymmetric international financial order – that is, the RMB is not an internationalized currency while US dollars and currencies from other developed countries are internationalized. This discussion naturally suggests that the condition for China to terminate its current strategic choice of an AOER is to internalize the RMB.

The first section of this chapter reviews the historical evolution of the current international monetary system. This allows us to see how the current asymmetric international financial order has been formed. Section 10.2 discusses the strategic choice of exchange regime by developing countries under this asymmetrical international financial order. Section 10.3 explores the risks, the urgencies and thus the paradox of RMB internationalization. Finally, Section 10.4 discusses the strategies that China might take on the road towards RMB internalization.

10.1 The exchange rate and exchange regime, the current international financial order and its historical evolution

The formation of any system has its own historical reasons, and the international monetary system is no exception. Historically, the international monetary system evolved from the gold standard to the Bretton Woods system, and to the recent

Jamaica system. The current international monetary system is established essentially on the Jamaica Agreement. Both the gold standard and the Bretton Woods can be regarded as being fixed exchange regimes. It was the Bretton Woods Agreement that allowed the US dollar to become a world currency.

The Bretton Woods system

At the Bretton Woods Conference in 1945, the United States, relying on its overwhelming edge obtained during the World War II, successfully propelled the US dollar to become the global reserve currency. Yet, according to the Bretton Woods Agreement, the United States promised to link the dollar to gold at the rate of $35 per ounce. This generous pledge gave the US dollar the de facto role of the gold standard – the standard to which every other currency was pegged. Thus, the US dollar took over the role that gold had played under the gold standard system. As a world currency, the US dollar was not only a common measure of value internationally, but also a common mean of payments in international trade and other international affairs (such as international aid, subscriptions to the United Nations and other international organizations, etc.). As a result, the US dollar emerged as the default reserve currency of central banks across nations.

The Bretton Woods pegged the US dollar to gold, while every other currency was pegged to the US dollar. Thus, what emerged was the "pegged rate" currency regime, a seemingly stable world monetary system. Under such a system, the Western world experienced an era of economic boom marked by rapid economic growth and low inflation. This period is often called the golden age of the world economy. Table 10.1 compares the rates of inflation and economic growth in some major Western countries between the era of the Bretton Woods system and the post-Bretton Woods era.

It needs to be noted that during this "golden age", US dollars flowed continuously to the rest of the world as the only global reserve currency, which effectively means that the US maintained a deficit in the balance of payments with the

Table 10.1 Growth rates and inflation rates of some major advanced countries: Bretton Woods era (1946–1970) versus post-Bretton Woods era (1974–1989)

	United States	United Kingdom	Germany	France	Japan	Canada	Italy
Inflation rate							
Bretton Woods era	2.4	3.7	2.7	5.6	4.5	2.7	3.8
Post-Bretton Woods era	5.6	9.4	3.3	8.8	2.6	7.3	12.9
Growth rate of GDP per capita							
Bretton Woods era	2	2.1	5.0	3.9	8.1	2.5	5.6
Post-Bretton Woods era	2.1	1.5	2.1	1.7	3.5	1.3	2.5

Data from Bordo (1995).

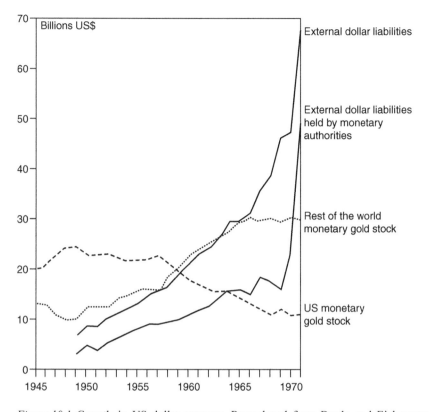

Figure 10.1 Growth in US dollar reserves. Reproduced from Bordo and Eichengreen (1993).

rest of the world. Figure 10.1 illustrates what happened, during this era, to the growth in US dollar reserves held by other countries (including their central banks).

The end of the Bretton Woods system and the establishment of the Jamaica system

Such a "pegged rate" currency system, with the US dollar at the center, however, was fated to be a failure. With increased uncertainties (such as the oil crisis, etc.) and the constant expansion of economic scale across nations, the dollar reserves held by the monetary authorities in the rest of the world continuously built up. Yet, due to the scarcity of mineral gold, the increase in gold production cannot be manipulated. Thus, when the outflow of US dollars was accelerated, the US-held gold reserves no longer appeared to be large enough to maintain the dollar at the fixed peg of $35 per ounce. This caused the holders of US dollars in the rest of the world to lose faith in the US commitment. Consequently, they began to convert their dollar reserves into gold reserves, which inevitably depleted the US gold pool (see Figure 10.1). Eventually, the United States had to dishonor its former pledge after an unsuccessful devaluation of the dollar. This, in effect, means the collapse of the Bretton Woods system.

The Jamaica Agreement of 1976 came hard on the heels of the demise of the Bretton Woods system. This laid the foundation for the post-Bretton Woods international monetary system. The biggest amendment by the Jamaica Agreement to its predecessor, the Bretton Woods system, is contained in the new code of conduct by which the exchange rate system is arranged. Contrary to the "pegged rate" currency regime implemented by the Bretton Woods system (i.e., where member countries could not change their par value without approval from the IMF), the Jamaica system allows a free choice of currency regime – that is, member countries are entitled to determine the exchange rate regime (including the floating exchange regime and the fixed exchange regime) appropriate to their own national conditions.

The international pattern of currency regime under the Jamaica system

The current international pattern of currency regime is based on the principle of free choice established by the Jamaica system. Overall, most developed economies, such as the US, Japan and the Eurozone countries, have adopted a floating exchange regime, while China, along with many other developing countries, has gone to the other extreme by choosing a fixed or manageable floating exchange regime. Table 10.2 shows the distribution of the exchange regimes across countries as of December 2006.

As indicated above, there are a total of 25 countries (regions) plus the Eurozone area (12 countries) that have chosen a floating exchange regime. Most of them are developed countries. Other countries (regions) either have no independent legal currency (29 countries), or implement a currency board system (7 countries),[2] whereas the remaining 109 countries in general can be understood to have a fixed exchange regime in a traditional sense (including managed floating).[3]

Currency manipulator

Although the Jamaica Agreement provided countries with access to a free choice of exchange regime according to their own national situation, their freedom was bound by an invisible fetter – the prevention of "a currency manipulator". In 1977, less than a year after the Jamaica Agreement was enacted, the Executive Board of the IMF (composed of members from developed countries) adopted a decision entitled the "Surveillance over Exchange Rate Policies" (known as the "1977 Decision"), stating that "each member shall avoid manipulating exchange rates or the international monetary system in order to prevent effective balance of payments adjustment or to gain an unfair competitive advantage over other members."[4]

Table 10.2 International pattern of the exchange regime as of December 2006

Exchange rate regime		Countries (regions)
Exchange arrangements with no separate legal tender	Another currency as legal tender (9)	Panama, Timor-Leste, Ecuador, Kiribati, Marshall Islands, Micronesia, Palau, El Salvador, San Marino
	ECCU (6)	Antigua and Barbuda, Dominica, Grenada, Saint Kitts and Nevis, Saint Lucia, Saint Vincent and the Grenadines
	CFA franc zone (14)	Benin, Burkina Faso, Togo, Guinea-Bissau, Côte d'Ivoire, Mali, Niger, Senegal, Equatorial Guinea, Congo, Gabon, Cameroon, Chad, Central Africa
	Eurozone (12)	Ireland, Austria, Belgium, Germany, France, Finland, The Netherlands, Luxembourg, Portugal, Spain, Greece, Italy
Currency board arrangements (7)		Estonia, Bulgaria, Bosnia and Herzegovina, Djibouti, Lithuania, Brunei, Hong Kong (China)
Other conventional fixed peg arrangements	Against a single currency (47)	United Arab Emirates, Aruba, Egypt, Ethiopia, Antilles, Barbados, Bahamas, Pakistan, Bahrain, Belarus, Bolivia, Belize, Bhutan, Eritrea, Cape Verde, Guyana, The Netherlands, Honduras, Zimbabwe, Qatar, Comoros, Kuwait, Latvia, Lesotho, Lebanon, Rwanda, Maldives, Malta, Macedonia, Mauritania, Namibia, Nepal, Sierra Leone, Seychelles, Saudi Arabia, Swaziland, Suriname, Solomon Islands, Trinidad and Tobago, Turkmenistan, Venezuela, Ukraine, Syria, Iraq, Jordan, Vietnam, China
	Against a composite (5)	Fiji, Libya, Morocco, Samoa, Vanuatu
Pegged exchange rates within horizontal bands (6)		Denmark, Cyprus, Slovakia, Slovenia, Tonga, Hungary
Managed floating with no pre-determined path for the exchange rate (51)		Algeria, Afghanistan, Argentina, Angola, Papua New Guinea, Paraguay, Burundi, Dominican Republic, Russia, Gambia, Colombia, Georgia, Kazakhstan, Haiti, Kyrgyzstan, Guinea, Ghana, Cambodia, Czech Republic, Croatia, Kenya, Laos, Liberia, Romania, Madagascar, Malawi, Malaysia, Mauritius, Mongolia, Bangladesh, Peru, Myanmar, Moldova, Mozambique, Nigeria, Serbia and Montenegro, Sao Tome and Principe, Sudan, Sri Lanka, Tajikistan, Thailand, Tunisia, Guatemala, Uruguay, Uzbekistan, Singapore, Jamaica, Armenia, Yemen, India, Zambia
Independently floating (25)		Albania, Australia, Brazil, Iceland, Poland, Philippines, Democratic Republic of Congo, South Korea, Canada, United States, Mexico, South Africa, Norway, Japan, Sweden, Switzerland, Somalia, Tanzania, Turkey, Uganda, New Zealand, Israel, Indonesia, UK, Chile

Table from IMF's website (www.imf.org/external/np/mfd/er/2006/eng/0706.htm)

Obviously, such a seemingly fair provision is targeted at those developing economies with a fixed (or manageable floating) exchange regime: in accordance with this provision, developing countries should not devaluate their domestic currency when setting their exchange policy. But what is interesting is that, if we examine the currencies of developing countries, we find that those developing countries with a fixed (or manageable floating) exchange regime have often set their exchange policy in a way that allows devaluation of their domestic currencies. Table 10.3 lists the ratios of market exchange rates of US dollar to the exchange rates computed by real purchasing power parity (PPP) in 2003.

As listed in Table 10.3, almost all developing countries have a market exchange rate that is significantly greater than the exchange rate computed by purchasing power parity, implying that the ratio is much higher than unity. This means that their currencies have fallen in value. Meanwhile, all the developed countries have the ratios that are close to or less than unity. In this sense, almost all developing countries are "currency manipulators".

10.2 The choice of AOER for developing countries

As noted earlier, under the Jamaica system, developing countries tend to select a fixed (or manageable floating) exchange regime while developed countries are prone to choose a floating exchange regime. In addition, the currencies in developing countries are often devaluated despite the provision against a "currency manipulator" set by the IMF. Why, then, would developing countries choose a fixed (or manageable floating) exchange regime? Why do they dare to challenge IMF's provision against a "currency manipulator"? Next, we will make an analysis of this.

Asymmetric international financial order

In the system of the gold standard, a currency's value is supported by the specific amount of gold it represents. Thus it makes sense to view any currency as an international currency, with the international role of each currency on the same footing as other currencies. The Bretton Woods system was a system in which the dollar was pegged to the gold standard, and other currencies pegged to the dollar. Even though the international monetary system of this "dual peg" pushed the dollar to supreme international status, other currencies were still fixed to the gold standard in an indirect way. In this sense, as long as the "dual peg" could be maintained and the currencies across countries were freely convertible according to the "dual peg", a country's currency could still be seen as an international currency.

However, the era of paper money came on the heels of the breakdown of the Bretton Woods system. The Jamaica system is contingent on the fact that a country's currency is not gold-based, and hence the polarization of currencies has emerged: the currencies issued by developed countries have higher credit by virtue of their powerful political and economic advantages, so their currencies

Table 10.3 Ratios of market exchange rates of the US dollar to the exchange rates calculated by the real purchasing power parity in 2003

North Korea	180.6	Mauritius	3.81	South Africa	2.47	Grenada	1.54
Uzbekistan	10.97	Solomon Islands	3.81	Tonga	2.46	Jamaica	1.52
Tajikistan	9.28	Iran	3.76	Namibia	2.39	Slovenia	1.51
Burundi	8.42	Republic of Guinea-Bissau	3.62	Cuba	2.38	Seychelles	1.46
Belarus	7.79	Eritrea	3.56	Lithuania	2.37	Bahrain	1.45
Guinea	7.61	Bolivia	3.55	Jordan	2.36	Lebanon	1.43
Ethiopia	7.05	Tanzania	3.52	Honduras	2.36	South Korea	1.43
Nepal	6.94	Turkmenistan	3.51	Guatemala	2.34	Kuwait	1.42
Ukraine	6.58	Mongolia	3.49	Fiji	2.34	Cyprus	1.40
Moldova	6.58	Thailand	3.47	Vanuatu	2.33	Congo (Brazzaville)	1.40
Bulgaria	6.50	Bulgaria	3.47	Ecuador	2.33	Hong Kong (China)	1.40
Mozambique	6.38	Argentina	3.41	Kiribati	2.30	Mexico	1.38
Armenia	6.15	Comoros	3.41	Estonia	2.24	Singapore	1.36
Swaziland	6.05	Colombia	3.40	Belize	2.20	Portugal	1.34
Malawi	5.95	Djibouti	3.39	El Salvador	2.19	Serbia and Montenegro	1.34
Papua New Guinea	5.94	Sierra Leone	3.35	Dominica Island	2.18	Bahamas	1.28
Rwanda	5.93	Cameroon	3.30	Peru	2.17	Puerto Rico	1.20
India	5.72	Republic of North Africa	3.22	Samoa	2.15	New Zealand	1.19
Bangladesh	5.67	Senegal	3.21	Gabon	2.15	Israel	1.17
Vietnam	5.57	Morocco	3.17	Oman	2.14	Australia	1.11
Sri Lanka	5.43	Mali	3.17	Brunei	2.12	Canada	1.10
Kazakhstan	4.96	Bhutan	3.13	Panama	2.08	Greece	1.08
Paraguay	4.87	Côte d'Ivoire	3.08	Trinidad and Tobago	2.07	Spain	1.08
Pakistan	4.84	Dominican Republic	3.05	Micronesia	2.04	Netherlands Antilles	1.06
Indonesia	4.77	Algeria	3.03	Bosnia and Herzegovina	2.04	United Arab Emirates	1.04
Cambodia	4.73	Cape Verde	2.98	Equatorial Guinea	2.03	United States	1.00
Uganda	4.68	Malaysia	2.97	Yemen	2.02	Italy	0.97
Egypt	4.68	Iraq	2.93	Costa Rica	1.98	Qatar	0.96
Ghana	4.63	Central African Republic	2.88	Venezuela	1.98	Austria	0.94
Mauritania	4.57	Uruguay	2.88	Slovakia	1.90	United Kingdom	0.93

Country	Ratio	Country	Ratio	Country	Ratio	Country	Ratio
Laos	4.51	Kenya	2.85	Syria	1.89	France	0.92
Azerbaijan	4.49	Chile	2.83	Czech Republic	1.86	Germany	0.91
Congo (DRC)	4.48	Sudan	2.80	Suriname	1.82	Belgium	0.90
Nicaragua	4.43	Brazil	2.80	Botswana	1.81	Luxembourg	0.86
Philippines	4.43	Liberia	2.78	Poland	1.80	Netherlands	0.85
Sao Tome and Principe	4.40	Benin	2.76	Macao, China	1.80	Sweden	0.81
Burkina Faso	4.38	Albania	2.71	Turkey	1.76	Finland	0.80
China	4.18	Togo	2.68	Hungary	1.74	Iceland	0.76
Lesotho	4.13	Maldives	2.65	Antigua	1.73	Japan	0.76
Niger	4.10	Nigeria	2.63	Barbados	1.72	Denmark	0.76
Russia	4.10	St. Vincent Island	2.62	Malta	1.71	Ireland	0.74
Afghanistan	4.09	Madagascar	2.59	Croatia	1.67	Norway	0.71
Gambia	4.08	Romania	2.56	St. Lucia	1.67	Switzerland	0.70
Zimbabwe	4.04	Zambia	2.55	Saint Kitts and Nevis	1.66	Bermuda	0.65
Chad	3.96	Macedonia	2.53	Saudi Arabia	1.65		
Somalia	3.81	Latvia	2.48	China Taiwan	1.64		

Data from the PWT (Penn World Table), at http://pwt.econ.upenn.edu/. *Table 10.3* Ratios of market exchange rates of the US dollar to the exchange rates calculated by the real purchasing power parity in 2003 have developed into international currencies; the currencies issued by developing countries are not international currencies because they are economically backward. The demise of the Bretton Woods system has done little to weaken the position of the US dollar as the most important international currency (the world currency). Driven by inertia, people (especially in developing countries) still deem the dollar the world's main reserve currency, and in spite of the emergence of the euro, it is still difficult to shake the dollar's status in the world economy.

The difference between international and non-international currencies is what mainly separates developed countries from developing countries in the international economic arena. International currency is a currency that is internationally recognized to act as a yardstick of value, means of payment and medium of exchange, on the premise that the currency is freely convertible. Non-international currency is generally not recognized in the international community, and cannot be converted into an international currency in the international foreign exchange market. Of course, there is no clear dividing line between international and non-international currencies. In general, a fixed index is adopted to represent the degree of internationalization. The index is usually calculated by placing weight on such indicators as circulation scope, circulation volume, payments in international trade, international loans (or debts), international investment, international bonds and the share in official international reserves. If the index of the dollar's internalization is set to 100, then that of the euro is close to 40, of the yen is 28.2, and of the RMB is little more than 2 (see Table 10.4).

What separates international currencies from non-international currencies forms the typical asymmetrical feature of the international financial order. The question is, does this asymmetrical order of international finance mean that developing countries have to strategically choose the accumulation-oriented exchange regime?

Perspective from economic security

An international currency can be used for international payments (or can be converted into another international currency for international payments at a very low cost). Thus, a country that issues an international currency does not need foreign exchange reserves. Indeed, to a developed economy, the rule of foreign exchange reserve is no longer important. However, when a country's currency is

Table 10.4 Indices of the internationalizing degree of the dollar, yen, euro, and RMB

	Circulation scope	Circulation volume	Trading payment	Loan payment	International bond	International investment	Official reserves	Total
Dollar	100	88.7	80	99.5	44	19.5	64	100
Euro	88.5	0.9	20	4	19	39.8	6	39.4
Yen	73	0.4	5	1	23	4	20	28.2
Yuan	6.6	1.1	0	0	0	0	0	2

not internationalized, that country must use other currencies (i.e., international currencies) to pay for imports and international debts. Thus, accumulating enough international currencies to meet a variety of risks becomes an important and unavoidable objective when the country engages in the international market.

Such accumulation is just like the savings behavior of a regular family. Although families have income and expenditure in every period, in general they will save part of their income in case of risks and uncertainties in the future. Despite its annual exports and imports, which incur the inflows and outflows of international currencies, a country whose home currency is not internationalized will inevitably save a portion of the international currencies earned in order to safeguard its economic security. This forms the country's so-called international currency reserves.

The size of a country's international currency reserves will first hinge on the scale of the economy: the larger the economy, the more resources (such as oil, etc.) are needed to maintain its economic operation.[5] This also means that, as a rapidly rising economy, China's international currency reserves should be rising, too. The size of international currency reserves will also increase with the increase in risks and uncertainties in the international market, such as the frequent occurrence of financial crises, oil crises and "hot money" flows.

Given the rise of China's economic scale and the amplified risks and uncertainties in the international market, the reserve of international currencies necessary for China to maintain its economic security will continue to increase.

Now we shall examine how China and other developing countries accumulate their international currency reserves. Obviously, China's balance of payments needs to be in disequilibrium (in surplus): only when its balance of payments is in surplus can the net inflow of US dollars occur, which makes it possible for China to accumulate more US dollars. On the other hand, for the balance of payments to register a surplus the RMB must be devaluated, which can be achieved by the People's Bank of China (PBC) continuously bidding up for US dollars at the Foreign Exchange Trading Center in Shanghai.

To sum up, because developing countries issue a currency that is not internationalized, they are faced with more international financial risks when compared with developed countries. In order to maintain their economic security, developing countries need to accumulate international currency reserves with the constant expansion of their economic size. This suggests that they should devaluate their home currencies to create a surplus in the balance of payments. This devaluation can be achieved when their central banks go to the foreign exchange markets (usually set in their domestic territories) to bid up for international currencies.

Perspective from optimal resource allocation

Next, we will examine the choice of an accumulation-oriented exchange regime (AOER) for developing countries in terms of optimizing resource allocation and promoting economic growth.

A developing economy is often a dual economy, in which there are huge unused economic resources, such as surplus labor (Lewis, 1954). There is no doubt that an AOER will be more conducive to promote exports. It may also attract more foreign direct investment because of the fact that the devaluation of home currency makes investment resources (such as raw materials and labor) cheaper compared with the international market. An economy with huge unused economic resources could count on exports and foreign direct investment to digest those idle resources, thereby improving the efficiency of resource allocation and increasing the overall welfare of their residents.

Indeed, the existence of huge idle resources in developing countries itself indicates that the allocation of economic resources is not optimized either at home or abroad. In other words, both domestic and world economies fall into typical non-Pareto efficiency. Theoretically, this means that there is some room for improving the overall efficiency in resource allocation. The exchange rate regulates worldwide resource allocation in the same way as relative price does. Accordingly, whether or not a currency regime is reasonable should not only be contingent on whether it creates a balance of payments, but also on whether it benefits resource allocation within the world economy.

10.3 The paradox of RMB internationalization

Prerequisites for floating

Given the previous analysis, we have found that the adoption of an accumulation-oriented exchange regime (AOER) by China is a natural response of a developing country to the current asymmetrical international financial order. Further, it is in line with the principle of optimal resource allocation within the worldwide economy. However, such a response has led to China facing increasing pressure from the international community – especially the US. Pressure from the international community has forced the Chinese government to make some concessions regarding the appreciation of the RMB (although the Chinese government does not admit this openly). However, this does not mean that the Chinese government will completely abandon the AOER. Only under the following two conditions may China completely give up the AOER and let the exchange rate fully float:

- China has already or will soon run out of surplus labor;
- the RMB has been internationalized, and has become one of the world's major currencies.

We have every reason to believe that China will continue to grow rapidly further down the road, so in the foreseeable future China will witness its surplus labor gradually becoming absorbed. But internationalizing the RMB is a Herculean task for China.

The enormous risk in capital account liberalization

The main obstacle to RMB internationalization is liberalization of the capital account in China (Gao and Yu, 2010). According to standard theory, convertibility (including current account convertibility and capital account convertibility) is a necessary condition for a currency to be internationalized. Convertibility increases the liquidity of the RMB and RMB-denominated assets, and thus reduces the risk of holding, thereby increasing people's willingness to hold the RMB and RMB-denominated assets. Non-convertibility is a major threat to internationalize a currency (Mundell, 2003).

At the end of 2007, according to the classification by the International Monetary Fund (IMF), there were 12 items, of a total of 43, under the capital account that were fully convertible or only subject to a very small limit in China; 16 items were partly convertible; and 15 items were totally unconvertible.[6] This means that half of China's capital account is still controlled.

Appropriate control of the capital account is an effective means of hedging against international financial contagion. Capital account openness involves a huge risk for China, whose currency is still not internationalized. "China's financial market is like a little bathtub, which is not big enough for major international financial sharks to splash in" (Huang, 1998). According to the statistics from International Financial Services London (IFSL), in April 2009, the average daily trading volume at the global foreign exchange market was about 3.1 trillion US dollars. Even this huge number had reduced by 24 percent compared to April 2008.[7]

Another reason why the capital account cannot be liberalized is because of the existence of "hot money". A large share of China's international currency reserves springs from the inflows of "hot money". This "hot money" comes in partly through legal channels, such as in the name of Qualified Foreign Institutional Investors (QFIIs), while most flows into China through illegal means.

How much "hot money" has flowed into China? It's a question for which nobody knows the answer. Scholars have measured it in various ways, with the results varying widely. For instance, according to a study from the Chinese Academy of Social Sciences in 2008, the total of "hot money" inflows into China surged to $1.2 trillion between 2003 and the first quarter of 2008, with total profits of $0.55 trillion of "hot money"; the sum of the two is $1.75 trillion – about 104 percent of China's foreign exchange reserves by the end of March 2008.[8]

So-called "hot money" will flow out, of course, and its impact on the international currency reserves of China lies in the moment of its outflow. Prior to its outflow, we cannot identify the risk. This means that the threat from "hot money" against China's national economic security is covert. The existence of a large amount of "hot money" implies that China's capital markets cannot be fully liberalized. Once capital markets are fully opened and while RMB internationalization cannot be achieved in the short term, China's national economic security will face enormous risks.

The urgency of RMB internationalization

Although RMB internationalization is a Herculean task that involves many risks, China has many reasons to speed up the process.

A low degree of RMB internationalization that cannot be matched with the position of a large economy

As the largest developing country, China has seen its overall economic scale ranked second in the world. However, the RMB, the currency issued by China, has a very low degree of internationalization (see Table 10.4). The low degree of RMB internationalization does not match China's position as a large economy.

The constant expansion of strategic rigid demand

With the constant expansion of the Chinese economy, the strategic rigid demand of China (such as for oil, iron ore, etc.) is growing. For instance, China's oil imports rose to 218.38 million tonnes in 2009, with its dependence on oil imports rising to 56 percent. In recent years, China's annual spending on oil imports alone has been as high as more than $100 billion while its proportion of total imports is also continuously increasing (see Figure 10.2).

However, the frightening thing is that the pricing of oil, iron ore and other strategic resources is not set by China, though China is already a super-buyer in the international market (the second in oil, the first in iron ore, etc.). At the same time, the prices of these resources are showing a fluctuating upward trend. In

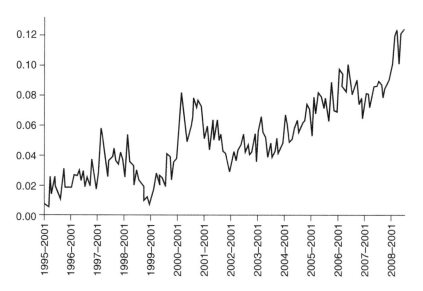

Figure 10.2 The share of net oil imports in total imports of China, 1995–2009. Monthly data available at www.cei.gov.cn/.

2000, the price of crude oil was about $30 per barrel. It skyrocketed to $140 in 2007. Influenced by the financial crisis of 2008, it slumped to approximately $40 a barrel. It then climbed again to $80 a barrel. We can imagine that oil prices in the near future will soar again, given the speculation of international financial capital.

The above analysis allows us to see that, on the one hand, with the constant expansion of the Chinese economy the strategic rigid demand of China (such as for oil, iron ore, etc.) is growing; on the other hand, the pricing of those strategic resources is not set by China while their prices are showing an upward trend (though fluctuating). As a non-international currency, the RMB cannot directly purchase oil and other strategic resources: China must use its painstakingly accumulated international currency to make purchases. This means that if the RMB is not internationalized, China will always be exposed to the shocks of oil and other strategic resources. To safeguard against this risk, China has continuously to accumulate more international currency with its economic expansion. However, China's accumulation of international currency is cuases the Chinese economy a variety of huge stresses from both the domestic economy and the international community. Related discussions follow.

An unsustainable ability to accumulate more foreign exchange

As pointed out in Chapter 8, the growth rates of real exports over the past 30 years have usually been at higher levels, often at 20 percent and rising to a peak of 60 percent. On average, the rate was about 14.06 percent between 1991 and 2009. However, an unavoidable question is: How can markets in developed countries whose expansion is only at 2–3 percent absorb the exports from China, whose expansion rate is nearly 14 percent? If China were a small country, there would be less pressure for it to keep exporting to developed countries at high speed. However, China is now a large country. From the perspective of trade balance, China's future exports should also be growing at the rate of 2 percent or 3 percent, otherwise trade friction will be frequent. Since exports are the main channel to creating foreign exchange, a decline in export growth for China must also mean a decline in the ability to create more foreign exchange. Thus, if the RMB cannot internationalized, China's economic security and financial risks will be significantly increased.

The external pressure of RMB internationalization

The so-called external pressure does not refer to the pressure imposed by the international community to internationalize the RMB. Perhaps, in their own interests, developed countries that issue international currencies may not want the RMB to be internationalized. The so-called external pressure refers to their frequent criticism of China's accumulation-oriented exchange regime (AOER), which, as discussed earlier, necessarily means a surplus of international payments caused by RMB devaluation. China's AOER has met with more and more opposition from developed countries. However, the only way China can give up accumulating greater reserves of international currencies is to let the RMB itself be an international currency.

The pressure from huge foreign exchange reserves

Since the RMB is not internationalized, China has to rely on accumulating more international currency to safeguard its economic security. Currently, China's international currency reserves have reached nearly $3 trillion. Such huge reserves bring the following pressures. First, the huge foreign exchange reserves, mainly in US dollars, bring the risks of management. After the financial crisis, the Federal Reserve implemented a quantitative easing monetary policy. This devaluated the dollars and dollar-denominated assets held by the PBC, and can be regarded as a loss of investment in foreign assets. Second, the huge foreign exchange reserves purchased by the PBC often indicate a huge injection of monetary base in the domestic economy, and thus create the problem of excessive liquidity. This indeed leads to difficulties in demand management in China's monetary policy (see discussion in Chapter 7).

The paradox of RMB internationalization

The above analysis shows that the non-internationalized RMB leaves China at high risk of international payments. Meanwhile, there is also wide demand from the international community for China to reform its exchange regime. This has put further pressure on China to promote RMB internationalization. However, in accordance with existing theories, China's capital account convertibility is one of the premises of RMB internationalization. Yet the small bathtub of China's financial markets cannot be deemed a great place for international financial sharks to splash in. Coupled with the possible existence of huge inflows of "hot money" at this stage, liberalization of China's capital account will be confronted with even greater risks. Thus we see that there is a dilemma in the process of RMB internationalization: RMB non-internationalization places China in financial jeopardy, but RMB internationalization requires liberalization of the capital account, which will put China at a greater risk. This is the current paradox of RMB internationalization.

10.4 The road to RMB internationalization

While no one can deny that opening capital account can make help to promote RMB internationalization, whether the capital account in China should be opened is still a controversial issue. Indeed, whether capital account is liberalized or not, RMB internationalization still depends on the admission from international community while it is the strength of Chinese economy underlies such admission. In this sense, the process of RMB internationalization can be started, even if China's capital account is not completely open.

Current strategies of RMB internationalization

The year 2009 is considered to have been the beginning of RMB international-ization. The RMB settlement of cross-border trade is being promoted on a trial basis, and currency swaps have been greatly expanded. RMB internationalization is slowly being carried forward in accordance with the step-by-step strategy of "liberalization, regionalization and internationalization".

The currency swap is considered an important step towards RMB inter-nationalization. The financial crisis in 2008 contributed to bilateral currency swaps between China and some neighboring countries as well as other develop-ing countries. At the request of the monetary authorities of some countries and regions, such as Hong Kong, Korea, Malaysia, Belarus, Indonesia, Argentina, Iceland, Singapore, and others, the PBC has signed agreements of bilateral cur-rency swap with the monetary authorities of those countries and regions totaling 803.5 billion RMB yuan.

RMB settlement of cross-border trade is currently another important tool to promote RMB internationalization. It will improve the function of the RMB as a medium of exchange. Since July 2009, there has been rapid development in the scale of RMB settlement: by the end of 2009, RMB settlement of cross-border trade only totaled 3.6 billion RMB yuan; in the first half of 2010, that amount reached 70.6 billion RMB yuan. Yet the rapid development of aggregate data does not reveal the structural risks involved in RMB settlement of cross-border trade. Cross-border trade can be divided into two parts: imports and exports. For export, RMB settlement means that foreign importers pay the exporters from China in RMB. For import, RMB settlement implies that foreign exporters *may* accept RMB payments. It becomes apparent that when it comes to RMB settle-ment, imports are much more important than exports. From the standpoint of preventing international payment risks, RMB internationalization can be a sub-stantive progress only when the import trade is settled in RMB.

The possible next step: bond strategy and bond market opening

The key of RMB internationalization is to expand the international demand for the RMB. The demand for money can always be divided into two types: transaction demand and asset demand. The RMB settlement of cross-border trade can be deemed as expanding the RMB international demand for the purpose of transaction.

To expand the RMB international demand, asset demand must also be con-sidered, and is perhaps even more important. The RMB deposited in accounts outside China (because of RMB settlement of cross-board trades) needs appro-priate investment products, and the international "hot money" that wants to flow into China also needs its own legal place to invest. Therefore, China should provide enough RMB-denominated bonds to meet international asset demand for RMB, for which treasuries can be regarded as a core component.

Since the Chinese economy is still booming, the international community has every reason to expect RMB appreciation. Therefore, as long as the interest rate of RMB-denominated bonds is not too low, they will be attractive investment products. When foreign investors (including the central banks of countries) are holding RMB-denominated bonds in large amounts, RMB will be internationalized in a substantive way.

It should be noted that such a bond strategy can also be understood as opening the bond market in China and its related item of RMB convertibility under the capital account. Therefore, it is consistent with the step-by-step liberalization of the capital account in China. Finally, the financial status of the Chinese government, as indicated in Chapter 9, is healthy. This bond strategy will not cause a debt problem for the Chinese government.

Historically, developed economies have capitalized on the fixed exchange regime (Bretton Woods system) to enhance their economic and technological strengths; to achieve the internationalization of their sovereignty currency; and to establish an international financial order in their own favor. Then, under the guise of promoting freedom, developed countries not only legalize the floating exchange regime, but also impose a forced interference in the free choice of developing countries regarding their exchange regimes. Under this asymmetrical, unfair international financial order, developing countries will inevitably choose an accumulation-oriented exchange regime (AOER) to prevent international financial risks, safeguard their domestic economy and catch up with developed countries.

In some senses, RMB's internationalization should be a prerequisite for the RMB to be finally floating. If the US wants China to speed up the reform of the exchange regime towards floating, it should help China to speed up the process of internationalizing the RMB.

Discussion and questions

1   Explain the following concepts: fixed exchange rate regime, floating exchange regime, manageable floating exchange regime, accumulation-oriented exchange regime, international currency and non-international currency.
2   Do you consider RMB to be an international currency? Why, or why not? Do you think the RMB is depreciated or not? Why, or why not? What is the current exchange regime of the RMB? Why?
3   How was the exchange rate across countries decided under the Bretton Woods system? Why did the Bretton Woods system finally collapse? What benefits did the United States obtain from the Bretton Woods system?
4   What is the Jamaica system? How was the exchange rate across countries decided under the Jamaica system? What is the basic distribution of current exchange rates and exchange regimes across the world, especially between developing and developed countries?
5   What is a currency manipulator? Do you think China is a currency manipulator?
6   Explain briefly why countries with non-international currencies choose an AOER.

7 What are the prerequisites for the RMB to be fully floating? Why?

8 Explain why China needs to promote RMB internationalization.

9 Do you think RMB internationalization will be easy? What might the risks involved in RMB internationalization be? What do we understand by the paradox of RMB internationalization?

10 What is "hot money"? How does "hot money" flow into China? How much "hot money" do you think there is in China? What impact does it have on the Chinese economy?

11 Evaluate the current strategy for RMB internationalization. What might China do in the next step to promote RMB internationalization?

Appendix A

A review of Keynesian and neoclassical economics

This appendix introduces two contemporary main schools of economics: neoclassical economics and Keynesian economics. We believe that the major difference between the two schools springs from their different understandings of the market economy. First, we will give a critical review of neoclassical economics. The purpose of the review is not to deny the inherent logical consistency and integrity of neoclassical theory, but rather to reveal a behavior with regard to expectation of economic agents assumed in its theoretical framework – that is, the so-called "full-confidence expectation". The whole system of neoclassical economics hinges on this assumption with regard to expectation. However, whether this assumption is in line with the reality of modern market economies (especially the market economy in China) is debatable. At the same time, Keynesian economics can, to a large extent, be understood as a revolution against this neoclassical assumption. We go on to discuss Keynesian economics and respond to some criticism of Keynesian theory. We hope this will help in understanding why Keynesian economics is more suitable for the Chinese economy.

A.1 Full-confidence expectation

The neoclassical theory depends on the equilibrium of demand and supply. For a given product, we are told there are two corresponding curves, demand and supply curves, which reflect the "desired" demands and supplies of firms or households at different given prices (including non-equilibrium prices). Typically, the demand curve is downward sloping while the supply curve is upward sloping. The intersection of the two curves is called "equilibrium". At equilibrium, supply is equal to demand, and thus the market is cleared. When the market is not at equilibrium (i.e., supply is not equal to demand), the price will automatically be adjusted towards equilibrium. This type of market behavior applies not only to a general product market, but also to a factor (such as labor) market.

What neoclassical economists pride themselves on is that both the demand and the supply curves can be deduced from an optimization process of economic agents. Hence, they are often deemed to reflect the basic characteristics of individual behavior: rationality and selfishness. In other words, the theory is established on a solid micro-foundation. To offer a deeper insight, it is necessary for us to examine how individuals make decisions with regard to demand and supply under the neoclassical system.

Decision of households

First, we will examine the decision process of a household. For the given price p_i, $i = 1, 2, \ldots, n$; where p_i is the price of commodity i, a household will choose the demand x_i^d to give

$$\max U(x_1^d, x_2^d, \ldots, x_n^d) \tag{A.1}$$

subject to

$$p_1 x_1^d + p_2 x_2^d + \ldots + p_n x_n^d \leq y \tag{A.2}$$

where $U(\cdot)$ denotes the utility function and y represents the income for the household. The solution to this optimization problem gives rise to the following demand function of the household with respect to product i:

$$x_i^d = D_i(y, p_1, p_2, \ldots, p_n) \tag{A.3}$$

Here, we need to make two remarks. First, generally, we are often told that the income y is given. Yet from the general equilibrium model of neoclassical economics, we find that the income is generated from the household supply of factors (such as labor). To put it simply, we may assume that the factor supply from the household is given in the form of endowments. Thus, the income of y can be defined as

$$y = w_1 l_1^s + w_2 l_2^s + \ldots + w_m l_m^s \tag{A.4}$$

where w_j ($j = 1, 2, \ldots, m$) is the price of the factor j, and l_j^s represents the supply of the factor j.

Second, when making economic decisions, the household does not take into account whether the given prices p_i and w_j are equilibrium prices.

Decision of firms

Now we turn to a firm that produces i. The decision-making process of the firm can be expressed as follows. For the given product price p_i and factor price w_j, the firm will choose the factor demands l_j^d and the product supply x_i^s to give

$$\max p_i x_i^s - (w_1 l_1^d + w_2 l_2^d + \ldots + w_m l_m^d) \tag{A.5}$$

subject to

$$x_i^s = F(l_1^d, l_2^d, \ldots, l_m^d) \tag{A.6}$$

where $F(\cdot)$ signifies the firm's production function. The solution to this optimization problem can allow us to derive the firm's demand and supply functions with respect to factor j and product i:

$$l_j^d = d_j(p_1, w_1, w_2, \ldots, w_m) \tag{A.7}$$

$$x_i^s = s_i(p_1, w_1, w_2, \ldots, w_m) \tag{A.8}$$

This decision process indicates that the firm, when making its decisions, also ignores the question of whether the given prices p_i and w_j are at equilibrium or not.

Full-confidence expectation

The previous discussion on the decision-making process of households and firms can lead to the following facts.

First, whether households or firms, their optimization processes include two types of decision-making: demand and supply. Also, these two types of decisions are made simultaneously. Given the market prices for products and for factors (regardless whether they are at equilibrium or not), firms will make the decision to supply its output and will also make the decision regarding demand for factors. Similarly, households will make the decision about demand for consumption, and will also make the decision regarding supply factors.

Second, for the same economic agent, the effectiveness of his or her decision depends on whether both supply and demand can be realized. For instance, the effectiveness of decisions by households depends not only on whether they can purchase the amount of products they desire under the given price p_i, but also on whether their factor supplies (or endowments) can really be employed under the given factor price w_j.

Third, both product prices and factor prices are given in the whole process of decision-making. Households and firms do not consider whether those given prices are equilibrium prices or not.

Fourth, the so-called decision-making is only a process that determines individuals' willingness. A decision does not mean a transaction, and only a transaction can reflect the effectiveness of a decision. A decision without a transaction does not carry any practical significance.

Fifth, although the demand and supply decisions of the same individual are made simultaneously in the model, there is a certain time lag between the two transactions corresponding to these (i.e., sale and purchase) in reality.

From the above analysis, we thus find that there inherently exists an assumption on the behavior of an agent's expectations underlying the equilibrium analysis of neoclassical theory. We may call this assumption "full-confidence expectation".

Definition: Full-confidence expectation refers to the expectation behavior that can be expressed as follows. Given the market prices of products and factors (regardless of whether they are at equilibrium or not), individuals (households or firms) expect that they can sell (or purchase) the quantity of products (or factors) as much as they want.

Here, we need to note that the so-called "quantity ... as much as they want" means the optimal quantity that a household (or a firm) obtains through its optimization process. Let's take that quantity for a firm as an example (see Figure A.1).

Suppose that for the possible different production functions, firms have different supply curves, such as S_1, S_2 or S_3 as in Figure A.1. Obviously, they are derived from the firms' optimization process (see equations (A.5) and (A.6)). Thus, given the market price P, the quantities the firms are willing to supply can be expressed as Q_1, Q_2 and Q_3. In particular, when there are constant returns to scale so that the firm's marginal cost is constant, the firm's supply curve can be shown as S_4 in the figure. In this case, the optimal quantity (or the quantity as much as the firm wants) goes to positive infinity. According to the assumption of full-confidence expectation, no matter how much the optimal output is (or even goes to positive infinity), firms expect that they can all be sold out.

It is apparent that the full-confidence expectation is not suited to an economy with large volatility, risks and uncertainties, and incomplete information. Such an economy is precisely what is envisaged and studied by Keynesian economics.

It should be noted that the assumption of "full-confidence expectation" does not attract enough attention from economists. However, we can find some similar thoughts in the vast economic literatures. For example, Weintraub (1977: 4) called the simultaneity of individual's decision-making on demand and supply an "anomaly". Clower (1965) referred to the household's income as defined by

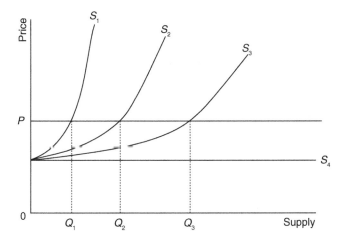

Figure A.1 The optimal quantities of firms.

neoclassical economics as "notional income" (see equation (A.4)), and the corresponding consumption demand as "notional demand", so that it can distinguished from the effective demand as proposed and used by Keynes in his economic analysis.

Walras' tâtonnement process

We already know that, in neoclassical economics, individuals, when making decisions, expect that their willingness in demand and supply (derived from their optimization) can be realized regardless of whether the current market prices are at equilibrium or not. At the same time, we also note that the realization of the willingness in demand and supply depends on market transactions. If the market transactions often render economic decisions unable to be realized, then we have reason to believe that individuals will change their way of decision-making. For this reason, study of the transacting process is key to evaluating the effectiveness of neoclassical economics.

In the vast economic literature, it is not difficult to discover that Walras (1874) made a significant contribution to the study of the market exchange process. More surprisingly, individuals' demand and supply decisions, as described previously, can be fully embodied in the exchange model proposed by Walras. So it is necessary to introduce Walras' exchange process.

Assume that there is only one market in the economy that we are considering. This means that all commodities and production factors must be exchanged in this market. There are many market participants: buyers and sellers. However, when they come to the market, they find it difficult to exchange goods with each other because they cannot determine the transaction price in the first place. Fortunately, there is an auctioneer (or a market manager) in the market, whose role is to call out the "bids" and "offers" until the equilibrium price is reached.

All traders must comply with the following rules: when the auctioneer quotes prices, traders should truthfully fill out, in the form issued by the auctioneer, the quantity of products that they are willing to buy or sell, even if they know the current quoted prices are not necessarily the equilibrium prices, or even if they know that this quoting process needs to be repeated many times. The forms, after being filled in, must be delivered to the auctioneer.

When the auctioneer obtains the completed forms, he will compute the supplies and demands at the current quoted prices and adjust the prices accordingly: when the demand for a certain product is greater than its supply, the price increases; otherwise the price decreases. As a result, the auctioneer can quote a new set of prices and wait for a new round of forms to be filled and submitted by the traders.

Walras argued that if the traders follow the rule as described above while the process is repeated again and again, the auctioneer will eventually quote a set of equilibrium prices at which all product supplies will be equal to their demand.[1]

It is easy to see that in this trading process the traders can offer their supplies and demands according to the current quoted prices, unfettered by concerns as to whether these prices are at equilibrium or whether their submitted supplies and demands can eventually be realized. They know that only after the equilibrium prices have been quoted can transactions be conducted. If trading does occur in this way, the full-confidence expectation might be reasonable: the trader will be able to assume that their demands and supplies will be realized at the quoted prices since he or she knows that if not, the prices will be re-quoted until equilibrium is reached.

It should be noted that the price quotation as discussed above is merely a process of determining the equilibrium price. It does not involve how to proceed with the transaction following the determination of equilibrium prices. Indeed, even after equilibrium prices have been determined, traders may still find it difficult to search for suitable trading partners among many traders, so the trading process is far from complete. Related issues will be discussed later in this appendix.

This trading process may be counted as only one of many traditional trading modes in reality. It is, however, difficult to find a trace of it in today's society. As Nell (1983: 113) noted, now nobody deems this process, regarded by Edgeworth as "noisy and unconvincing dynamics", to be a true reflection of market transactions.

A trap for neoclassical economics

Now let us move away from the Walrasian exchange market and come to an economy filled with risks, uncertainties and imperfect information, though there might also be many opportunities and temptations. In such a society, we may reasonably assume that individuals do not have "full-confidence expectation".

When individuals come to such a society, they will be engaged in two types of trades: buying and selling. For an individual, which one should come first? Neoclassical economics does not provide an answer. Implicitly, the theory assumes that the individual makes the demand and supply decisions simultaneously. Weintraub (1977: 4) once regarded "the simultaneity" as one of the anomalies of neoclassical system, but did not provide a solution. Even Benassy (1982) was ensnared. In Chapter 4, he distinguishes the time ordering of an agent's different decisions. Through this manner, he appropriately illustrates the "spill-over effect" caused by an "initial disturbance" transmitted from market to market. Yet, in Chapter 7, he gives up this distinction and works again on the simultaneity. Though he believes that "in reality agents visit markets sequentially" (p. 63) working on simultaneity, in his mind, is "*absolute standard in all multimarket equilibrium model and it will simplify the exposition, as we shall not have to formalize the ordering of the markets*" (p. 63).

However, this "standard" is misleading. In practice, agents cannot visit all markets simultaneously. Next, we will attempt to answer the question "which one should come first?" First, let us consider the case if the individual (household or firm) buys first. For this situation to be possible, the following two conditions must be satisfied:

- the individual must have sufficient financial resources to cover the purchase;
- the individual must expect that the goods or services related to the purchase must be sold out.

Obviously, if the individual does not have full-confidence expectation, the second condition cannot be met. In this case, even if the individual has sufficient financial resources (such as using loans, etc.) to pay for the purchase, he or she will still be first engaged in sales activities (such as obtaining contracts and orders). In an economy filled with uncertainties, even though firms have sufficient funds, they will not buy raw materials and employ labor to produce products that they have no confidence will sell in the market. Similarly, if households do not know whether they will be employed or how much they will be paid, they will not plan and engage in spending.

Thus, in an economy filled with uncertainties, we can predict that individuals will be first engaged in sales activities. But if all traders sell first, where does the demand come from? If nobody was to place a demand first, the economy would not operate. For neoclassical economics, this is a trap set by Keynes, who emphasized uncertainties in an economy. The problem cannot be resolved within the neoclassical system. What we need is a methodological revolution!

A.2 The theory of effective demand – Keynesian revolution

We have seen that neoclassical economics is established on an assumption with regard to agent's expectation behavior, namely "full-confidence expectation". We also noted that such an assumption is not suited to an economy imbued with volatility, uncertainties and incomplete information. This is the economy that is envisaged and studied by Keynesian economics. Next, we will review Keynesian economics. To give readers an intuitive understanding of Keynesian theory, especially the theory of output determination, we will follow Walras and invent a story about trading.

The trading at Javits Center – a made-up story

The economy that we consider here is highly decentralized. However we could imagine a special place, perhaps called the "trader center", where all possible traders have to come to express their desired transactions. This idea does not mean, as Walras imagined, that all traders will get together "standing face to face" (Walras, 1954: 41) to follow the order from the auctioneer. Indeed, there is no need for the auctioneer at all. We can imagine that the trade center is divided by various rooms (or plots), each one corresponding to a particular commodity. We can suppose that the room (or plot) is rented, either individually or jointly, by the producers who produce that commodity. We can further assume that firms that produce the same type of products are asked to put their rooms (or plots) together in order to ensure the prices are set open to the public (although their production bases are scattered throughout the country). In practice, a place of this kind is very much similar to, for example, New York's Javits Center, where various trade fairs take place. All these mean that although our economy is highly decentralized, it is also highly efficient in the sense that information can easily be transmitted, and therefore searching for a potential trading partner is relatively easy.

In order to facilitate our analysis, let us assume a particular Monday with the following characteristics:

1   All business contracts (including those between firms and firms, and between firms and households) have expired, so all business activities stopped last Friday.
2   Each firm has a certain amount of inventory, leaving it with no intention to purchase additional inputs (including labor) or to produce additional output if there are no new orders.
3   Each household has sufficient daily necessities and a certain amount of deposits and cash.

In this case, firms come to the center for two purposes. First, they must sell their inventories or get additional orders for their products; second, they must purchase extra inputs for production. However, since the contracts or orders for their products are no longer there and inventory is sufficient, their primary task is to sell. That is, they must initially stay in their rooms or plots waiting for the arrival of buyers. Only when they have obtained a new order (or their inventories have reduced to a certain degree) will they consider purchasing extra inputs or employing labor.

As for householders, their employment contracts have expired; whether they will get a new job in the future is still unknown, but they have sufficient daily necessities. Therefore, they also come to the center initially to sell their labor services. If they succeed in obtaining a new employment contract, they may use their pocket money to buy some luxury goods to enjoy at home.

As might be imagined, in this case the whole trading center would be dead and silence, because each individual is waiting for the arrival of buyers. But if everyone is waiting for a buyers to come first, then how will trading start?

In order to break the silence, a special trader is needed to arrive. What makes him or her special lies in the fact that this trader has comes to the center not for selling but only for buying, or buying first. Are there such traders, in reality? Yes! They are the investors, governments or exporters. Investment is a long-term business, and its return is obtained in the long run. There is no need to take orders as a necessary condition. On the other hand, there is also a period of time required for investment to be transformed into production capacity. For governments and exporters, their purpose in visiting the trade center is also simply to buy rather than to sell. Therefore, a special name is given to the three items of expenditure (i.e., investment, government spending and exports): "autonomous demand".

Now consider an investor who comes to, say, a plot belonging to a construction company, to express that he wants to have a building constructed and thus, as a result, a contract (order) is made between him and the construction company. The manager of the company will then get busy. He will calculate the inputs, including labor, steel, and other raw materials, etc., needed for producing that building, and hence a visit is arranged to these various input markets. His visits will generate a series of other exchanges (contracts): those who sell their outputs to (or get contracts with) the construction company as suppliers will also visit their own input markets as demanders. Therefore, more exchanges will follow. The trading center now becomes crowded. We can expect that the process will continue until it moves to its endpoint. The existence of such an endpoint indicates that the sequence of reflections created by our initial investor will finally converge to zero.

We might call this endpoint an equilibrium. It is not the usual demand–supply equilibrium; it is an equilibrium (in the Nash sense) corresponding to our initial investment. In practice an "endpoint" may never exist, since more investors and other autonomous demanders will arrive in succession before the end of the reflections created by the previous investor. Furthermore, the time taken by the sequence of reflections due to a certain autonomous demand may be very long. All these indicate that the trades, which seem to be carried in a disordered random fashion in our daily life, intrinsically proceed in an orderly way: they are the reflections or multiplier effects due to certain (not necessarily one type of) previous autonomous demands – though it is always difficult, actually impossible, to distinguish which reflection (or trade) is attributed to which autonomous demand.

> Definition: We define the reaction arising from a certain autonomous demand (expressed as a series of induced demand) as the multiplier effect of that autonomous demand.

The above description can be imagined as an example of how trades are carried on in a market. It is a demand-determined economy, and the auctioneer that is required in Walras' tâtonnement process need not exist. Although this example is extremely simple and highly abstract, it does, we believe, reflect the essential feature of the way our market operates. This is the essence of output determination in Keynesian economics, which has often been known as the theory of "effective demand" or the theory of "multiplier".

Money circulation at Javits Center

The preceding description of the trading process at the Javits Center can also be seen as money circulation in the real sector of an economy.

Many studies on monetary economics treat money as a stock, and thus use the traditional demand–supply approach to determining the money stock equilibrium. However, money as a medium of exchange is also a flow. It is circulated among different agents. So, how is money circulated?

Research on money circulation can be traced back to Wicksell's (1936) *Interest and Prices*. For this reason, our discussions will start with Wicksell's most famous "trilemma".

Let us first turn back to Walras' tâtonnement process. Suppose our mysterious auctioneer has adjusted all prices to their equilibrium. Hence he has completed his mission and steps down from his stage. It now remains for the trade to be executed. To look at the issue more clearly, we may assume that there are three individuals in the market: A, B and C. A has a product A that is needed by B, B has a product B that is needed by C, and C has a product C that is preferred by A (see Figure A.2). How are these exchanges carried out in this case?

First, we note that if there is no money, it will be very difficult to proceed with the exchanges because what A needs is not provided by B though the product that B needs is provided by A. Second, even if we assume that all of the above traders have sufficient money, there is still one problem: who will buy (or pay) first? General traders, such as A, B and C in this case, come to the market not only for purchases, but also for sales. Thus, if there is some uncertainty in the economy, we have no reason to believe that any of them will be the first to buy: if A first buys the product from B, and C does not buy the product from A, then A may be in trouble. But if no one wants to purchase first, the transaction cannot be started, and money will not flow. This brings us back to the beginning of the Monday at the Javits Center, discussed above.

Wicksell's trilemma once again confirms that in order to conduct transactions, there must be a special type of trader who comes to the market only for the purpose of buying, not selling, or just for the purpose to spend money. As noted above, investors, among other autonomous demanders, are such special traders. Indeed, once investors (among other autonomous demanders) have invested, their money is injected into the market and becomes the starting point of money circulation in the real sector of the economy (see Figure A.3). Here, the so-called real sector of the economy is composed of the product market and the labor market. It does not include financial and money markets.

Now let's look at Figure A.3. The payment of an investment, say I, can be thought of as being a starting point of the whole voyage of money circulation. This amount of money, which is also equal to v_1, flows out from the account of the investor to that of the corresponding seller. This will realize the production of the first-round enterprises, and hence a certain amount of profit will be generated. The enterprises may retain a part of the profit in their deposit accounts as their own saving sf_1, which is therefore withdrawn from circulation in the real

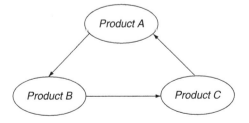

Figure A.2 Wicksell's "trilemma".

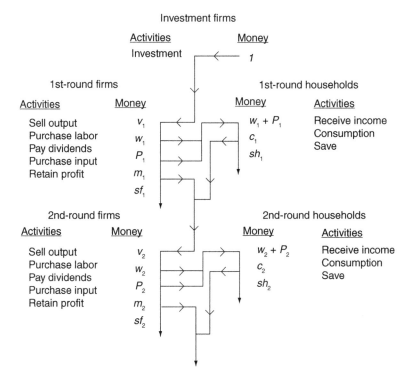

Figure A.3 Money circulation in the real sector of the economy.

sector of the economy. The rest of the money, including the dividends p_1, the payments to labor w_1 and the payments to the second-round firms for purchasing material m_1 will be continuously circulated. Of these, m_1 flows into the account of the second-round firms, and w_1 and p_1 into the account of the first-round households as consumer income. Again, part of this income will flow into the account of second-round firms as the payment for consumption c_1; the other part will be retained as household saving sh_1 in their deposit accounts, and hence withdrawn from the circulation. Now, the total amount of money flowing into the accounts of second-round firms is $m_1 + c_1$, which is also equal to v_2. A part of them, sf_2, will be retained, and hence withdrawn from the circulation; the other will continuously flow out.

The circulation process continues but, since in each round a certain amount of money is withdrawn from the circulation as savings, the money in circulation will be continuously contracted. We can expect that if there is no further additional money (such as through investment) injected into the economy, the money in circulation will finally converge to zero. This implies that the total amount of saving (which is the money withdrawn from the circulation) is equal to the total amount of investment (which is the money injected into the circulation at the beginning).

Here, we note that the preceding discussions on monetary circulation only concern the real sector of an economy. At the same time, we assume that the investor has sufficient funds for to pay for the investment. Where, then, do these funds come from? Stated another way, how is the investment financed? It is the money circulation in the financial sector of the economy that makes this possible. For further discussion about monetary circulation in the financial sector, see Gong (2005: Chapter 14).

Basic hypothesis

An intuitive understanding of Keynesian theory with regard to output determination (or the theory of effective demand) has been presented above through a simple, abstract story on trading. We have seen that such a trading process also means money circulation in the real sector of an economy. We must keep in mind that the Keynesian theory of output determination reflected in this trading process is different from neoclassical economics, according to which output is determined by the production capacity via production function. As depicted in Figure A.1, the output that a firm is willing to sell (or the optimal output) is apparently derived from its production function. In neoclassical macroeconomics, this can be expressed as follows: the aggregate output is determined by the aggregate production function (such as the Cobb–Dauglass production function). Yet, according to Keynesian effective demand theory, aggregate output is determined by aggregate demand.

The Keynesian theory of effective demand is based on the following assumptions:

Hypothesis 1. Households make consumption decisions based on realized income rather than notional income. Similarly, firms' decision-making on the produced output is constrained by the market demand.

Here we would like to mention that the so-called market demand for firms can be reflected in orders, contracts, or estimated demand under the conditions of sufficient information. This method of decision-making mirrors how the economic uncertainties that Keynes repeatedly stresses affect individuals' behavior in their decision-making. It is the uncertainties that make households and firms lack confidence about the future, leading them to be careful when making decisions. The demand proposed by households and firms under the aforementioned circumstances can be interpreted as effective demand, which is essentially different from the notional demand advocated by neoclassical economics.

Hypothesis 2. Generally, firms have enough production capacity to meet the market demand. This also means that excessive capacity exists under the normal circumstances. Hence, the realization of aggregate demand is not subject to the constraints from the supply side of the economy.

Here, it's necessary to take the concept of production capacity one step further. First, if the data from the United States and other Western countries are examined, the capacity utilization (or utilization rate of capital equipment) generally hovers around 80 percent in the manufacturing sector, never exceeding more than 100 percent. Second, there is a great flexibility in computing capacity utilization, as it obviously depends on the operating time of capital equipment. If computed according to the operation scheme of 40 hours per week as 100 percent utilization, then, taking into account overtime work, the greatest possible capacity utilization can be much higher than 100 percent. This indicates that there is almost no such thing in reality as a demand being constrained by production capacity.

Hypothesis 3. Firms' decisions on prices and output are separated from each other. Prices can be considered as given in the process of firms' determination of output.

Many textbooks assume that price is constant when discussing Keynesian theory. This presents the impression that the whole theory of the Keynesian system is based on price rigidity, which can lead to the economy being in disequilibrium. Without price rigidity, demand and supply can be adjusted so that the economy can be in disequilibrium. However, the Keynesian theory of output determination is not affected by whether prices are permitted to fluctuate. Here, the main point is that the decision-making processes of price and output are separated so that when the firm is making its output decision the price has already been set down and announced publicly, as at the Javits Center. Price theory in Keynesian economics will be discussed below.

A.3 The micro-foundation of Keynesian economics

We have seen that Keynesian theory of output determination (or effective demand) is established on a challenge to the "full-confidence expectation" inherent in the neoclassical system. According to this theory, output determination can be understood as a multiplier process, which can also be expressed as a process of market trading. Compared with the trading process embodied in neoclassical theory (i.e., Walras' tâtonnement process), the trading process at the Javits Center, as discussed previously, seems much closer to the reality. At the same time, money circulation in the real sector of the economy can be well explained by such a process.

However, Keynesian economics is also criticized by economics professionals – especially by neoclassical economists. The major criticism is that Keynesian theory lacks micro-foundations. Here, the so-called micro-foundation criticism refers to the fact that many behavior equations in the system of Keynesian economics are not derived from optimization. This form of analysis is often seen as being contrary to the basic behavior characteristics of economic agents proposed by Adam Smith, which means economic agents are always pursuing maximization of their own self-interest when engaged in economic activities. Although the "weakness" of lacking micro-foundations did not cause much attention from economics professionals prior to the 1970s, it has begun to receive more and more interest with the development of economic research.

So, does Keynesian theory really lack micro-foundations? Indeed, the so-called "lack" does not mean "non-existence". Differently speaking, it is very likely that the micro-foundations of Keynesian economics have not been found yet and needs to be revealed through further economic research. And this is precisely where the charm of economics lies! In effect, it is the study of the micro-foundations of Keynesian macroeconomics that has caused the formation of the new Keynesian system, one of the two major schools in economics today.[2] Next, we will introduce research by new Keynesians on the micro-foundations of Keynesian economics.

Sticky pricing – the price-setting theory of Keynesian economics

As stated above, the output and price are determined separately in Keynesian economics. Here, we will first discuss how prices are set. In new Keynesian economics, this is expressed by the theory so-called "sticky pricing", which has indeed been the major contribution by new Keynesians in recent years.[3]

First, we note that the firms discussed here must be monopolistic or monopolistically competitive, rather than perfectly competitive. A perfectly competitive firm has full confidence that its optimal output can be sold out at a given price. Also, a perfect competitive firm can only be a price-taker rather than a price-setter. Therefore, when examining price-setting behavior, we are dealing with the firms that are monopolistic or monopolistically competitive. At the same time, monopolistic or monopolistically competitive firms make decisions according to the market demand curve they confront. This is consistent with the effective demand theory that firms' outputs are determined and constrained by market demand.

Assume that initially the demand curve expected by a firm is D_0 (see Figure A.4). Note that, as for a firm, its real demand curve is unknown. Accordingly, it can only make decisions according to the expected demand curve. If the marginal cost curve for the firm is MC and the marginal revenue curve is MR_0, as in Figure A.4, then the optimal price set by the firm is initially P_0. As might be imagined, when the firm sets the optimal price P_0, it will show the price publicly, such as by printing it on menus, price tags and advertisements.

Suppose now that at price P_0, the actual demand is Q_a rather than Q_0 as expected. The firm in this case has reason to adjust its expected demand curve to D_a so that the new optimal price should become P_1. Now we want to know whether the firm would adjust its price to P_1.

It should be noted that price adjustment is not without costs. Such costs include not only the menu cost, such as the costs required for reprinting the price

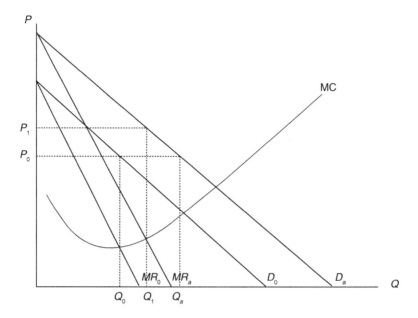

Figure A.4 The sticky pricing of new Keynesians.

tag (or menu), but also the possible reputation cost caused by the change in price. Obviously, reputation cost has much to do with the amplitude and frequency of adjustment. The greater the amplitude of adjustment, the more the reputation cost is. For instance, consumers might be able to accept a 5 percent increase in price, but they may find it difficult to put up with a 100 percent increase in price. At the same time, the greater the frequency of adjustment, the more the reputation cost is. Occasional adjustment can be tolerated by customers, but a firm infamous for frequent changes in price would eventually be abandoned by customers. When the adjustment cost arrives at a certain level, a profit-maximizing firm will not adjust its price at all, even if it knows the current price is not optimal.

Thus, in the sticky pricing model of new Keynesians, when confronted with the changes in market demands firms may delay their price adjustment, which means the price may be sticky: price adjustment is neither timely nor necessarily optimal.

Bounded rationality – determination of output

Next, we would like to discuss the micro-foundations of output determination in Keynesian economics. We know that, according to Keynesian theory, output is determined by demand. Here, we want to show that such a theory of output determination, i.e., the effective demand theory, is also rational, or can be expressed by an optimization model. However, as pointed by Gong and Semmler

(2006), the "rationality" here should be viewed as "bounded rationality", since an additional constraint, the demand constraint, is added into the optimization model. It is this constraint that enables agents to have no full-confidence expectation, and thus to become more realistic compared to the agents assumed by neoclassicals.

Given the product and factor prices P and W, as well as the market demand Y^d, the firm's problem with regard to output determination, according to Keynesian theory, can be written as:

$$\max PY - WL \tag{A.9}$$

subject to

$$Y = f(L) \tag{A.10}$$

$$Y \leq Y^d \tag{A.11}$$

where Y stands for the output that firms want to produce, and $f(\cdot)$ denotes the production function. The capital stock is assumed to be given, and thus labor is the only factor that needs to be chosen for production. It is apparent that without the constraint (A.11), the problem is exactly like the neoclassical problem of the output decision.

Before we solve this problem, it is necessary to explain the price P given above. As depicted earlier, in Hypothesis 1, according to Keynesian theory the decisions of price and output are separated. We also described how price is determined within a new Keynesian model of sticky pricing. Therefore, we can assume that the price given in this output decision problem has been determined and announced in the way described by the previous sticky pricing model. At the given price, the firm carries out a decision on output. Hence, although our model (A.9)–(A.11) looks like an output decision model for a perfectly competitive firm except the demand constraint (A.11), we still should not consider the firm as a perfectly competitive firm; the firm's monopoly status is reflected in its ability to set price.

Let us put the constraint (A.11) aside temporarily and thus return to the standard model of neoclassical analysis. Since the production cost here only comes from labor whose determination is given by $L = f^{-1}(Y)$, the cost function of firms can be written as

$$c(Y) = Wf^{-1}(Y) \tag{A.12}$$

Substituting it into the objective function (A.9), we can obtain the first-order condition:

$$P = MC(Y) \tag{A.13}$$

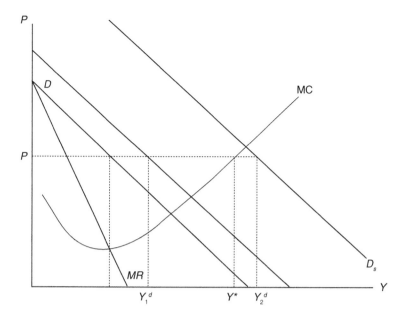

Figure A.5 Bounded rationality.

where *MC* is the marginal cost: $MC(Y) = c'(Y)$ and $c(Y)$ is given by equation (A.12). Equation (A.13) shows that if we do not consider the demand constraint (A.11), the optimal output is given at the condition that the marginal cost equals the price. Let us denote this optimal output as Y^*. We can regard this optimal output as the neoclassical output, which is without boundaries, or not subject to the demand constraint. As discussed previously, only when the firm has full confidence will it consider producing output Y^*.

Now, let us examine what will happen after adding the constraint (A.11). At this point, the firm has no confidence to sell Y^* and therefore its output supply is constrained by the market demand Y^d. Figure A.5 indicates how the firm makes decisions on output in this case.

In Figure A.5, we assume that the demand curve initially expected by the firm is given by D. Given this expected demand curve, the marginal revenue curve is derived as MR The price set and announced by the firm is given by P. If the firm has full confidence, its output will be Y^* that meets the first-order condition (A.13).

Next, assume that at the price P announced by the firm, the actual market demand is Y_1^d, that is $Y^d = Y_1^d$. It's clear that $Y^d < Y^*$ at this point. The constraint (A.11) shows that the actual production must be less than or equal to Y^d, so the firm will choose Y^d as its output supply. But if we assume that at the price P announced by the firm the actual market demand is Y_2^d, that is, $Y^d = Y_2^d$ (note that in this case $Y^d > Y^*$), the firm will choose Y^*, since the marginal cost is larger than the marginal revenue when production exceeds Y^*.

The previous analysis thus indicates that the solution to the decision problem (A.9)–(A.11) can be written as:

$$Y = \begin{cases} Y^d & Y^d \leq Y^* \\ Y^* & Y^d > Y^* \end{cases}$$

where Y^* meets equation (A.13).

The assumption of excess capacity

Here, we would also like to note that if we follow the tradition that supply is defined as the amount of output that a firm is willing to sell at a given price, then in Figure A.5 the supply is Y^* when the price is given at P. This seems to suggest that in the case of monopolistic competition, the market is generally over-supplied. Only when the firm excessively underestimates its market demand when setting price does supply have the potential to fall short of demand. For instance, the actual market demand curve is D_s as in Figure A.5, but the firm underestimates it as D. Note that in this case, the supply by the firm is Y^* while the demand is Y_2^d.

The preceding analysis corroborates our earlier Hypothesis 2, which implies that firms are generally in the situation of excessive capacity (supply). Here, we can see that this excessive supply is clearly inseparable from firms' monopolistic behavior of setting prices. Thus, the micro-foundations of Keynesian economics cannot be established on a perfectly competitive economy; rather, monopoly or monopolistic competition is what envisaged by Keynesian economics.

Appendix B
Behavior analysis of investment

In Appendix A, we provided a behavior analysis on output and price for the firm in the economy envisaged by Keynesian economics. In this appendix, we will present a behavior analysis on investment, the most important variable that has impacted on the Chinese economy over the past 30 years. We note that such a behavior analysis is completely missing in neoclassical economics, since the analytical system of neoclassical economics does not require an independent investment function: once output is determined by production function, investment is simply arranged to be equal to saving. However, in Keynesian economics, investment is a crucial variable and must be independent and autonomous. Therefore, behavior analysis of investment becomes necessary.

We will first discuss investment in the absence of loans and other financial constraints. The resulting investment function will be directly used in Appendix C, where Harrodian economy is investigated. Then we will introduce credit constraints so as to derive the investment function compatible with contemporary Chinese economy. This function will receive econometric testing, and be directly used in Appendix D, where a macro-dynamic model of contemporary Chinese economy is presented.

B.1 The existence of optimum capacity utilization

To discuss investment in the absence of loans and other financial constraints, let us first build a theorem on the existence of optimal capacity utilization. The existence of such an optimum indicates that firms make investments in order to achieve optimal capacity utilization. We use a dynamic optimization model to derive the theorem.

In the standard microeconomic theory of short run analysis, production costs can be divided into two categories: fixed cost and variable cost. In general, the average cost falls with the rise in output due to the presence of fixed cost; when the output nears the maximum production capacity, the average cost begins to rise. When considering investment, however, the fixed cost no longer exists because what we do is to change capacity. In this case, we shall assume that average cost is a non-decreasing function of capacity utilization.[1]

Given this assumption, we consider a representative firm i, $i = 1, 2, \ldots, n$. It has a cost function at time t:

$$C_{i,t} = c_i(U_{i,t})Y_{i,t}, \quad c_i > 0 \tag{B.1}$$

where $C_{i,t}$ is the total cost of firm i at time t, $Y_{i,t}$ denotes the firm's output measured in monetary units,[2] and c_i represents the firm's average cost, which is a function of capacity utilization. Here, $U_{i,t}$ can be written as

$$U_{i,t} = \frac{Y_{i,t}}{A_i K_{i,t}} \tag{B.2}$$

where $K_{i,t}$ is the capital stock at time t, and A_i refers to the level of technology. For the given cost function expressed by equation (B.1), the firm's profits can be written as

$$\pi_{i,t} = Y_{i,t} - c_i\left(\frac{Y_{i,t}}{A_i K_{i,t}}\right)Y_{i,t} - I_{i,t}$$

where $I_{i,t}$ stands for the investment of firm i at time t.

Investment can be used to create the future production capacity. Hence, we assume that there is a sequence of expected demands about the future $E\{Y_{i,t+j}\}_{j=0}^{\infty}$ given to firm i, when the firm makes an investment decision at time t. As a result, the firm's problem with regard to investment can be expressed as the selection of an investment sequence $\{I_{i,t+j}\}_{j=0}^{\infty}$ as

$$\max_{\{I_{i,t+j}\}_{j=0}^{\infty}} E\sum_{j=0}^{\infty} \beta^j\left[Y_{i,t+j} - c_i\left(\frac{Y_{i,t+j}}{A_i K_{i,t+j}}\right)Y_{i,t+j} - I_{i,t+j} \right] \tag{B.3}$$

subject to

$$K_{i,t+j} = (1 - d_i)K_{i,t+j-1} + I_{i,t+j} \tag{B.4}$$

where E is the expectation operator, β is the discount factor, and d_i stands for the depreciation rate. Obviously, equation (B.4) can be understood as the capital accumulation. It must be noted that although this decision-making will generate a sequence of investment $\{I_{i,t+j}\}_{j=0}^{\infty}$, only investment $I_{i,t}$ will be implemented by the firm at time t.

The Euler equation of this optimization problem composed of (B.3) and (B.4) can be written as follows:

$$E\left[Y_{i,t+j}\frac{Y_{i,t+j}}{A_i K_{i,t+j}^2}\left(\frac{Y_{i,t+j}}{A_i K_{i,t+j}}\right) \right] + \beta(1 - d_i) - 1 = 0$$

By replacing $Y_{i,t+j}/(A_i K_{i,t+j})$ in the above with equation (B.2), we obtain

$$E\left[U_{i,t+j}^2 c_i(U_{i,t+j})\right] = \frac{1}{A_i}[1 - \beta(1 - d_i)] \tag{B.5}$$

The optimal capacity utilization can be derived from equation (B.5) as long as $c'(\cdot) \neq 0$. Since the right side of equation (B.5) is represented with all parameters, we can find that the optimal capacity utilization is time-invariant.[3] We can denote U_i^* as the solution to the optimum capacity utilization.

B.2 Investment without financial constraint

Given the optimal capacity utilization U_i^*, we can derive the optimum investment. Because the investment is made to achieve U_i^*, the optimal investment at time t, denoted as $I_{i,t}^*$, should be subject to

$$\frac{EY_{i,t}}{A_i[(1 - d_i)K_{i,t-1} + I_{i,t}^*]} = U_i^*$$

where the left side of the equation is the expected capacity utilization. From this equation, we can derive

$$I_{i,t}^* = \frac{1}{A_i U_i^*} EY_{i,t} - (1 - d_i)K_{i,t-1} \tag{B.6}$$

Now we suppose that the cost function, technology and depreciation rate are identical among all i's. Thus, the optimal capacity utilization will be the same across all i's. This identical assumption is very common in the representative agent model, which will allow us to get rid of the subscript i. Dividing both sides of equation (B.6) by K_{t+1}, (B.6), under the identical assumption, can be rearranged as

$$\frac{I_t}{K_{t-1}} = \frac{1}{AU^*} \frac{EY_t}{K_{t-1}} - (1 - d) \tag{B.7}$$

To make our analysis tractable, it is assumed that there is a linear relation between the expected demand and the past demand, that is, $EY_t = eY_{t-1}$, where e is a parameter. Given the linear relation, we can derive social investment function without financial constraints from (B.7) as

$$I_t / K_{t-1} = -(1 - d) + \xi U_{t-1} \tag{B.8}$$

where $\xi = e/U^*$. This function will be used in Appendix C, where the Harrodian economy will be presented.

B.3 Investment with financial constraint

Next, we shall introduce a credit constraint into the model. Let us first examine the impact of interest rate on investment in China. As discussed in Chapters 1 and 6, compared with OECD countries the real interest rate in China is very low. Meanwhile, there are still some soft budget constraints on many firms (especially state-owned enterprises), implying that interest rate cannot be an effective constraint on investment, such as in leaving the investment lower than the optimum represented by (B.6). Effective investment constraint often stems from the amount of loans available for firms to obtain.

Now suppose that our representative firm can obtain the loan of $\Delta M_{i,t}$ from state-owned commercial banks. We already know that if firms are not restricted by loans, their investment will be equal to $I_{i,t}^*$, as expressed by (B.6). This means that the firm's investment with financial constraint can be written as

$$
I_{i,t} = \begin{cases} I_{i,t}^* & I_{i,t}^* < \Delta M_{i,t} \\ \Delta M_{i,t} & I_{i,t}^* \geq \Delta M_{i,t} \end{cases}. \tag{B.9}
$$

Let ΔM_t be the total amount of growth in the monetary base. Thus, the total amount of loans generated by ΔM_t can be expressed as $(\gamma-1)\Delta M_t$, where $\gamma>1$ can be regarded as the money multiplier $\gamma>1$. We can regard $(\gamma-1)\Delta M_t$ as the total amount of loans offered by the state-owned commercial banks.

Next, let us examine credit allocation by the state-owned commercial bank system $\{\Delta M_{i,t}\}_{i=1}^n$, where

$$
\Delta M_{i,t} = l_i(\gamma-1)\Delta M_t \tag{B.10}
$$

and $l_i \in [0, 1)$. Under this loan scheme, firms' investment decisions are expressed in terms of equations (B.6), (B.9) and (B.10). Adding all the $I_{i,t}$ values together, we get the total investment I_t:

$$
I_t = \sum_{i=1}^n I_{i,t} \tag{B.11}
$$

According to l_i obtained by the firm, we find out that for some firms their investments are restricted by loans, that is, $I_{i,t}=\Delta M_{i,t}$; for others, their investments are optimal, namely, $I_{i,t}=I_{i,t}^*$. Arranging the serial number i's so that the investments of the first n_1 firms are constrained by loans, we thus can rewrite equation (B.11) as

$$
I_t = \varphi \Delta M_t + \sum_{i=n_1+1}^{n-n_1} \left[\frac{1}{A_i U_i^*} EY_{i,t} - (1-d_i)K_{i,t-1} \right] \tag{B.12}
$$

where

$$
\varphi = (\gamma-1)\sum_{i=1}^{n_1} l_i > 0
$$

According to the identical assumption among the firms, we can substitute U^*, A and d for U_i^*, A_i and d_i to get rid of the subscript i ($i = 1, 2, \ldots, n$). Equation (B.12) can then be rearranged as

$$I_t = \varphi \Delta M_t + \frac{1}{AU^*} \sum_{i=n_1+1}^{n-n_1} EY_{i,t} - (1-d) \sum_{i=n_1+1}^{n-n_1} K_{i,t-1}$$

Dividing both sides of the above equation by the total capital stock K_{t-1}, we thus get

$$\frac{I_t}{K_{t-1}} = \varphi \frac{\Delta M_t}{K_{t-1}} + \frac{1}{AU^*} \frac{EY_t}{K_{t-1}} \varsigma_y - (1-d)\varsigma_k \qquad (B.13)$$

where Y_t is the total demand, and parameters ς_y and ς_k can be interpreted as the proportions of demand and capital stock of $n - n_1$ firms in Y_t and K_{t-1}, namely,

$$\varsigma_y = \frac{\sum\limits_{i=n_1+1}^{n-n_1} EY_{i,t}}{EY_t}, \varsigma_k = \frac{\sum\limits_{i=n_1+1}^{n-n_1} EY_{i,t} - 1}{EY_{t-1}}$$

We assume that both of them are time-invariant.

To make our analysis tractable, we impose two linear relations: one is between the total money supply and total capital stock (i.e., $K_{t-1} = vM_{t-1}$); the other exists between expected aggregate demand and past aggregate demand (i.e., $EY_t = eY_{t-1}$),[4] where both v and e are parameters. Given the two linear relations as depicted above, the investment function (B.13) can now be rewritten as

$$I_t / K_{t-1} = \xi_i + \xi_u U_{t-1} + \xi_m m_t \qquad (B.14)$$

where $m = \Delta M_t / M_{t-1}$ represents the growth rate of money supply, $U_t = Y_t / AK_t$ is the capacity utilization at the macro level, and the parameters of ξ_i, ξ_u and ξ_m are subject to

$$\xi_i = -(1-d)\varsigma_k, \xi_u = e\varsigma_y / U^*, \xi_m = \varphi / v$$

This aggregate investment function will be used in Appendix D, where a macro-dynamic model of contemporary Chinese economy is presented.

Appendix C

The Harrodian economy and the existence of a destabilizing mechanism

As explained in Chapter 7, the coexistence of stabilizing and destabilizing mechanisms along with external shocks brings about business cycles such as we have observed in the economy. We also pointed out that if the force from a destabilizing mechanism is larger than that from a stabilizing mechanism, then business cycles (perhaps initiated by some external shocks) cannot be damped or self-corrected. In this case, the counter-cyclic policies from governments are essential for the economy to be stabilized. Among the variants of destabilization mechanisms, Harrod's knife-edge puzzle, generated from investment behavior, might be the most important. In this appendix, we offer a mathematical analysis of Harrod's model to explore this destabilization mechanism.

C.1 The Harrodian economy

The following equations might be considered as the structural form of the product market in the Harrodian economy[1]:

$$Y_t = \frac{1}{s} I_t \tag{C.1}$$

$$Y_t^p = AK_t \tag{C.2}$$

$$U_t = \frac{Y_t}{Y_t^p} \tag{C.3}$$

$$K_t = (1-d)K_{t-1} + I_t \tag{C.4}$$

$$I_t / K_{t-1} = -(1-d) + \xi U_{t-1} \tag{C.5}$$

where Y_t is output (which can also be understood as aggregate demand in a demand determined economy), I_t is investment, Y_t^p is potential output, K_t is capital stock, and U_t is capacity utilization.

The meanings of these equations (C.1)–(C.5) are all straightforward: equation (C.1) explains the determination of output by multiplier ($1/s$); equations (C.2) and (C.3) are the definitions of potential output and capacity utilization, respectively; equation (C.4) describes the accumulation of capital stock; and, finally, equation (C.5) is an investment function without financial constraint, as described in Appendix B. Apparently, the key variable here is the investment I_t: investment creates not only capacity in the product market via (C.2) and (C.4), but also demand via a multiplier (see equation (C.1)). We will find that it is the behavior of investment that creates a destabilizing mechanism for the economy.

C.2 The warranted rate of growth

In the Harrodian economy, as depicted above, the balance of the product market is reflected in the comparison of Y_t and Y_t^p. The so-called warranted rate of growth is the growth rate at which demand–supply equilibrium is warranted in the product market. We shall now derive this growth rate.

Dividing both sides of (C.4) by K_{t-1}, we obtain

$$k_t = -d + \frac{I_t}{K_{t-1}} \tag{C.6}$$

Here, $k_t \equiv (K_t - K_{t-1})/K_{t-1}$ is the growth rate of capital stock, which should also be the growth rate of potential output Y_t^p (since A is constant). Now let $Y_t = Y_t^p$ (or $U_t = 1$). From (C.1) and (C.2), we obtain

$$\frac{1}{s} I_t = A K_{t-1} \tag{C.7}$$

Expressing I_t/K_{t-1} in terms of (C.7), we obtain from (C.6)

$$k_t = -d + sA \tag{C.8}$$

The right side of equation (C.8) is composed of parameters and therefore is time-invariant. Thus, when the product market is at demand–supply equilibrium, the economy will grow at a constant rate $k_t^* = -d + sA$. Harrod called this rate the warranted rate of growth.[2]

Apparently, the economy growing at the warranted rate is an ideal state. A deviation from that state means disequilibrium at product market.

C.3 The puzzle of the knife-edge: the existence of the destabilization mechanism

Having arrived at the concept of warranted rate of growth, Harrod began to examine whether the economy can by itself converge to the state at which the product market is in equilibrium or the economy is growing at the warranted rate. According to Harrod, this does not seem to occur. On the contrary, as long as the economy deviates from the state of equilibrium in the product market, the deviation will be larger and larger.

For example, when there is a certain degree of overheating in the economy, investment will increase to meet the increased demand (or insufficiency in capacity). Yet investment not only increases capacity, but also the aggregate demand. Since $A<1$ and $1/s>1$,[3] we find that for the economy as a whole the increased demand will be larger than the increased capacity. This will overheat the economy further, and thus impel the firms to invest more. On the other hand, if there is excess capacity, firms will reduce their investment. Yet the reduction in investment will reduce aggregate demand too. Again due to $A<1$ and $1/s>1$, the reduction in aggregate demand will be larger than the reduction in capacity. Therefore, excess capacity will be enlarged. Harrod called this problem a knife-edge problem.

Mathematically, the knife-edge problem essentially means that the system of Harrod's model is unstable. This instability can be formalized as follows. From equations (C.1)–(C.3), we have

$$U_t = \frac{I_t}{sAK_{t-1}}$$

Substituting the investment function (C.5) into the above, we obtain

$$U_t = -\frac{1-d}{sA} + \frac{\xi}{sA}U_{t-1} \qquad \text{(C.9)}$$

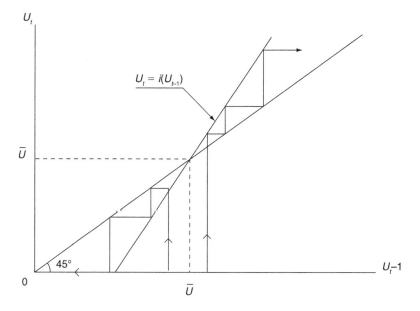

Figure C.1 The trajectory of U_t: @eqn_243_0001.tif@

Denote $\overline{U}$ as the steady state of U_t. We can then find from the above that

$$\overline{U} = \frac{1-d}{\xi - sA}$$

For $\overline{U}$ to be positive so that it is economically meaningful, we request that $\xi > sA$. But this indicates that $\xi/(sA) > 1$. Therefore, the dynamic system as expressed in (C.9) is unstable. Figure C.1 shows the trajectory of U_t.

Appendix D

A macro-dynamic model of contemporary Chinese economy – an overshooting perspective of "deflationary expansion" in China

In this appendix, we will introduce a macro-dynamic model of contemporary Chinese economy based on the theoretical preparation through Appendix A to Appendix C. The model is essentially the same as that presented in Gong and Lin (2007, 2008). It has some Keynesian features: the output is determined by demand via the multiplier process. Given such a method of output determination, an autonomously (or independently) determined investment is introduced that plays a key role in business cycles (via the destabilizing mechanism) and economic growth. At the same time, prices and wages are adjusted slowly as depicted in the Keynesian sticky pricing model. That price and wage adjustment along with the monetary policy that will also be introduced can be regarded as a stabilizing mechanism of the Chinese economy. It is the coexistence of stabilizing and destabilizing mechanisms that triggers the business cycles in China. As pointed out previously, such a macro-dynamic model with Keynesian features will be better suited to explaining contemporary Chinese economy.

In order to investigate whether the model accords with contemporary Chinese economy, we have conducted some econometric tests on the model. At last, we will offer an explanation for "deflationary expansion" – one of the mysteries in Chinese economy.

D.1 Structural form of the model

Output and investment

Consider a closed economy in which output is driven by investment. Time is discrete, and is indexed by t, $t = 1, 2, \ldots$ To simplify our analysis, we may assume that the relation between output and investment is linear so that we can write

$$Y_t = \theta I_t, \theta > 1 \tag{D.1}$$

Above, Y_t and I_t refer to output and investment in period t. Equation (D.1) is similar to equation (C.1), with $\theta = 1/s$.

Following the discussion in Appendix B, we shall write the investment function as

$$I_t \,/\, K_{t-1} = \xi_i + \xi_u U_{t-1} + \xi_m (m_{t-1} + p_{t-1}) + \mu_t, \quad \xi_u, \xi_m > 0 \tag{D.2}$$

where K_t is the capital stock, U_t is the capacity utilization, m_t is the growth rate of the money supply, p_t is the inflation rate and μ_t can be regarded as a shock. Note that here $m_t - p_t$ can be regarded approximately as the growth rate of the real money supply. Compared to (B.14) in Appendix B, we here adopt real money growth rather than nominal money growth as an impact on investment. Meanwhile, we also introduce the shock μ_t into the investment function. Rather than assuming μ_t to be purely stochastic, we shall assume that μ_t follows:

$$\mu_t = \rho \mu_{t-1} + \varepsilon_t, \quad \rho \in (0,1) \tag{D.3}$$

where ε_t is an independently and identically distributed (i.i.d.) innovation.

The capacity utilization U_t is defined as

$$U_t = \frac{Y_t}{A K_{t-1}}. \tag{D.4}$$

This indicates that the capital stock in period $t-1$ is measured at the end of period $t-1$ (or at the beginning of period t) so that it provides the production capacity for period t.[1]

Prices and wages

Next, we will discuss how price is determined. We shall not assume that the price will be determined at the level that can clear the market at every period. This is particularly true to China, since China is still a transitional and developing economy. Following the dual Philip curves of price and wage, as discussed in Flaschel, Gong and Semmler (2001) and Fair (2000), we may consider the following price and wage dynamics:

$$w_t = \alpha_w + \alpha_p p_t + \alpha_n (N_t - \bar{N}) + \alpha_x x_t, \quad \alpha_p, \alpha_n, \alpha_x > 0 \tag{D.5}$$

$$p_t = \beta_p + \beta_w w_t + \beta_u (U_t - \bar{U}) - \beta_x x_t, \quad \beta_w, \beta_u, \beta_x > 0 \tag{D.6}$$

where w_t is the growth rate of nominal wage rate, N_t is the employment rate, x_t is the growth rate of labor productivity, and $\bar{N}$ and $\bar{U}$ can be regarded as the normal levels of N_t and U_t, beyond which inflation in wage and price will be accelerated. Evidently, our expression of price and wage dynamics is based on the fairly symmetric assumptions on the causes of price and wage inflation. Both of them are driven on the one hand by a demand pressure component given by $U_t - \bar{U}$ and $N_t - \bar{N}$, and on the other hand by a cost push term measured by p_t, w_t and x_t in the right-hand side of (D.5) and (D.6).

Labor market

With regard to the employment rate N_t, we could write it as

$$N_t = \frac{n(Y_t,\ldots)}{L_t^s} \tag{D.7}$$

where L_t^s is the labor supply and $n(\cdot)$ is the demand for labor, which is a function of output Y_t, among others. Due to the current dual structure of the Chinese economy, we would expect that L_t^s could be enormous compared to the demand for labor. This will affect the significance of the parameter α_n in wage equation (D.5). Details will be provided when we turn to the empirical estimation of our dynamic model.

Monetary policy

We know that the government in China has set up a yearly target for money growth, which can be regarded as a major macroeconomic policy for demand management and growth promotion. Once the target has been set up, the monetary authority employs the credit plan as its principle instrument to implement the target. Although in most cases the credit plan is only indicative, due to the state ownership of banks in China the credit supply from the state banks may not deviate very much from the credit plan.

In the formulation of the money supply function, we shall consider that the government may have a stable (or long-term) target of growth rate in the money supply, in addition to the short-term target of the inflation rate. We denote this long-term target as g. This target is somehow related to the desired economic growth under some acceptable inflation rate (or the desired growth rate in nominal GDP) that the government wants to achieve. Given such a target, the yearly money supply will be adjusted according to actual economic performance:

$$m_t - m_{t-1} = \pi_p(\bar{p} - p_{t-1}) + \pi_m(g - m_{t-1}) \qquad \pi_p, \pi_m > 0 \tag{D.8}$$

where $\bar{p}$ can be regarded as the short-term inflation target, which empirically can be computed as a sample mean of p_t. This formulation indicates that the change in money supply will first respond to whether inflation in the previous year was below or above the target inflation rate $\bar{p}$. Second, the change in the money supply also responds to whether the actual money supply in the past year was below or above the long-term target. If it was below the long-term target, the growth rate of money supply in this year will increase.

Apparently, this formulation of the money supply rule reflects the strong attention of the government to using the money supply (or cheap and easy credit) to promote economic growth.

D.2 Estimation of parameters

The model constructed here involves four key behavior functions: (D.2), (D.5), (D.6) and (D.8). To verify their relevance to China, we provide a simple regression for these four behavior functions by employing annual data from the *China Statistical Yearbook*, except for the capacity utilization U_t, which is computed by Gong and Yang (2002).

We should mention that for China, these annual data are the only data source before 1998. The estimation here is rather unsophisticated due to the lack of data sources with more frequency. Table D.1 records the estimated parameters, while Figure D.1 shows the match of the estimation with the observation.

We first discuss the parameters in Set 5, named "other parameters." They are estimated with the method of moments by matching the first moments of the corresponding data. Note that here, $\bar{x}, \bar{p}$ and $\bar{U}$ are, respectively, the sample means of x_t, p_t and U_t. The data for estimating θ and A are implied by (D.1) and (D.4).

The estimation equations for the four behavior functions take the form

$$I_t / K_{t-1} = \xi_r + \xi_u U_t + \xi_m (m_{t-1} - p_{t-1}) + \mu_t, \qquad \mu_t = \rho \mu_{t-1} + \varepsilon_t \tag{D.9}$$

$$w_t = \alpha_w + \alpha_p p_t + \alpha_x x_t + \delta_t \tag{D.10}$$

Table D.1 Estimates of parameters (numbers in parentheses are the standard errors)

Set 1	Investment function	$\xi_1 = -0.1571 \ (0.1225)$ $\xi_u = 0.4010 \ (0.1739)$ $\xi_m = 0.1087 \ (0.0367)$ $\rho = 0.8547 \ (0.0776)$ $DW = 1.9102$
Set 2	Wage equation	$\alpha_w = 0.0785 \ (0.0156)$ $\alpha_p = 0.6301 \ (0.1690)$ $\alpha_x = 0.3141 \ (0.1274)$ $DW = 1.6453$
Set 3	Price equation	$\tilde{\beta}_p = -0.4640 \ (0.1276)$ $\beta_w = 0.6732 \ (0.1462)$ $\beta_u = 0.5895 \ (0.1702)$ $\beta_x = 0.1446 \ (0.1211)$ $DW = 1.6919$
Set 4	Money supply function	$\kappa_0 = 0.1058 \ (0.0529)$ $\kappa_1 = -0.3589 \ (0.2611)$ $\kappa_2 = 0.5674 \ (0.2357)$ $DW = 1.3917$
Set 5	Other parameters	$\theta = 3.2069 \ (0.4019)$ $A = 0.4760 \ (0.0552)$ $\bar{x} = 0.0536 \ (0.0961)$ $\bar{p} = 0.0600 \ (0.0707)$ $\bar{U} = 0.7500 \ (0.0577)$

Data from Research Group of RMB Internationalization (2006).

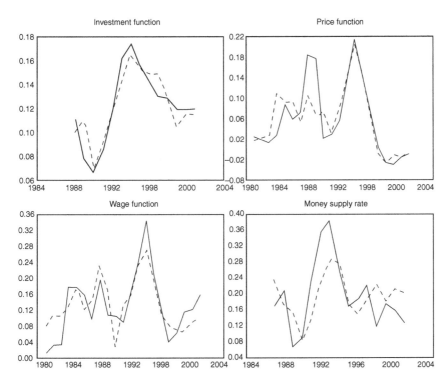

Figure D.1 Matching the observations (solid lines, sample data; dashed lines, simulated data).

$$p_t = \tilde{\beta}_p + \beta_w w_t + \beta_u U_t - \beta_x x_t + \xi_t \tag{D.11}$$

$$m_t = \kappa_0 + \kappa_1 p_{t-1} + \kappa_2 m_{t-1} + \eta_t \tag{D.12}$$

where ε_t, δ_t, ζ_t and η_t are all assumed to i.i.d. innovations. We apply the Cochrane-Orcutt procedure to estimate the investment function (D.9), while the OLS method is directly applied to (D.10), (D.11) and (D.12).

We should note several points here. First, most estimates directly respond to the structure parameters as discussed in the structure form of the model except for $\tilde{\beta}_p$, here in Set 3, and the parameters in Set 4. Other structural parameters, such as β_p, π_p, π_m and g, can be computed from the following restrictions:

$$\tilde{\beta}_p = \beta_p - \beta_u \bar{U}, \kappa_0 = \pi_p \bar{p} + \pi_m g, \kappa_1 = -\pi_p, \kappa_2 = 1 - \pi_m$$

From these we can obtain

$$\beta_p = -0.0218, \pi_p = 0.3589, \pi_m = 0.4326, g = 0.1947$$

Note that here the computed g is close to the sample mean of the growth rate of money supply (M1), which is 0.2006.

Second, we have dropped the employment rate $N_t - \bar{N}$ as the explanatory variables in the equations of wage (D.10). The estimate α_n with respect to $N_t - \bar{N}$ is statistically insignificant. The estimate is -0.0946 while the standard error is 2.3076. As discussed previously, the labor supply in China (as in many developing countries) seems to be unlimited due to the enormous labor surplus from the rural areas. This indicates that we could assume $L_t^s = +\infty$. Given this, we obtain $N = 0$ and $\bar{N} = 0$.

D.3 Analysis

In this section, we provide a dynamic analysis of the model that we constructed in the previous section. Our first task is to transform the structure form of the model into an intensive form, which can be expressed as a standard dynamic system in discrete time.

The intensive form of the model

The following is the proposition regarding our transformation.

Proposition 1: Let $i_t \equiv I_t / K_{t-1}$. Assume that $L_t^s = +\infty$ and x_t is fixed at $\bar{x}$. The structural form of the model (D.1)–(D.8) when ignoring ε_t in (D.3) can be transformed into the following standard three-dimensional system:

$$i_t = \xi_0 + \xi_1 i_{t-1} + \xi_m m_{t-1} + \rho \mu_{t-1} \tag{D.13}$$

$$m_t = \pi_0 - \pi_p \alpha_1 i_{t-1} + (1 - \pi_m) m_{t-1} \tag{D.14}$$

$$\mu_t = \rho \mu_{t-1} \tag{D.15}$$

where

$$\xi_0 = \xi_i - \xi_m \alpha_0, \xi_1 = \xi_u(\theta / A) - \xi_m \alpha_1, \pi_0 = \pi_p \bar{p} + \pi_m g - \pi_p \alpha_0$$

$$\alpha_0 = \frac{\beta_p + \beta_w \alpha_w + \beta_w \alpha_x \bar{x} - \beta_u \bar{U} - \beta_x \bar{x}}{1 - \beta_w \alpha_p}, \quad \alpha_1 = \frac{\beta_u \theta}{(1 - \beta_w \alpha_p) A}$$

The proposition is proved in the latter part of this appendix. For our non-stochastic dynamic analysis, μ_t can be regarded as an investment shock to the economy, if the initial condition μ_0 is not zero. Since we do not have enough information to specify the dynamics of x_t, we have set it to be constant. The assumption $L_t^s = +\infty$ captures the seemingly unlimited supply of labor reserved in the rural areas of China.

The steady state of the model

The steady state of our dynamic system is well established in the following proposition.

Proposition 2: The system composed of (D.13)–(D.15) has an unique equilibria $(\bar{i}, \bar{m}, \bar{\mu})$ at which

$$\bar{m} = g \tag{D.16}$$

$$\bar{i} = \frac{1}{1-\xi_1}(\xi_0 + \xi_m g) \tag{D.17}$$

$$\bar{\mu} = 0 \tag{D.18}$$

The proof of this proposition is trivial by setting $i_t = i_{t-1} = \bar{i}$, $m_t = m_{t-1} = \bar{m}$ and $\mu_t = \mu_{t-1} = \bar{\mu}$ in (D.13)–(D.15).

The stability of the model

It should be noted that although the system is three-dimensional, μ is autonomously determined via (D.15). Therefore, we shall first, for our stability analysis, focus on the system composed of (D.13) and (D.14) only. This indicates that we are considering an economy in which the initial condition of μ_t, denoted as μ_0, is equal to zero. The following is the proposition regarding the stability of our dynamic system.

Proposition 3: Let J be a Jacobian matrix evaluated at the steady state of the dynamic system composed of equations (D.13)–(D.14), with $\mu_0 = 0$ and $\lambda_{1,2}$ the two eigenvalues of J. Suppose that $1 - \beta_w \alpha_p > 0$ and $\xi_1 - \pi_m < 1$. Then there exists a π_p denoted as π_p^* such that in the neighborhood of π_p^*,

1   $\lambda_{1,2}$ are complex conjugate;
2   The modulus of the complex conjugate denoted as $|\lambda_{1,2}|$ can be either below or above 1 depending on the castellation of the structure parameters. In particular,
   a   When $\pi_p < \pi_p^*$, $|\lambda_{1,2}| < 1$;
   b   When $\pi_p = \pi_p^*$, $|\lambda_{1,2}| = 1$;
   c   When $\pi_p > \pi_p^*$, $|\lambda_{1,2}| > 1$.

3   $\dfrac{d|\lambda_{1,2}(\pi_p)|}{d\pi_p}\Big|_{\pi_p = \pi_p^*} = 0$

Proof of this proposition will be given in the latter part of this appendix.

We should note that the assumption that $1-\beta_w\alpha_p>0$ is well satisfied, given the estimates recorded in Table D.1. However, $\xi_1-\pi_m<1$ is not satisfied. According to our estimates, we compute ξ_1 as 1.9517, which is larger than $1+\pi_m$. Yet by a small change in some parameter, this assumption could be satisfied. For example, if we adjust β_u to 0.3207, which is 80 percent of our estimate, ξ_1 becomes 1.4114 and, therefore, the assumption is satisfied. Figure D.2 provides a simulation with β_u adjusted to 0.3207 while all the other parameters are kept as the same as in Table D.1.

With this proposition, one finds that the equilibrium (i_t, m_t) may exhibit cyclical behavior. It can either be attracting or repelling, depending on the castellation of the structure parameters. For instance, it may depend on the magnitude of π_p (given other structure parameters). In particular, the system undergoes a Hopf bifurcation at $\pi_p=\pi_p^*$, and therefore it permits the limit cycles.[2] In the case of Figure D.2, the cycles are explosive and therefore the equilibrium (i_t, m_t) is repelling. This indicates that π_p, as we have estimated, is larger than the bifurcation π_p^*. In the next subsection, we will explore the case when π_p is less than π_p^*.

D.4 An overshooting perspective of "deflationary expansion" in China

Given the analytical result as expressed in the last subsection and the estimated parameters as reported in Table D.1, we shall conduct some numerical simulations

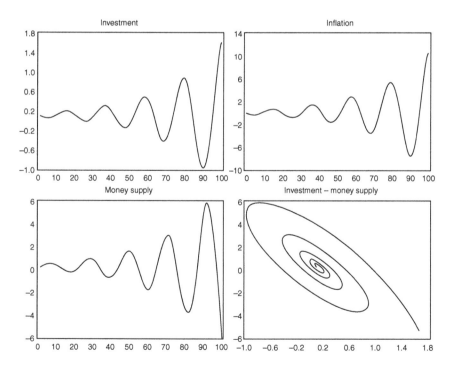

Figure D.2 Model simulation: the unstable case.

based on which one may explain the deflationary problem that has occurred recently in the Chinese economy. In this exercise, the only further adjustments on the structural parameters are β_p and π_p, which we set to -0.065 and 0.2405, respectively. The adjustment on β_p allows us to obtain a more reasonable steady state in the inflation rate. Meanwhile, the adjustment on π_p will make the modulus of the complex conjugate less than 1 (or make π_p less than the bifurcation π_p^*). Given the standard deviations reported in Table D.1, we find that such adjustments (including β_u adjusted to 0.3207) are all within the interval of statistical significance. Note that the equilibrium here is attracting, since we have adjusted π_p below the bifurcation π_p^* and therefore the system is inherently asymptotically stable. However, even in this case deflation could still occur when there is an overshoot in investment.

Such an overshoot may have been stirred up in 1992. At that time, the economy in China had just been recovering from the shadow of the Tiananmen Square affair. Deng's speaking tour in the South of China in 1992 had re-established China's development strategy toward a more open and market-oriented economy. It thus brought an overshoot in investment in the following year. To verify such an overshoot, we can look at the residue from the estimation of our investment function (D.9). As one can find in Figure D.3, there is a sharp increase in the residue (the observed negative predicted) in 1993. This indicates that the overshoot in investment did occur in 1993.

To replicate the economic impact of such an overshoot, we can consider the initial condition in our simulation as follows. We consider the initial investment i_0 to be composed of two parts: one is the shock in investment represented by μ_0,

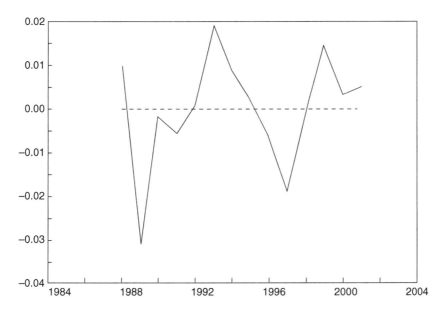

Figure D.3 Residue from the estimation of investment function.

another is the investment following its regular path as if there were no shock. We may consider the second part of i_0 to be slightly below the steady state of it, since the economy had just been in recovery. Here, we assume it was 98 percent of $\bar{\imath}$. For μ_0, we consider three numbers: 0.0006, 0.0003 and 0, indicating no shock. Since the second part of i_0 is below the steady state of i_t, we shall set the initial condition of money supply m_t, for all three cases, to be above its steady state $\bar{m}$, indicating that the government was still wanting to pull the economy out of recession by following its regular money supply rule (D.8). Here, we assume m_0 to be 104.5 percent of $\bar{m}$. Figure D.4 provides a simulation for such initial conditions. In particular, given the two shocks represented by the two positive μ_0's, we obtain two impulse response curves: the solid line represents the trajectory generated from the larger shock with $\mu_0 = 0.0006$, while the dashed line is from the small shock with $\mu_0 = 0.0003$. The dotted line is for the case of no shock.

Clearly, without the investment shock the economy might have continuously remained in a slump (or below its steady state value) for the next few periods, though it was recovering slowly. This is represented by the dotted line with $\mu_0 = 0$. The shock in investment represented by the positive μ_0's generates an investment boom over the subsequent periods. Such an investment boom, represented by a strong sequential increase in investment (see panel (a) in the figure) not only indicates a strong sequential increase in growth rate of GDP, but also brings a sequential increase in capacity utilization (see panel (c) in the figure). The sequential increase in capacity utilization will accelerate inflation over subsequent periods (see panel (b) in the figure).

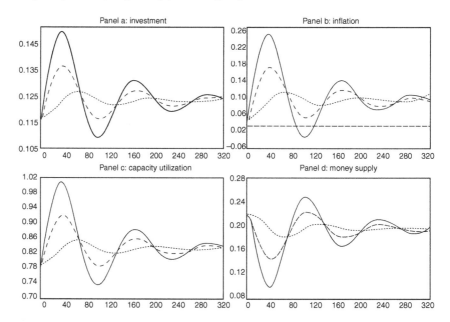

Figure D.4 Impulse response curves to shocks (solid line, larger shock; dashed line, small shock; dotted line, non-shock).

Once inflation began to accelerate, the government exercised a contraction policy by reducing the money supply. We thus can find a sequential decrease in the money supply (see panel (d) in the figure), which at its lowest point was only about 10 percent. Such a contraction in money supply finally slowed down the investment (see panel (a) for the sequential decrease in investment after reaching a peak at about 15 percent). Yet the economy had already established a huge capacity from the previous investment boom era. Consequently, when investment (and thus demand) was slowed down, the economy experienced serious over-capacity (see panel (c) for the sequential decrease in capacity utilization after reaching a peak at about 100 percent) and subsequently the price went down too (see panel (b)). We should note that such a variation in simulated series is consistent with the time series variation as observed in Figure 7.2.

It is interesting to note that if the shock is not large enough, for instance, $\mu_0 = 0.0003$, or if there is no shock, the system does not generate enough volatility and thus deflation may not occur (see the dashed and dotted lines in panel (b)). It is in this sense that the overshoot in 1993 served as a fundamental reason for the deflation problem that started in 1997.

D.5 The proof of Propositions 1 and 3

The proof of Proposition 1

By the definition of i_t, (D.2) can be written as

$$i_t = \xi_i + \xi_u U_{t-1} + \xi_m m_{t-1} - \xi_m p_{t-1} + \mu_t \tag{D.19}$$

We now examine the capacity utilization U_t and inflation rate p_t. In accordance with equation (D.4), when Y_t is given by equation (D.1), we find that U_t is the linear function of i_t:

$$U_t = (\theta / A) i_t . \tag{D.20}$$

When $x_t = \bar{x}$, equations (D.5) and (D.6) imply that

$$p_t = \beta_p + \beta_w (\alpha_w + \alpha_p p_t + \alpha_x \bar{x}) + \beta_u (U_t - \bar{U}) - \beta_x \bar{x}$$

By substituting (D.20) into the above equation and rearranging it, the equation can be rewritten as

$$p_t = \alpha_0 + \alpha_1 i_t \tag{D.21}$$

where α_0 and α_1 are given by Proposition 1. Substituting equations (D.3), (D.20) and (D.21) into (D.19) while ignoring ε_t, we thus get (D.13), as in the proposition. At the same time, substituting (D.21) into (D.8), we get (D.14) as in the proposition. In order to obtain (D.15) as in the proposition, we simply need to ignore ε_t.

The proof of Proposition 3

At the steady state $(\bar{i}, \bar{m})$, the Jacobian matrix of the system (D.13)–(D.14) can be written as

$$J = \begin{bmatrix} \xi_1 & \xi_m \\ -\pi_p \alpha_1 & 1 - \pi_m \end{bmatrix}$$

Thus, the eigenvalues $\lambda_{1,2}$ can be derived from the following equation

$$\lambda^2 - a_1 \lambda + a_2 = 0$$

where

$$a_1 = \xi_1 + 1 - \pi_m, a_2 = (1 - \pi_m)\xi_1 + \xi_m \pi_p \alpha_1$$

We first note that π_m and π_p do not have an impact on α_1 and ξ_1. Meanwhile, the assumption $1 - \beta_w \alpha_p > 0$ implies that $\alpha_1 > 0$. Let us now derive the bifurcation π_p^* on the assumption that the eigenvalues $\lambda_{1,2}$ are complex conjugate. This can be done by assuming that the modulus $|\lambda_{1,2}|$ (which is a_2) equals 1, that is,

$$(1 - \pi_m)\xi_1 + \xi_m \pi_p \alpha_1 = 1$$

By solving this equation for π_p, we thus obtain

$$\pi_p^* = \frac{1 - (1 - \pi_m)\xi_1}{\xi_m \alpha_1} \tag{D.22}$$

Given π_p^*, we now start to prove that $|\lambda_{1,2}|$ is a pair of complex conjugates. This requires that $\alpha_1^2 - 4a_2 < 0$, that is

$$(\xi_1 + 1 - \pi_m)^2 - 4[(1 - \pi_m)\xi_1 + \xi_m \pi_p^* \alpha_1] < 0 \tag{D.23}$$

Substituting (D.22) into the inequality (D.23), the requirement (D.23) becomes

$$(\xi_1 + 1 - \pi_m)^2 - 4[(1 - \pi_m)\xi_1 + 1 - (1 - \pi_m)\xi_1] < 0 \tag{D.24}$$

This inequality holds under the assumption $\xi_1 - \pi_m < 1$. We therefore prove 1 in the proposition. Next, due to

$$\frac{d|\lambda_{1,2}(\pi_p)|}{d\pi_p} = \xi_m \alpha_1 > 0 \tag{D.25}$$

we thus find that 2 and 3 in the proposition have also been proved.

Notes

1 Introduction

1 Qian (2003) and Tian (2005) have adopted this definition.
2 Here, we can have different interpretations on "self-interest". In fact, "self-interest", we refer to here, does not have good or evil characteristics.
3 Of course, whether the policy will be adopted still rests with the final choice of the government. In this sense, the role of economists is still in economic analysis.

2 Chinese economy before reform and opening up

1 Yu (2006: 1).
2 The Gold Yuan Certificate replaced the *fabi* in 1948.
3 Yang (1958: 13).
4 See Li and Zhang (1999: 3).
5 See Wu (1956: 56, 52, 161, 107, 105).
6 See the Central Finance Committee (1950).
7 See Lin, Cai and Li (1994).
8 It needs to be noted that "Hoffman theorem" is just an experiential inference. It does not tell us why factitiously prioritizing the development of heavy industry will be able to speed up the industrialization process. The related discussion is given in the fourth section of this chapter.
9 Lin, Cai and Li (1994).
10 In people's communes, everything was shared. Private kitchens became redundant, and everything in the private kitchen, such as tables, chairs, cooking utensils and pans, was contributed to the commune's kitchen. Private cooking was replaced by communal dining. Several families shared a big pot for meals.
11 Hu (1991).
12 Editorial Board of Chinese Encyclopedia: Economics (1988).
13 Cited from Wu (2003).
14 We note that an administrative organizational structure such as reflected in Figure 2.1 still remains in the contemporary Chinese economy to a large extent, though the relationship between governments and enterprises has changed considerably.
15 Wu (2003).
16 Wu (2006).
17 See Lin (2003), Lin and Sun (2003) and Lin and Liu (2008) among others.
18 The so-called soft budget constraint means that when companies encounter financial difficulties, they can be helped by external organizations to continue to survive. It is as opposed to a hard budget constraint. The soft budget constraint often occurs to those state-owned enterprises in traditional planned economies. The concept was first proposed by Kornai (1979, 1980).

19 See Jing and Sun (2008).
20 The concept of transaction costs was first put forward by Coase (1937).

3 Economic reform in China

1 The Four Asian Tigers or the Asian Tigers refer to Hong Kong, Singapore, South Korea and Taiwan. These were noted for maintaining exceptionally high growth rates and rapid industrialization between the early 1960s and 1990s. In the 21st century, all four tigers have been ranked as advanced and high-income economies.
2 See Yang (1998) for a detailed discussion.
3 A Chinese unit of area, 10 *fen* equals 66.66 m².
4 This practice of contracting farming work to households clearly ran contrary to the regulations of the day. *Regulations on the Work of Rural People's Communes* (published in December, 1978) clearly stated that "it's not allowed to contract farming work to households and divide up farming land for an individual work."
5 A Chinese unit of mass, 1 *jin* equals 500 g.
6 Deng (1994: 315–317).
7 Fengyang Flower Drum is a type of opera. It was originally performed by two sisters-in-law; one beat the drum, the other beat the gong and sang. The songs were about people's sad life in the past. Since the economic reform and opening up, the form and content of this art have developed greatly.
8 As mentioned earlier, the plan for agriculture output is only indicative rather than mandatory.
9 Cited from Lin and Ma (1999).
10 Zhang and Lu (2007: Chapter IV).
11 Cai (1999: 190).
12 This is mainly due to the 4 trillion yuan of planned investments from the government corresponding to the world financial crisis occurring in 2008.
13 It needs to be noted that here we do not offer the data for the service sector, but in fact there is a very high level of state-ownership in some service industries, such as banking. Later, in Chapter 6, we will discuss economic reform in the financial industry (including the banking industry) of China.
14 Related issues will be discussed in Chapter 6.

4 The data from China – what do they tell us?

1 Only a few countries, such as New Zealand, have recognized this.
2 Related data are not listed here; interested readers are directed to Samulson and Solow (1960).
3 See Mankiw (1990).

5 The high growth in contemporary Chinese economy

1 The neoclassical growth model is attributed heavily to Solow (1956).
2 See Barro (2000) and Barro and Sala-i-Martin (2003).
3 Kaldor (1961) once gave more facts regarding economic growth. Barro and Sala-i-Martin (2003) also conducted similar studies as well.
4 For more information about the excessive capacity in China, see www.gov.cn/zwgk/2009–09/29/content_1430087.htm.
5 We will talk about the issue of the RMB exchange rate in Chapter 10.
6 This section is aimed at economists and students who are majoring in economics. Other readers might wish to skip this section.
7 Appendix C provides a formal presentation with regard to Harrod's economy.
8 As shown at the beginning of Chapter 6 and in Appendix C, this instability is indeed

due to the dual rules of investment in simultaneously creating the demand and capacity in the product market.

9 For this type of model applied to the US economy, see Flaschel, Gong and Semmler (2001); to the German economy, see Flaschel, Gong and Semmler (2002); and to developing economies, such as China, see Gong and Lin (2007, 2008).

6 The financial system in contemporary Chinese economy

1 Data from China Banking Regulatory Commission (2009).
2 Data from Editorial Board of Almanac of China's Finance and Banking (2009).
3 Rankings are available at http://news.xinhuanet.com/world/2009-02/08/content_10781828.htm. In the ranking of global banks' market capitalization, the top 10 banks are: Industrial and Commercial Bank of China, China Construction Bank, Bank of China, the United Kingdom HSBC, JPMorgan Chase Bank, Wells Fargo, Spain's International Bank, Mitsubishi UFJ, Goldman Sachs, and China Bank of Communications.
4 From Deng (1993: 373).
5 Data from China Securities Regulatory Commission (2010).
6 Figures are calculated by referring to the data available at the websites of the China Securities Regulatory Commission (www.csrc.gov.cn/pub/newsite/sjtj/) and the People's Bank of China (www.pbc.gov.cn/).
7 See Zhou Qiren, "The market properties of the RMB exchange rate", *Economic Observer*, April 26, 2010.

7 The economic fluctuations in contemporary Chinese economy

1 A formal mathematical discussion of this destabilizing mechanism is provided in Gong (2001) and also in Appendix C of this book.
2 See Minsky (1982, 1986) for the idea of financial instability. Other typical works along this research line include Taylor and O'Connell (1985), Foley (1986, 1987), Franke and Semmler (1989, 1992), Delli Garttii, Gallegati and Gallini (1993), Delli Gatti and Gallegati (1994) and Flaschel, Franke and Semmler (1997: Ch 12) and Gong (2005).
3 See Keynes (1936).
4 See Gong Gang (2006a) for further information on the impact of bond investment on China's economy.
5 The quoted case comes from Xie, Zhou and Fang (2007), and some of the data from National Bureau of Statistics of China (2007).
6 According to the objective set in the Great Leap Forward, China had obviously "overtaken Britain and the United States".
7 Recently, the steel industry has not been one of the industries whose capacities are seriously excessive.
8 According to the latest report, (as of August 2010, after continuous reorganization and mergers, a central enterprise supervised by the State-owned Assets Supervision and Administration Commission (SASAC), which fulfills the responsibilities of investors, has been reduced to 123. This number does not include the financial and tobacco central enterprises under the supervision of other departments such as the China Banking Regulatory Commission (CBRC).
9 According to Brandt and Zhu (2000, 2001), the rotation of the credit plan from being "indicative" to being "mandatory" largely reflects China's business cycle.
10 Though has not been completely eliminated.
11 This effect is the same as the open market operation in the US. In the US, when the Federal Reserve adopts an open market operation, it uses US dollars to buy bonds and thereby injects the monetary base into the economy. The so-called monetary base (or

high-powered money) is the money injected directly by the central bank into the economy. According to economic theory, this will stimulate more money, such as the money created by the loan. Therefore, the total money supply to the society is usually interpreted as the multiplier, or a multiple of, the monetary base.

12 See Rawski (2002).
13 The aggregate demand curve is derived from the famous IS-LM model. The detailed illustration can be referenced in various textbooks of intermediate macroeconomics, such as Gong (2005).
14 See Bernanke (2002), Bordo and Lane (2004) and Cargill and Parker (2004).
15 See Gong (2002).
16 The data quoted here can be found in Chapter 6 of Cai and Lin (2003).
17 See Lin (2000, 2004).

8 Transformation to the second stage of economic development

1 Data from National Bureau of Statistics of China (2008) and the World Bank database.
2 Data from the Section of Industrial Transportation, National Bureau of Statistics of China, and the Bureau of Energy, National Development and Reform Commission (2007).
3 For instance, if the labor cost is cheap, there is no incentive to introduce production means with higher labor productivity.
4 The Gini coefficient is a measure of income and wealth inequality developed by an Italian statistician, Corrado Gini, in 1912. The data regarding the Gini coefficient of China are cited from He (2007), Li and Luo (2007) and Liu and Yu (2007), among others.
5 For a more detailed study on the subject of surplus labor in China, see Cai and Wang (2008), among others.
6 The data in these two figures come from Penn World Table (http://pwt.econ.upenn.edu/php_site/pwt_index.php).
7 Gong and Yang (2011) provides a more academic analysis of the transformation of these two proportions by building a dynamic macroeconomic model. The paper is available upon request.
8 The seminar work to treat technology as human capital is attributed to Lucas (1988). In addition, technology A may also include social infrastructure and management systems. See Barro (1990) and Barro and Sala-I-Martin (1992) for discussion.

9 Technological progress and human capital development

1 See Schultz (1961), Ben-Porath (1967), Becker (1975), and Lucas (1988), among others, for more classic articles and books on the theory of human capital.
2 Though the rate of return is declining with the increase in age.
3 See Nelson and Winter (1982), Pavitt (1984), Scherer (1984), and Gong (2001, 2006b), among others, for detailed studies.
4 In China.
5 From that perspective, the so-called transformation of the growth mode is somehow related to Schumpeter's concept of creative destruction.
6 See the discussion in Chapter 2.
7 According to National Bureau of Statistics in China (2009), for the years 2005 to 2009 the debt–GDP ratios in China were 17.64, 16.19, 19.59, 16.96 and 17.69, respectively.
8 It is often argued that debt can be distinguished as being explicit or implicit debt. By explicit debt we usually mean the debt issued by government directly, while implicit debt refers to non-statutory debt. There is no consensus on the components of implicit debt. For China, implicit debt once often referred to those non-performing assets of state-owned commercial banks. However, this has now been greatly reduced due to the restructuring and reform of the commercial banking system in China (see Chapter 6).

9 Indeed, as long as the growth rate of GDP is larger than the interest rate (as has been the case over the past 30 years in China), there is space for new governmental deficit without causing an increase in the debt–GDP ratio. That space (or the amount of deficit spending) will expand with the increase in the gap between the growth rate and the interest rate. It will also increase with the rise in the existing debt–GDP ratio. For a demonstration, see Gong and Chen (2007).

10 The reform of exchange regime and RMB internationalization

1 For the definition and implementation of AOER, see Section 6.3 of this book.
2 This is also a strict fixed exchange regime, but what's different from the standard fixed exchange regime is that the issuance of currency is backed by its foreign currency assets.
3 Managed floating also means the central bank's intervention in the foreign exchange market. The difference lies in the fact that the central bank's target rate is set within a band, rather than as a certain value.
4 See Section 1.(iii), Article IV of the IMF's Articles of Agreement, which is available at www.imf.org/external/pubs/ft/aa/aa04.htm#1.
5 Triffin (1947) put forward that reserves of foreign currencies should be consistent with the growth of international trade; the World Bank (1985) stated that "the ideal size of foreign reserves of developing countries should be sufficient to cover three months of imports", and to prevent payment risks and currency crisis.
6 See Gao and Yu (2010).
7 Data come from the People's Bank of China (2009a).
8 Data can be found at http://finance.ifeng.com/news/hgjj/200806/0626_2201_618918. shtml.

Appendix A: A review of Keynesian and neoclassical economics

1 It should be noted that Walras did not use mathematical methods to prove this conclusion. This work was completed by Arrow and Debreu, two modern mathematicians. Their outstanding contributions in this regard made them win the Nobel Prize in economics.
2 Another major school is new classical conomics. The study by this school is focused on creating macroeconomics based on the perfect competitive economy of neoclassical economics. The representative theory is the theory of the real business cycle (RBC). See Gong (2004) for more information.
3 For more classic articles on the price stickiness proposed by new Keynesians, see Calvo (1983), Rotemberg (1982), Mankiw (1985), Woodford (2003), Christiano, Eichenbaum and Evans (2005) among others.

Appendix B: Behavior analysis of investment

1 In effect, whether the average cost is an increasing or decreasing function of capacity utilization is no longer important. As will be indicated below, for the existence of the optimal capacity utilization, we simply assume that the first-order derivative of average cost cannot be zero.
2 It is also the firm's sales revenue. Here, we assume that expected price is constant when the firm makes an investment decision.
3 Though there may be multiple solutions.
4 This linear relationship has been given previously.

Appendix C: The Harrodian economy and the existence of destabilizing mechanism

1 For references, see Sen (1970) and Gong (2001), among others.
2 Note that in economic literature, the warranted rate is often defined as sA. This is the case when depreciation is ignored.
3 Note that $A < 1$ indicates that the investor may not get its return within one period even if the created capacity is fully utilized.

Appendix D: A macro-dynamic model of contemporary Chinese economy – an overshooting perspective to "deflationary expansion" in China

1 As pointed out in Appendix C, we can also define U_t as AK_t. This is will not change the basic properties of the model, but rather increase the non-linearity of the model, thus rendering analysis of the model more complex.
2 For the existence theorem of Hopf bifurcation in a two-dimensional discrete time-dynamic system, see Guckenheimer and Holmes (1986: 162).

References

Barro, R. J. (1990): Government Spending in a Simple Model of Endogenous Growth, *Journal of Political Economy*, 98: 103–125.

Barro, R. J. (2000): *Macroeconomics*, Cambridge, MA: MIT Press.

Barro, R. J. (2007): China Slowly but Steadily Push Forward Reform, in *The Two Possibilities of China's Future Economic Development in 10 Years – The World's Leading Economists' Viewpoints* (L. Ben, ed.), Beijing: Social Sciences Academic Press [in Chinese].

Barro, R. J. and Sala-I-Martin, X. (1992): Public Finance in Models of Economic Growth, *Review of Economic Studies*, 59: 645–661.

Barro, R. J. and Sala-I-Martin, X. (2003): *Economic Growth*, New York, NY: McGraw-Hill.

Becker, G. (1975): *Human Capital: A Theory and Empirical Analysis, with Special Reference to Education*, Chicago, IL: University of Chicago Press.

Benassy, J. P (1982): *Economics of Market Disequilibrium*, New York, NY: Academic Press.

Ben-Porath, Y. (1967): The Production of Human Capital and the Life Cycle of Earnings, *Journal of Political Economy*, 75: 353–359.

Bernanke, B. S. (2002): "Deflation: Making Sure It Does not Happen Here", Remarks at the National Economist Club, Washington, DC, www.federalreserve.gov/boarddocs/speeches/2002/20021121/default.htm.

Bernanke, B. S. (2008): "Remarks on the Economic Outlook", The International Monetary Conference, Barcelona, Spain, June 3, 2008 (this article can be found at www.federalreserve.gov/newsevents/speech/bernanke20080603a.htm).

Blanchard, O. (2000): *Macroeconomics*, New York, NY: Prentice Hall Inc.

Bordo, M. (1995): Is There a Good Case for a New Bretton Woods International Monetary System? *American Economic Review*, 85(2): 317–322.

Bordo, M. and Eichengreen, B. (1993): *A Retrospective on the Bretton Woods System*, Chicago, IL: University of Chicago Press.

Bordo, M. and Lane, J. L. (2004): "Good Versus Bad Deflation: Lessons from the Gold Standard Era", NBER Working Paper, No. 10329.

Brandt, L. and Zhu, X. D. (2000): Redistribution in a Decentralized Economy: Growth and Inflation in China under Reform, *Journal of Political Economy*, 108(2): 422–439.

Brandt, L. and Zhu, X. D. (2001): Soft Budget Constraint and Inflation Cycles: A Positive Model of the Macro-dynamics in China during Transition, *Journal of Development Economics*, 64: 437–457.

Cai, F. and Lin, Y. F. (2003): *The Chinese Economy*, Beijing: Chinese Financial and Economic Press [in Chinese].

Cai, F. and Wang, M. Y. (2008): A Counterfactual Analysis on Unlimited Surplus Labor in Rural China, *China & World Economy*, 16(1): 51–65.

Cai, J. W. (1999): *China's "Tango" at the end of the Century—Problems and Solutions*, Zhengzhou: Henan People's Press [in Chinese].

Calvo, G. A. (1983): Staggered Contracts in a Utility Maximization Framework, *Journal of Monetary Economics*, 12: 383–398.

Cargill, T. and Parker, E. (2004): Price Deflation, Money Demand and Monetary Policy Discontinuity: A Comparative View of Japan, China and United States, *North American Journal of Economics and Finance*, 15, 125–147.

China Banking Regulatory Commission (2009): *The Annual Report of the China Banking Regulatory Commission, 2008*, Beijing: China Banking Regulatory Commission.

China Securities Regulatory Commission (2010): *China Statistical Yearbook of the Securities and Futures* [in Chinese], Shanghai: Xue Lin Press.

Christiano, L., Eichenbaum, M. and Evans, C. (2005): Nominal Rigidities and the Dynamic Effects of a Shock to Monetary Policy, *Journal of Political Economy*, 113: 1–45.

Clower, R. W. (1965): The Keynesian Counterrevolution: A Theoretical Appraisal, in *The Theory of Interest Rates* (F. H. Hahn and F. P. R. Brechling, eds), London: Macmillan.

Coase, R. (1937): The Nature of the Firm, *Economics*, 4: 386–405.

Delli Gatti, D. and Gallegati, M. (1994): External Finance, Investment Expenditure, and The Business Cycle, in *Business Cycle: Theory and Empirical Methods* (W. Semmler, ed.), Dordrecht: Kluwer.

Delli Gatti, D., Gallegati, M. and Gardini, L. (1993): Investment Confidence, Corporate Debt and Income Fluctuation, *Journal of Economic Behavior and Organization*, 23: 161–187.

Deng X. P. (1993): *Selected Works of Deng Xiaoping*, Vol. 3, Beijing: People's Press.

Deng, X. P. (1994): *About Rural Policy Issues, Selected Works of Deng Xiaoping*, Vol. 2, Beijing: People's Press.

Editorial Board of Almanac of China's Finance and Banking (2009): *Almanac of China's Finance and Banking, 2009* [in Chinese].

Editorial Board of Almanac of China's Finance and Banking (2010): *Almanac of China's Finance and Banking, 2010* [in Chinese].

Editorial Board of Chinese Encyclopedia: Economics (1988): *Chinese Encyclopedia: Economics*, Beijing: Chinese Encyclopedia Publisher.

Fair, R. C. (2000): Testing the NAIRU Model for the United States, *Review of Economics and Statistics*, February, 64–71.

Finance Committee (1950): *Chinese Economic Bulletin, 1949* [in Chinese].

Flaschel, P., Franke, R. and Semmler, W. (1997): *Nonlinear Macrodynamics: Instability, Fluctuations and Growth in Monetary Economics*, Cambridge, MA: MIT Press.

Flaschel, P., Gong, G. and Semmler, W. (2001): A Keynesian Econometric Framework for Studying Monetary Policy Rules, *Journal of Economic Behavior and Organization*, 46: 101–136.

Flaschel, P., Gong, G. and Semmler, W. (2002): A Macroeconometric Study on Monetary Policy Rules: Germany and the EMU, *Jahrbuch für Wirtschaftswissenschaften*, 53: 1–31.

Foley, D. K. (1986): Stabilization Policy in a Nonlinear Business Cycle Model, in *Competition, Instability and Nonlinear Cycles* (W. Semmler, ed.), New York, NY: Spring-Verlag.

Foley, D. K. (1987): Liquidity–Profit Rate Cycles in a Capitalist Economy, *Journal of Economic Behavior and Organization*, 18: 363–376.

Franke, R. and Semmler, W. (1989): Debt-Financing of Firms, Stability and Cycles in a Dynamic Macroeconomic Growth Model, in *Financial Dynamics and Business Cycle: New Perspectives* (W. Semmler ed.), Armonk, NY: M. E. Sharpe.

Franke, R. and Semmler, W. (1992): Expectation Dynamics, Finance of Investment, and Business Cycle, in *Profits, Deficits and Instability* (D. B. Papadimitriou ed.), London: Macmillan.

Friedman, M. (1953): *Essays in Positive Economics*, Chicago, IL: University of Chicago Press.

Frisch, R. (1933): Propagation and Impulse Problems in Dynamic Economics, in *Economic Essays in Honor of Gustav Cassel*, London: Allen & Unwin.

Gao, H. H. and Yu, Y. D. (2010): The Meaning and the Conditions of RMB Internationalization, *International Economic Review*, Issue 1.

Gong, G. (2001): Product Innovation and Irregular Growth Cycles with Excess with Excess Capacity, *Metroeconomic*, 52: 428–448.

Gong, G. (2002): Cracking the Mystery of "Deflationary Expansion", *China Economic Research Center News*, Issue 127, Beijing: Tsinghua University [in Chinese].

Gong, G. (2004): Real Business Cycle: Theory, Empirics and Disputes, *China Economics Quarterly*, 3, 786–802 [in Chinese].

Gong, G. (2005): *Macroeconomics: Perspective from Chinese Economy*, Beijing: Tinghua University Press [in Chinese].

Gong, G. (2006a): The Studies on the Macroeconomic Effects of the Expansionary Fiscal Policy: On the Basis of Macro-econometric Model, *Journal of Quantitative & Technical Economics*, 12: 3–13 [in Chinese].

Gong, G. (2006b): Endogenous Technical Change: An Evolution from Process Innovation to Product Innovation, in *Time and Space in Economics* (T. Asada and T. Ishikawa, eds), Tokyo: Springer Verlag.

Gong, G. (2007): Resurrecting Keynesian Economics: Written at 70 Years Anniversary of the Publication of the "General Theory", *China Economics Quarterly*, 7(1): 1–26 [in Chinese].

Gong, G. (2008): *Contemporary Chinese Economy: the Third Voice*, Beijing: Higher Education Publisher [in Chinese].

Gong, G. and Chen, L. (2007): Supply Driven: On the Fiscal Policy for the Transformation of Growth Mode, *Nankai Economic Studies*, 2: 43–55 [in Chinese].

Gong, G. and Lin, J. Y. F. (2007): Overshooting the Explanation of "Deflationary Expansion" in China, *Economic Research*, 4: 53–66 [in Chinese].

Gong, G. and Lin, J. Y. F. (2008): Deflationary Expansion, an Overshooting Perspective to the Recent Business Cycles in China, *China Economic Review*, 19: 1–17.

Gong, G. and W. Semmler (2006): *Stochastic Dynamic Macroeconomics: Theory and Empirical Evidence*, New York, NY: Oxford University Press.

Gong, G. and Yang, G. (2010a): On the Evolution of Wage Proportion over National Income, *Management World*, Issue 5 [in Chinese].

Gong, G. and Yang, G. (2010b): C8/P4 The Inequality of Income Distribution in China: a Perspective from Functional Income Distribution, *China Social Science*, Issue 2 [in Chinese].

Gong, G. and Yang, G. (2011): "A Study on the Evolution of Consumption and Investment over GDP", Working Paper.

Gong, G. and Yang, L. (2002): "Estimates of Capacity Utilization in China", China Center for Economic Research Working Paper, No. 200216, Beijing: Tsinghua University [in Chinese].

Gong, G., Greiner, A. and Semmler, W. (2001): Growth Effects of Fiscal Policy and Debt Sustainability in the EU, *Empirica*, 28: 3–19.

Guckenheiner, J. and Hommes, P. (1986): *Nonlinear Oscillations, Dynamical Systems, and Bifurcations of Vector Fields*, New York, NY: Springer-Verlag.

Hale, D. and Hale, L. (2007): China to Take off, in *The Two Possibilities of China's Future Economic Development in 10 Years The World's Leading Economists' Viewpoints* (L. Ben, ed.), Beijing: Social Sciences Academic Press [in Chinese].

Harrod, R. F. (1939): An Essay in Dynamic Theory, *Economic Journal*, 49: 14–33.

Harrod, R. F. (1948): *Towards a Dynamic Economics*, London: Macmillan.

He, Y. (2007): Gini Coefficient: The Analysis on the History of Urban and Rural Policy, *China Information News*, April 11, 2007 [in Chinese].

Heckman, J. J. (2003): China's Investment in Human Capital, *Economic Development and Cultural Change*, 51: 795–805.

Hoffman, W. G. (1931): *The Growth of Industrial Economics* (German edn), 1958 (English translation), Oxford: Oxford University Press.

Hu, S. (1991): *Seven Years of Communist Party of China*, Beijing: Party History Publishing House.

Huang, D. (1998): *Towards Perfecting China's Financial System: Objectives and the Road*, Beijing: China Pricing Press [in Chinese].

Huggins, R., Izushi, H., Davis, W. and Luo, S. G. (2008): *World Knowledge Competitiveness Index 2008*, Cardiff: Center For International Competitiveness, Cardiff School of Management, University of Wales Institute.

Gilboy, J. (2007): The Mystery behind the Chinese Miracle, in *The Two Possibilities of China's Future Economic Development in 10 Years The World's Leading Economists' Viewpoints* (L. Ben, ed.), Beijing: Social Sciences Academic Press [in Chinese].

Jing, W. M. and Sun, J. Y. (2008): *Economic Transformation*, Beijing: Economic and Management Publishing House (in Chinese).

Kalbraith, J. K. (1985): *New Industrial State*, 4th edn, Boston, MA: Houghton Mifflin.

Kaldor, N. (1961): Capital Accumulation and Economic Growth, in *Theory of Capital: Proceedings of a Conference Held by the International Economics Association* F. A. Lutz and D. C. Hague, eds), New York, NY: St Martin's Press, pp. 177–222.

Keynes, J. M. (1936): *The General Theory of Employment, Interest Rate and Money*, London: Macmillan.

Kornai, J. (1979): Resource Constrained versus Demand Constrained System, *Econometrica*, 47(4): 801–819.

Kornai, J. (1980): *Economics of Shortage*, Amsterdam: North-Holland.

Lewis, S. A. (1954): Economic Development with Unlimited Supplies of Labour, *The Manchester School*, 22(2): 139–191.

Li, S. and Luo, C. L. (2008): Growth Forms and Employment and Income Gap: East Asian Experience and Implications for China, in *Promoting Social Harmony by Shared Growth* (J. Y. F. Lin, J. Z. Zhuang, M. Tang and D. Lin, eds), Beijing: China Planning Press [in Chinese].

Li, Z. Z and Zhang, R. J. (1999): *The Economic History of the People's Republic of China: 1949–1999*, Lanzhou: Lanzhou University Press [in Chinese].

Lin, J. Y. F. (2000): The Current Deflation in China: Causes and Policy Options, *Asian Pacific Journal of Economics and Business*, 4(2): 4–21.

Lin, J. Y. F. (2003): Development Strategy, Viability and Economic Convergence, *Economic Development and Cultural Change*, 51(2): 277–308.

Lin, J. Y. F. (2004): Is China's Growth Real and Sustainable? *Asian Perspective*, 28(3): 5–29.

Lin, J. Y. F. (2007): "Development and Transition: Idea, Strategy, and Viability", Marshall Lecture, Cambridge University, October 31–November 1, 2007.

Lin, J. Y. F. and Liu, P. L. (2008): Using the First Time Income Distribution to Achieve the Unite of Fairness and Efficiency and to Promote the Harmonious Development, in *Promoting Harmonious Society by Inclusive Growth* (J. Y. F. Lin, J. Z. Zhuang, M. Tang and D. Lin, eds), Beijing: China Planning Press [in Chinese].

Lin, J. Y. F. and Sun, X. F. (2003): The Theory of Strategy of Economic Development in Comparative Advantage, *International Economic Review*, Issue 11 [in Chinese].

Lin, J. Y. F., Cai, F. and Li, Z. (1994): *Chinese Miracle: Development Strategy and Economic Reform*, Shanghai: Shanghai People's Press [in Chinese].

Ling, Z. J. and Ma, L. C. (1999): *Cries: the Five Voices in China Today*, Guangdong: Guangdong People's Press [in Chinese].

Liu, M. Q. and Yu, J. T. (2008): The Study on Financial Structure and the Relationship between the Development of Small & Medium Enterprises and Income Distribution, in *Promoting Harmonious Society by Inclusive Growth* (J. Y. F. Lin, J. Z. Zhuang, M. Tang and D. Lin (eds), Beijing: China Planning Press [in Chinese].

Lucas, R. E. (1988): On the Mechanics of Economic Development, *Journal of Monetary Economics*, 22: 3–42.

Ma, K. and Cao, Y. S. (2002): *Transition from Planned Economy to Economic System in a Socialist Market*, Beijing: People's Press [in Chinese].

Mankiw, G. N. (1985): Small Menu Cost and Large Business Cycles: A Macroeconomic Model, *Quarterly Journal of Economics*, 100: 529–538.

Mankiw, G. N. (1990): A Quick Refresher Course in Macroeconomics, *Journal of Economic Literature*, 27: 1645–1660.

Miller, R. (2007): The High Growth and Low Inflation, What is Next?, in *The Two Possibilities of China's Future Economic Development in 10 Years The World's Leading Economists' Viewpoints* (L. Ben, ed.), Beijing: Social Sciences Academic Press [in Chinese].

Minsky, H. P. (1982): *Can "It" Happen Again?* Armonk, NY: M. E. Sharpe.

Minsky, H. P. (1986): *Stabilizing an Unstable Economy*, New Haven, CT: Yale University Press.

Mundell, R. A. (2003): *Selected Works of Mundell*, Beijing: China Financial Press [in Chinese].

National Bureau of Statistics in China (2004): *China Statistical Yearbook 2004*, Beijing: China Statistics Press [in Chinese].

National Bureau of Statistics in China (2006): *China Statistical Yearbook 2006*, Beijing: China Statistic Press [in Chinese].

National Bureau of Statistics in China (2007): *China Statistical Yearbook 2007*, Beijing: China Statistics Press [in Chinese].

National Bureau of Statistics in China (2008): *International Statistical Yearbook 2008*, Beijing: China Statistics Press [in Chinese].

National Bureau of Statistics in China (2009): *International Statistical Yearbook 2008*, Beijing: China Statistics Press [in Chinese].

National Bureau of Statistics in China (2010): *China Statistical Yearbook 2010*, Beijing: China Statistics Press [in Chinese].

Nell, E. J. (1983): Competition and Price-Taking Behavior, in *Growth, Profit and Property* (E. J. Nell, ed.), Cambridge: Cambridge University Press.

Nelson, R. R. and Winter, S. G. (1982): *Evolutionary Theory of Economic Change*, Cambridge, MA: Harvard University Press.

Obstfeld, M. and Rogoff, K. (1995): Exchange Rate Dynamics Redux, *Journal of Political Economy*, 103: 624–660.

OECD (2004): *Economic Outlook Database*, No. 75.

OECD (2006): *China Economic Research*, Beijing: China Renmin University Press [in Chinese].

Pavitt, P. (1984): Sector Pattern of Change, *Research Policy*, 13: 343–373.

Pejovich, S. (2000): *Property Economics – A Theory on Comparative Institutions*, Beijing: Economic Science Press [in Chinese].

People's Bank of China (2009a): *The Development Report of World Financial Market in 2009*, http://shanghai.pbc.gov.cn/publish/fzh_shanghai/2983/2010/20100915150514159846451/2010091515051415984 6451/20100915150514159846451_.html.

People's Bank of China (2009b): *The Development Report of China Financial Market in 2009*, www.pbc.gov.cn/publish/main/1049/2010/20100504223414158350746/2010050 4223414158350746_.html.

Qian, Y. Y. (2003): Understanding Modern Economics, in *Modern Economics and Economic Reform in China* (Y. Y. Qian, ed.), Beijing: China Renmin University Press [in Chinese].

Rawski, T. R. (2002): China's GDP Growth Accounting in Recent Years, *China Economics Quarterly*, 2(1): 53–62 [in Chinese].

Research Group of RMB Internationalization (2006): The Timing, Means and Strategies of Internationalization, *China Finance*, Issue 5 [in Chinese].

Romer, P. (1990): Endogenous Technical Change, *Journal of Political Economy*, 98: 71–102.

Rotemberg, J. (1982): Sticky Prices in the United States, *Journal of Political Economy*, 90: 1187–1211.

Samulson, P. and R. Solow (1960): Analytical Aspects of Anti-inflation Policy, *American Economic Review*, 50: 177–194.

Scherer, F. M. (1984): *Innovation and Growth: Schumpeterian Perspectives*, Cambridge, MA: MIT Press.

Schultz, P. T. (1961): Investment in Human Capital, *American Economic Review*, 51: 1–17.

Schultz, P. T. (2004): Human Resources in China: the Birth Quota, Returns to Schooling, and Migration, *Pacific Economic Review*, 9(3): 245–267.

Schumpeter, J. A. (1934): *The Theory of Economic Development: An Inquiry into Profits, Capital, Credit, Interest, and Business Cycle*, Cambridge, MA: Harvard University Press.

Schumpeter, J. A. (1942): *Capitalism, Socialism and Democracy*, republished by Routledge in 1994.

Sen, A. (1970): Introduction, in *Growth Economics* (A. Sen, ed.), Harmondsworth: Penguin Books Ltd.

Slutsky, E. E. (1937): The Summation of Random Causes as the Source of Cyclical Processes, *Econometrica*, 5: 105–46.

Solow, R. (1956): A Contribution to the Theory of Economic Growth, *Quarterly Journal of Economics*, 70: 65–94.

Taylor, L. and O'Connell, S. A. (1985): A Minsky Crisis, *Quarterly Journal of Economics*, 100: 871–886.

Tian, G. Q. (2005): The Basic Analytical Framework of Modern Economics and Research, *Economic Research*, Issue. 2 [in Chinese].

Triffin, R. (1947): National Central Banking and the International Economy, in *Essays in International Economic Equilibrium and Adjustment*, New York, NY: MacMillan.

Walras, L. (1874): *Elements D'économie Politique Pure*, Lausanne: Corbaz.

Weintraub, E. R. (1977): The Micro-foundation of Macroeconomics: A Critical Survey, *Journal of Economic Literature*, 15(1): 1–23.

Wicksell, K. (1936): *Interest and Prices*, 1898, English translation by R. F. Kahn, London: Macmillan.

Woodford, M. (2003): *Interest Rate and Prices*, Princeton, NJ: Princeton University Press.

World Bank (1985): *World Development Report 1985*, Beijing: China Financial and Economic Publishing House [in Chinese].

Wotezeer, J. (2008): China: the Optimal Growth Model, in *The Two Possibilities of China's Future Economic Development in 10 Years The World's Leading Economists' Viewpoints* (L. Ben, ed.), Beijing: Social Sciences Academic Press [in Chinese].

Wu, C. M. (1956): *Imperialism's Investment in Old China*, Beijing: People's Press [in Chinese].

Wu, J. L. (2006): *The Choice of China's Growth Model*, Shanghai: Shanghai Far East Publishing House [in Chinese].

Wu, L. (2003): Re-examination and Evaluation of China's Planned Economy, *Xinhua Digest*, Issue 11 [in Chinese].

Xie, Y. X., Zhou, J. and Fang, Z. W. (2007): To Improve the Competitiveness of Steel Enterprises is the Fundamental Way to Build Steel Power, in *China Steel News*, www.csteelnews.com/news/jianjie/25375.html [in Chinese].

Yang, J. B. (1958): *Eight Years of Economic Development in China*, Beijing: People's Press [in Chinese].

Yang, R. L. (1998): The Three-Stage Theory of Institutional Transformation – On the Innovative Behavior of Local Government System, *Economic Research*, Issue 1 [in Chinese].

Yu, J. S. (2006): *Development in Concussion – 30 Years of New Chinese Economy*, Central Literature Publishing House [in Chinese].

Zhang, Y. and Lu, D. (2007): *Contemporary Chinese Economy*, Renmin: China Renmin University Press [in Chinese].

Index

Page numbers in *italics* denote tables, those in **bold** denote figures.

For Product Safety Concerns and Information please contact our EU representative GPSR@taylorandfrancis.com Taylor & Francis Verlag GmbH, Kaufingerstraße 24, 80331 München, Germany

Batch number: 08165901

Printed by Printforce, the Netherlands